AF597493

AUSTRALIAN JOURNEY
East Coast

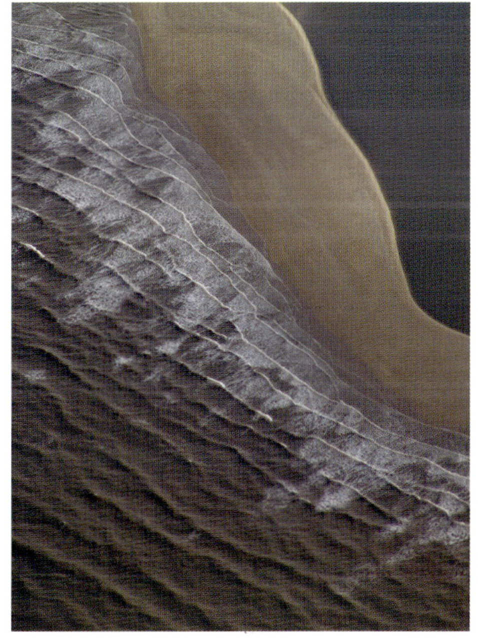

Debra Doenges Andrew Teakle

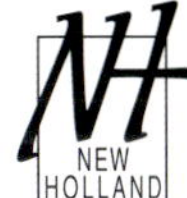

Dedication

This book is dedicated to all our dear friends. We cherish your love and support.

First published in Australia in 2007 by
New Holland Publishers (Australia) Pty Ltd
Sydney • Auckland • London • Cape Town

1/66 Gibbes Street Chatswood NSW 2067 Australia
218 Lake Road Northcote Auckland New Zealand
86 Edgware Road London W2 2EA United Kingdom
80 McKenzie Street Cape Town 8001 South Africa

Australian journey : east coast.

ISBN 9781741106282 (hbk.).

1. Coasts - Australia, Eastern - Pictorial works. 2.
Cities and towns - Australia, Eastern - Pictorial works. 3.
Photography, Artistic. I. Doenges, Debra. II. Teakle, Andrew.

919.400222

Publisher: Fiona Schultz
Designer: Debra Doenges and Andrew Teakle
Production Manager: Linda Bottari
Printer: Tien Wah Press (Malaysia) Pte Ltd

10 9 8 7 6 5 4 3 2 1

Cover: Bithry Inlet, Mimosa Rocks National Park, NSW, Debra Doenges
Title page: Coastal Patterns, Far North Queensland, Debra Doenges
Page 3: Jamison Valley, Blue Mountains National Park, NSW, Debra Doenges
Page 4: Rock in Kelp, Cape Schanck, Mornington Peninsula, VIC, Andrew Teakle

www.tesseraphoto.com www.tesseratravel.com

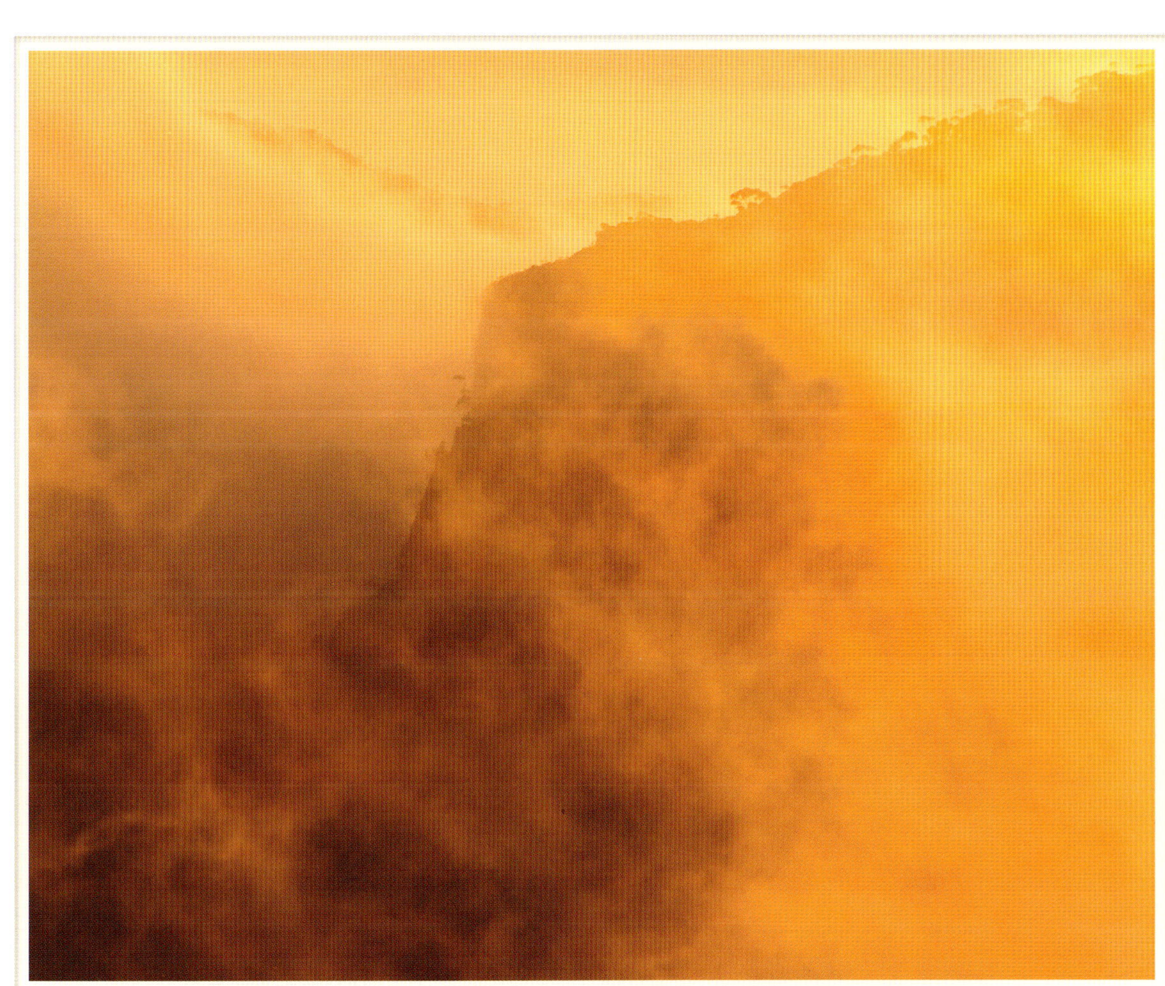

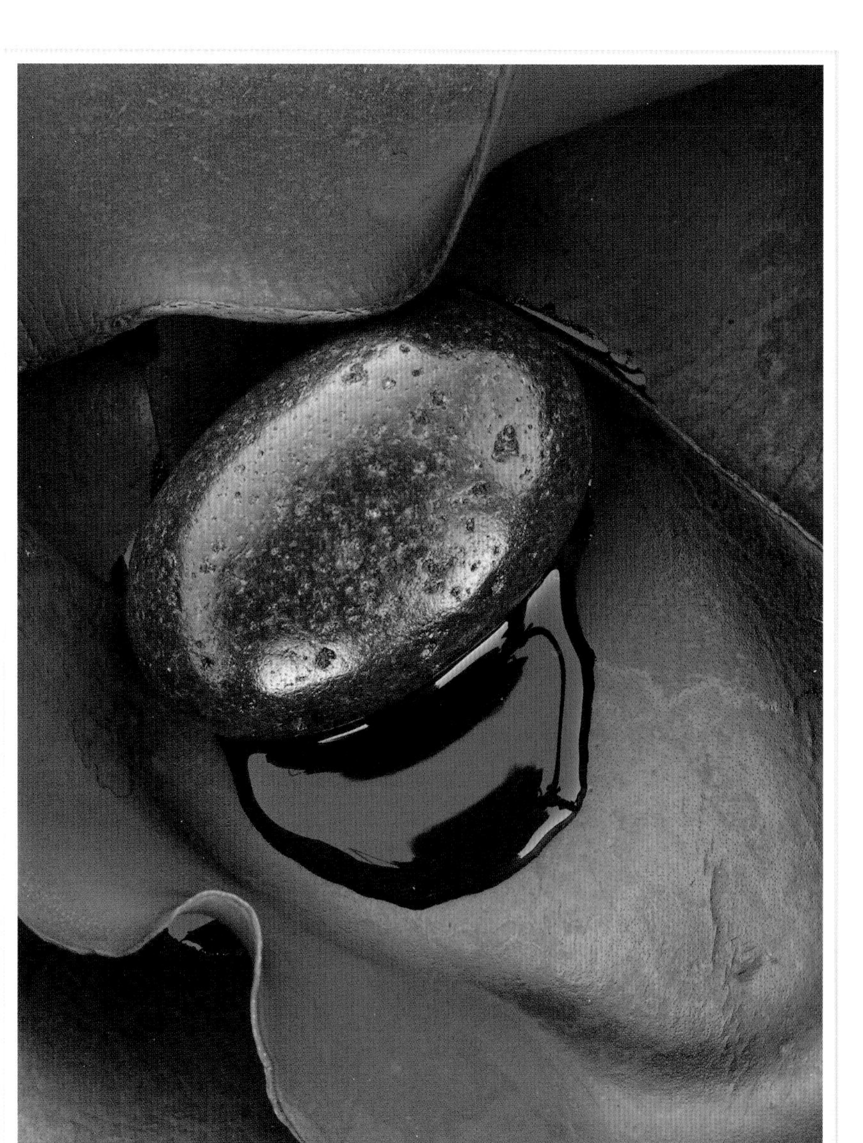

Introduction

Australia is a huge country filled with a myriad of delights. For a traveller, seeing all of the highlights of the sixth largest country in the world is no easy undertaking. Distances are great and large sections of the country have only rough tracks, if anything at all, rather than paved roads. In outback Australia, temperatures can be extreme and rainfall is low–except in the tropical north when the monsoon floods vast tracts of the Top End every year. This isolating and challenging environment, as opposed to the moister and less extreme temperature conditions near the coast, explains why 85 percent of the population lives within 50 kilometres of the ocean. Of this percentage, the majority live on the East Coast, between Melbourne in the south, Sydney in the middle and Brisbane in the subtropics.

The cities of Sydney and Melbourne take their place on the world stage as iconic destinations, dazzling with character, sumptuous food and sophistication. The coastal scenery of ranges from some of the most beautiful surf beaches in the world to rugged headlands and limestone cliffs. Lighthouses dot the coast, showcasing Australia's nautical history. The Great Barrier Reef, running more than 1,000 kilometres along the Queensland coast, is the most extensive reef system in the world: a living organism visible from space. The Great Dividing Range runs inland along the entire East Coast, giving birth to our largest rivers and boasting our highest mountains. Pockets of temperate, sub-tropical, and tropical rainforests dot these mountains and include ancient plant life such as the Antarctic Beech and the recently discovered Wollemi Pine. The Gold Coast in Southeast Queensland caters to the party crowd, providing beautiful beaches and theme parks by day and exotic nightspots after the sun goes down.

Australian Journey: East Coast transports you to many of the highlights of this section of the country. These 123 images have been selected from our many years of travels to reveal it at its best.

We hope you enjoy our favourite images of this vibrant and spectacular part of Australia.

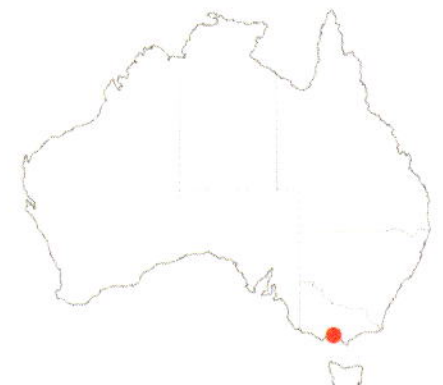

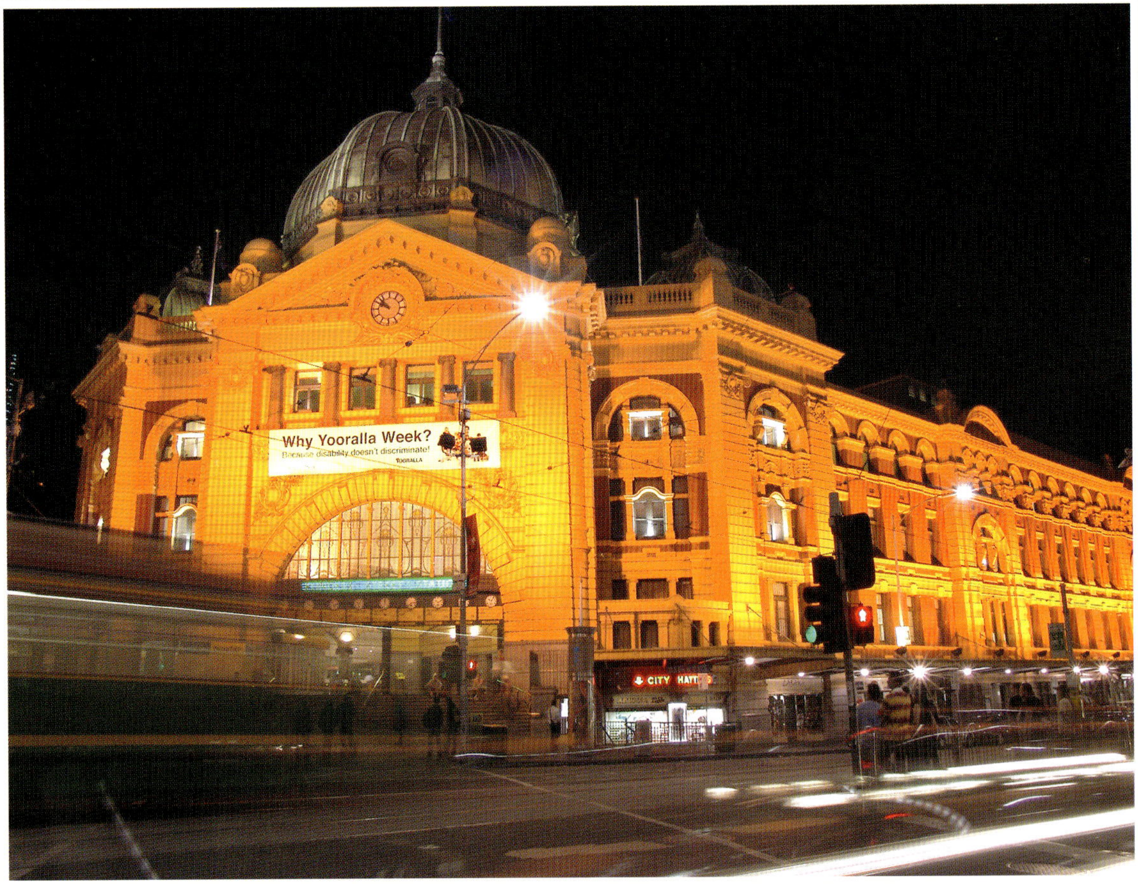

TRAM STREAKS BY FLINDERS STATION

Melbourne, VIC

Andrew Teakle & Debra Doenges

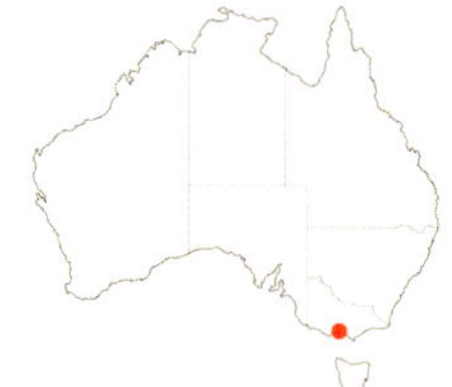

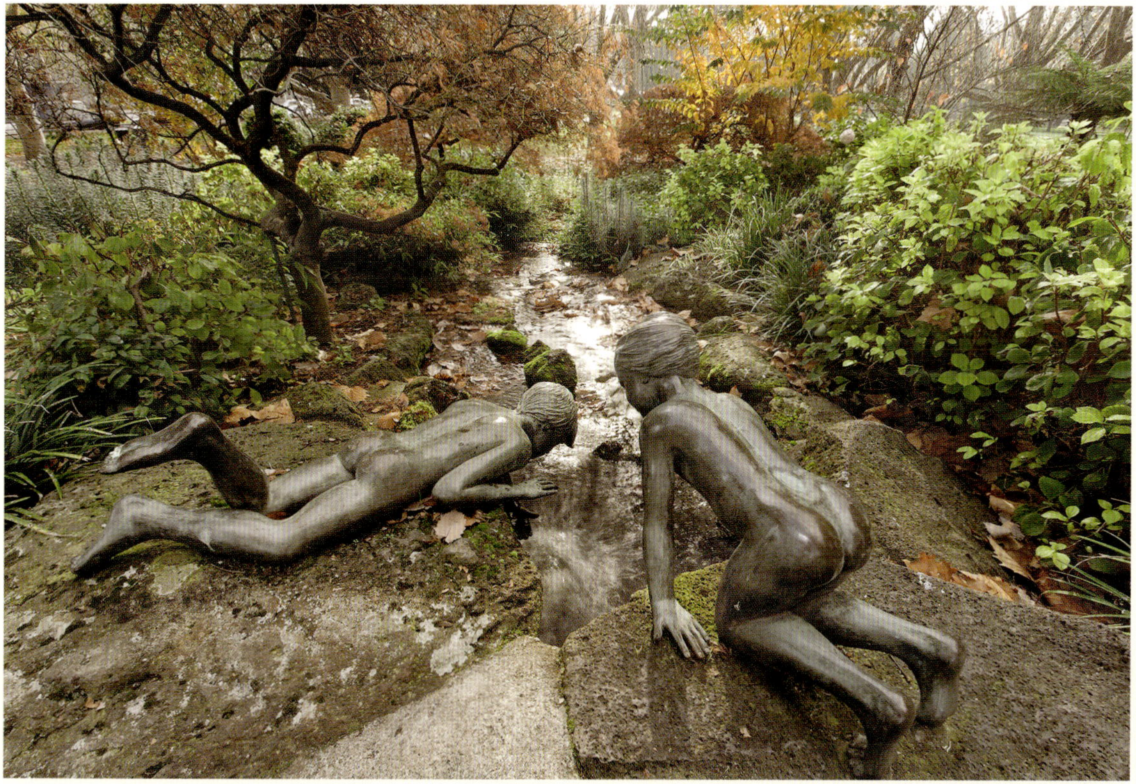

Andrew Teakle

QUEEN VICTORIA GARDENS

Melbourne, VIC

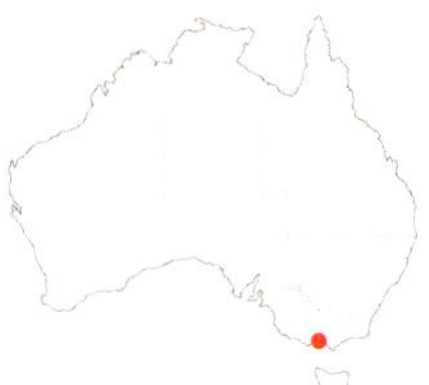

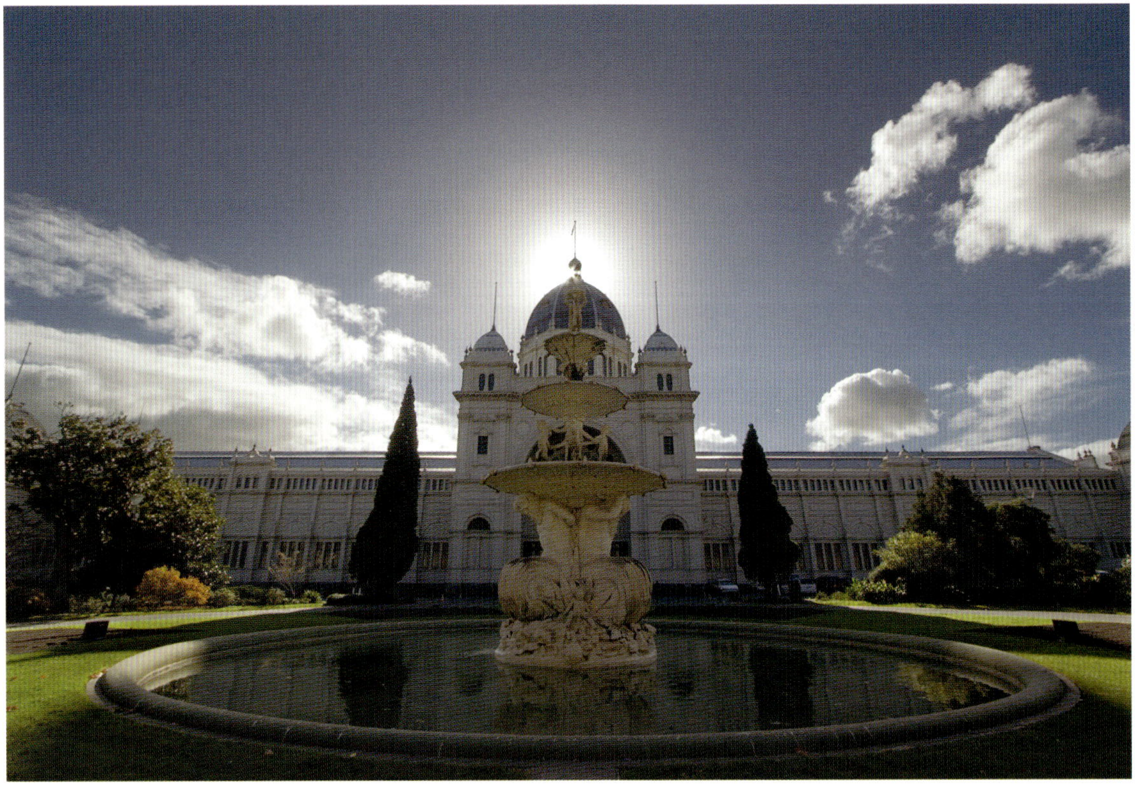

ROYAL EXHIBITION BUILDING
Melbourne, VIC

Andrew Teakle

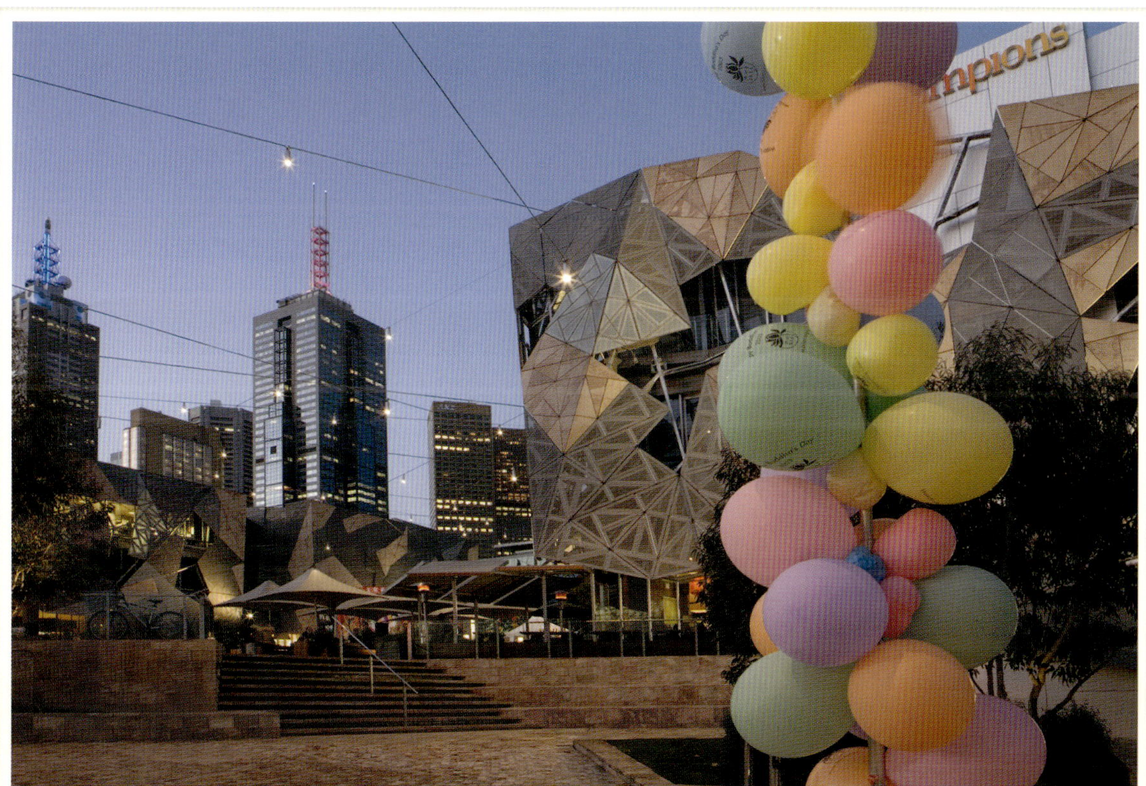

Debra Doenges

FEDERATION SQUARE
Melbourne, VIC

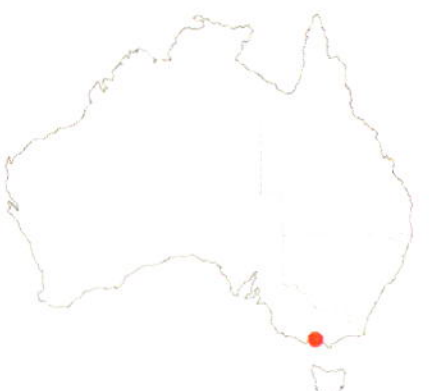

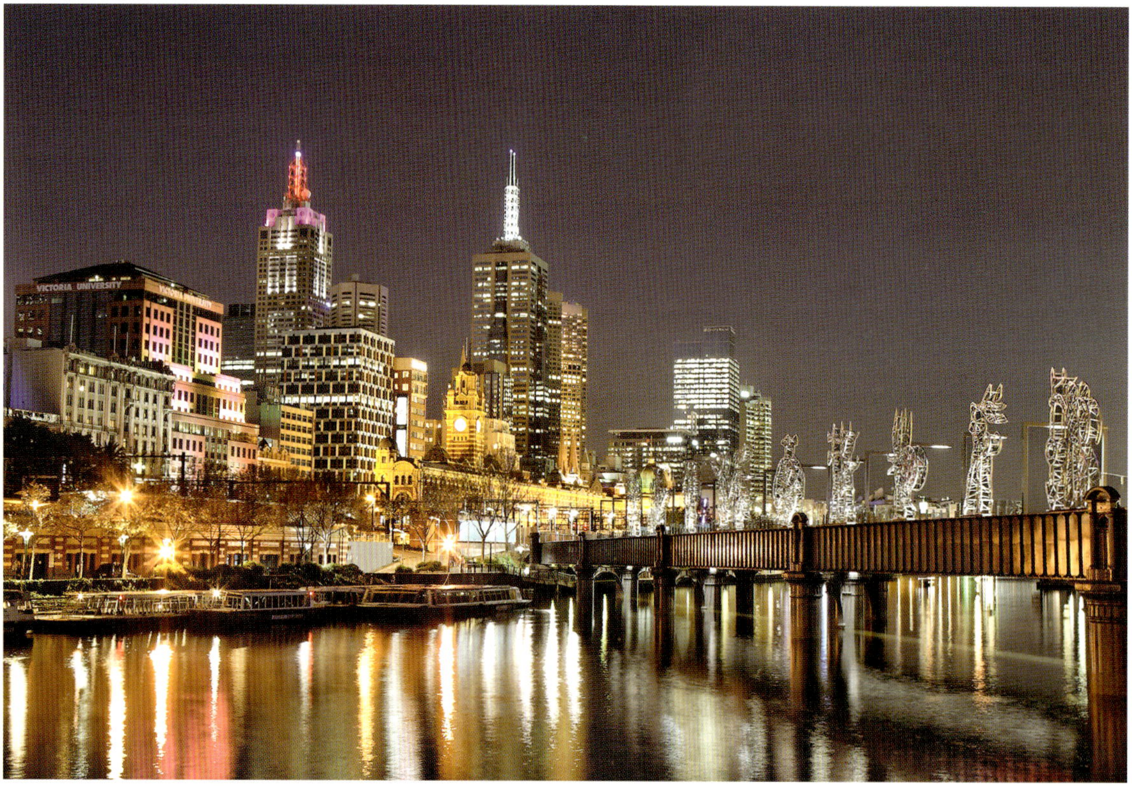

SKYLINE AT NIGHT
Melbourne, VIC

Andrew Teakle

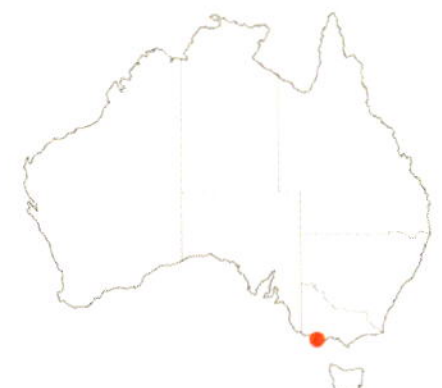

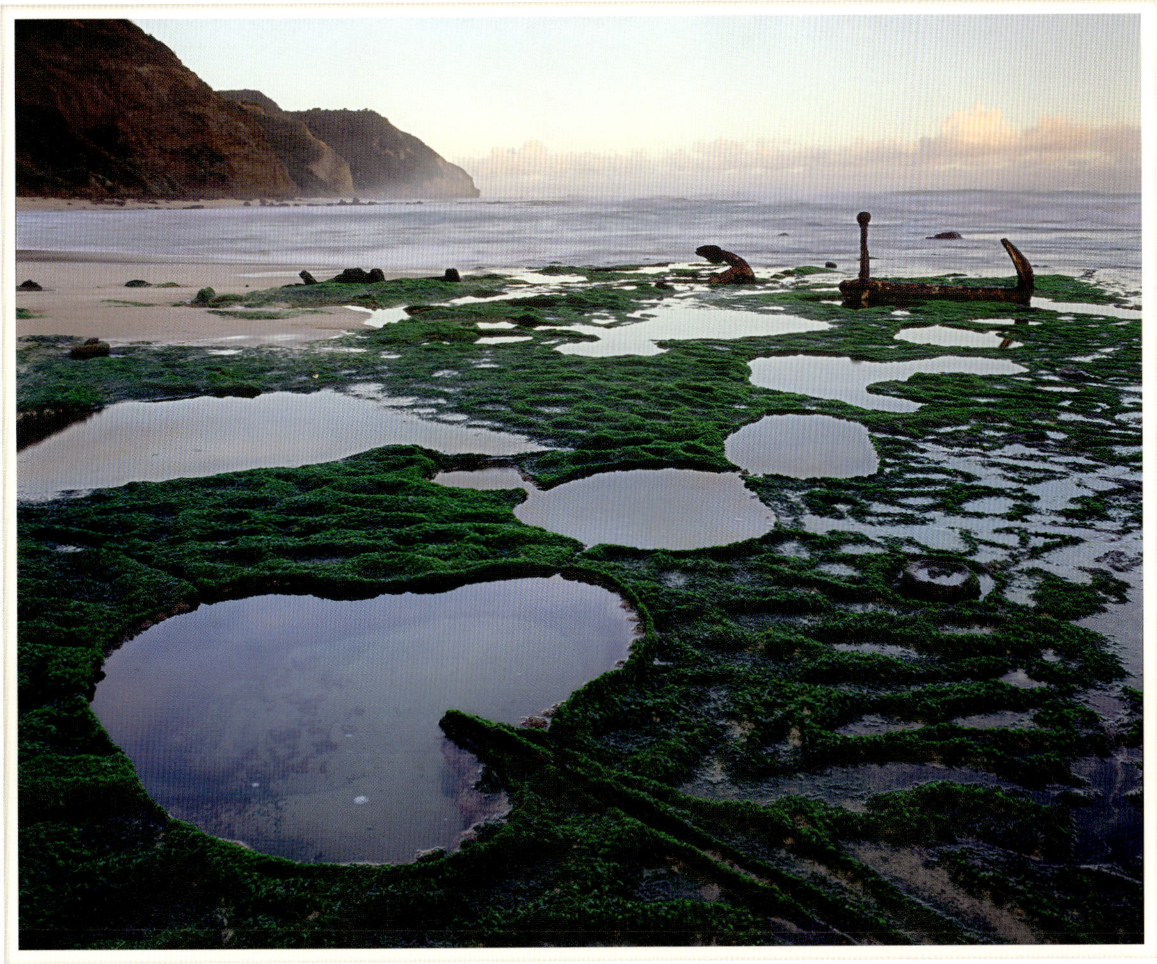

Debra Doenges

WRECK BEACH

Great Ocean Road, Port Campbell National Park, Vic

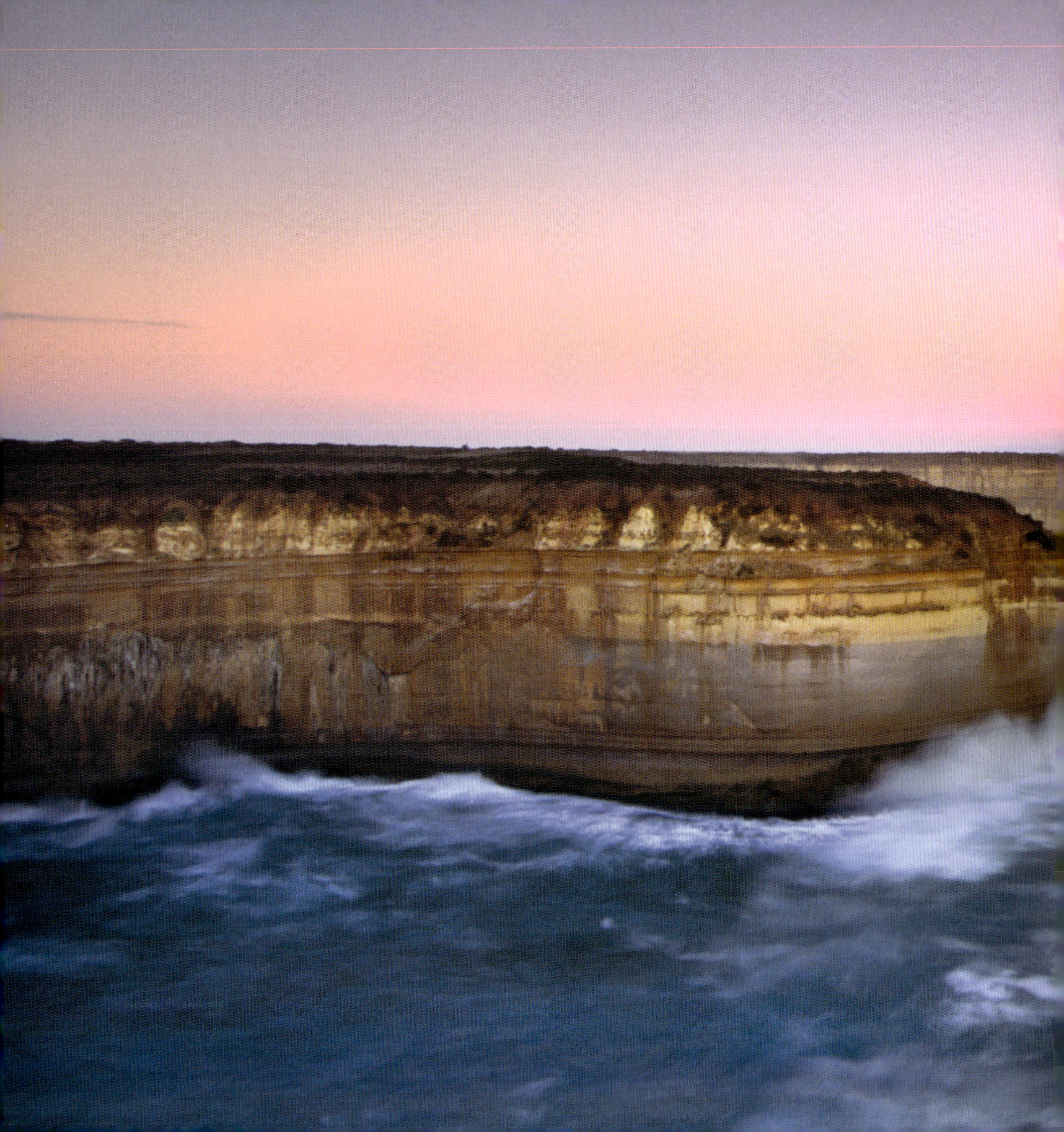

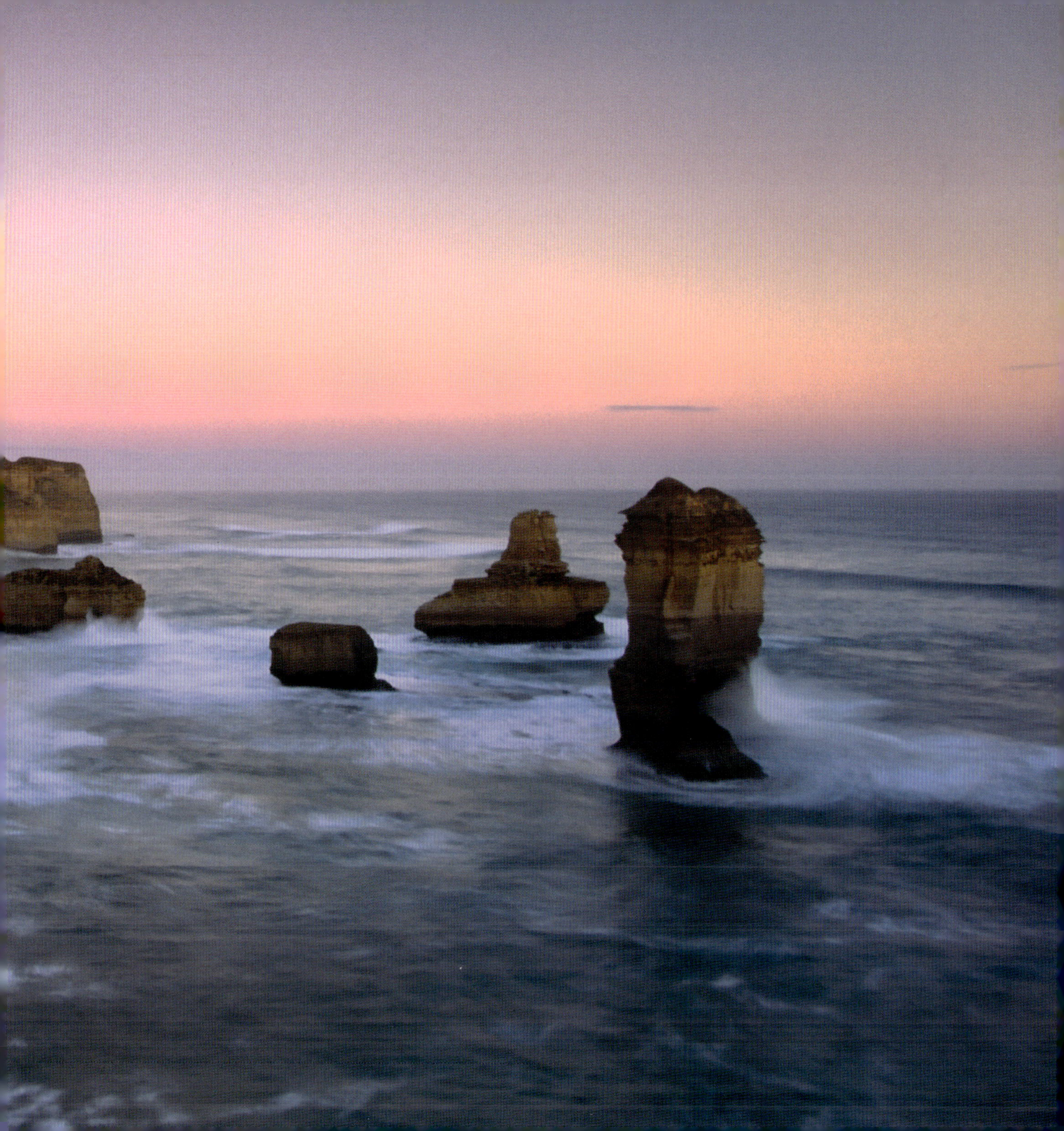

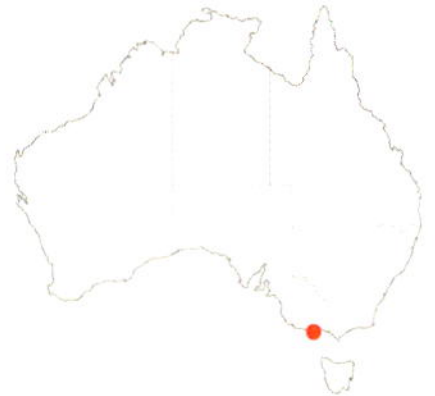

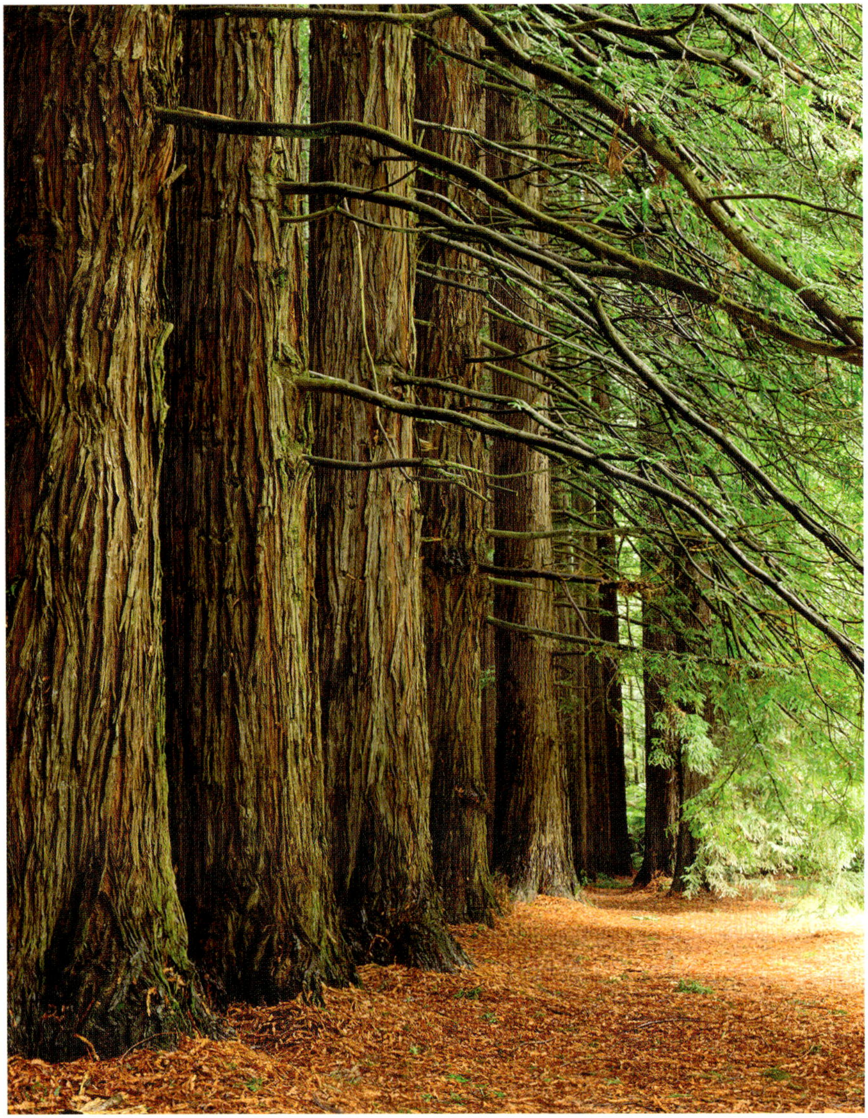

REDWOOD FOREST

Aire River, Otway Ranges, VIC

Debra Doenges

GREAT OCEAN ROAD

◀ Port Campbell National Park, VIC

Andrew Teakle

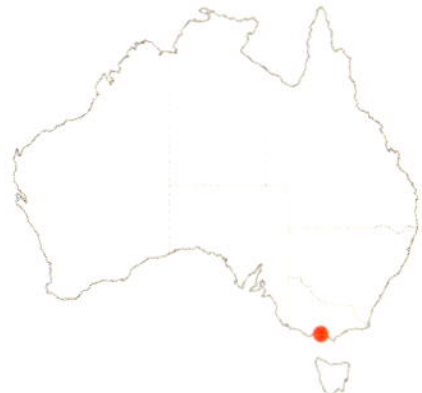

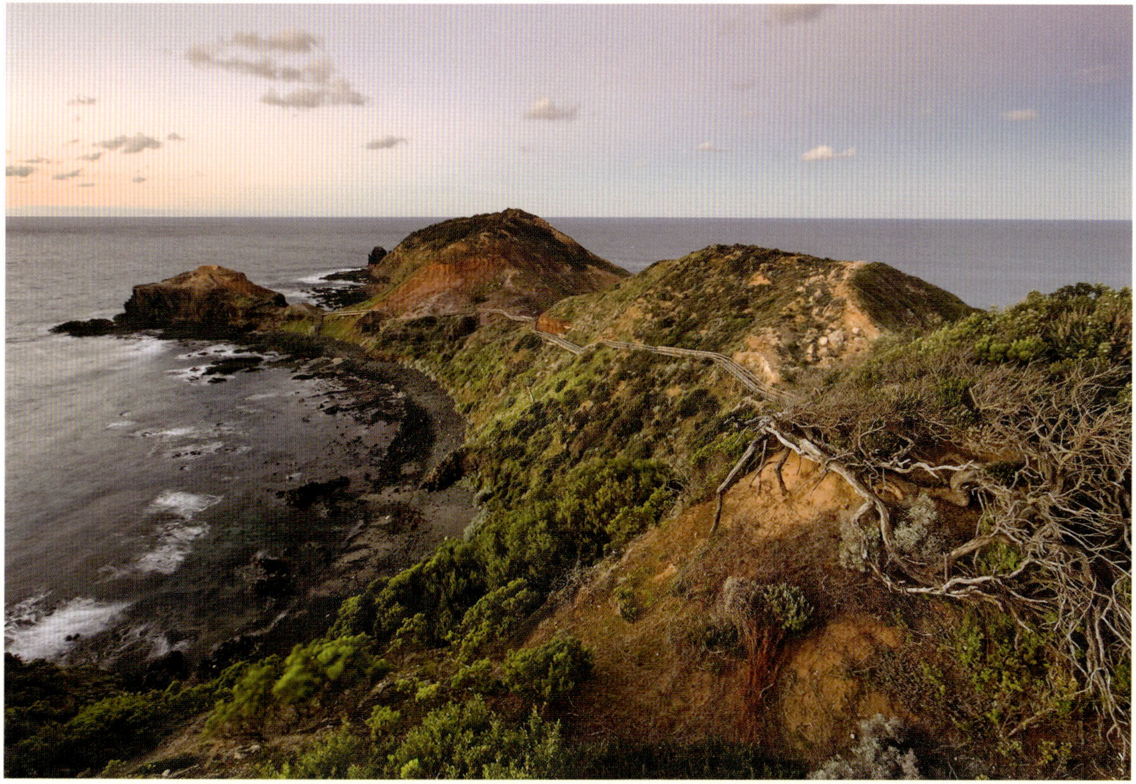

Andrew Teakle

CAPE SCHANCK

Mornington Peninsula, VIC

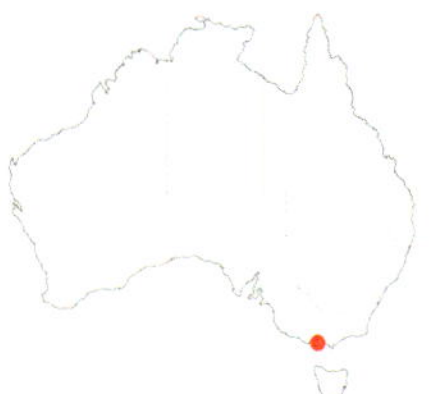

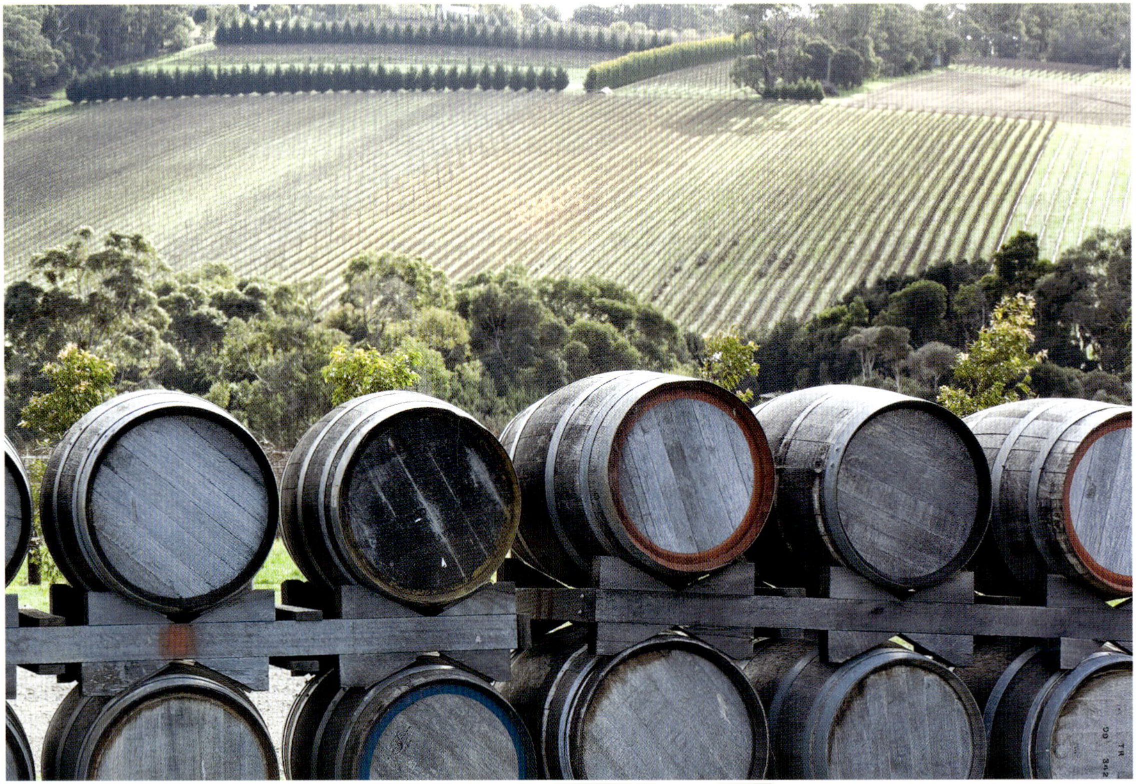

AUTUMN VINEYARD
Mornington Peninsula, VIC

Debra Doenges & Andrew Teakle

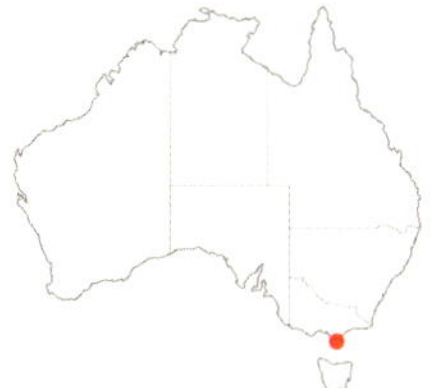

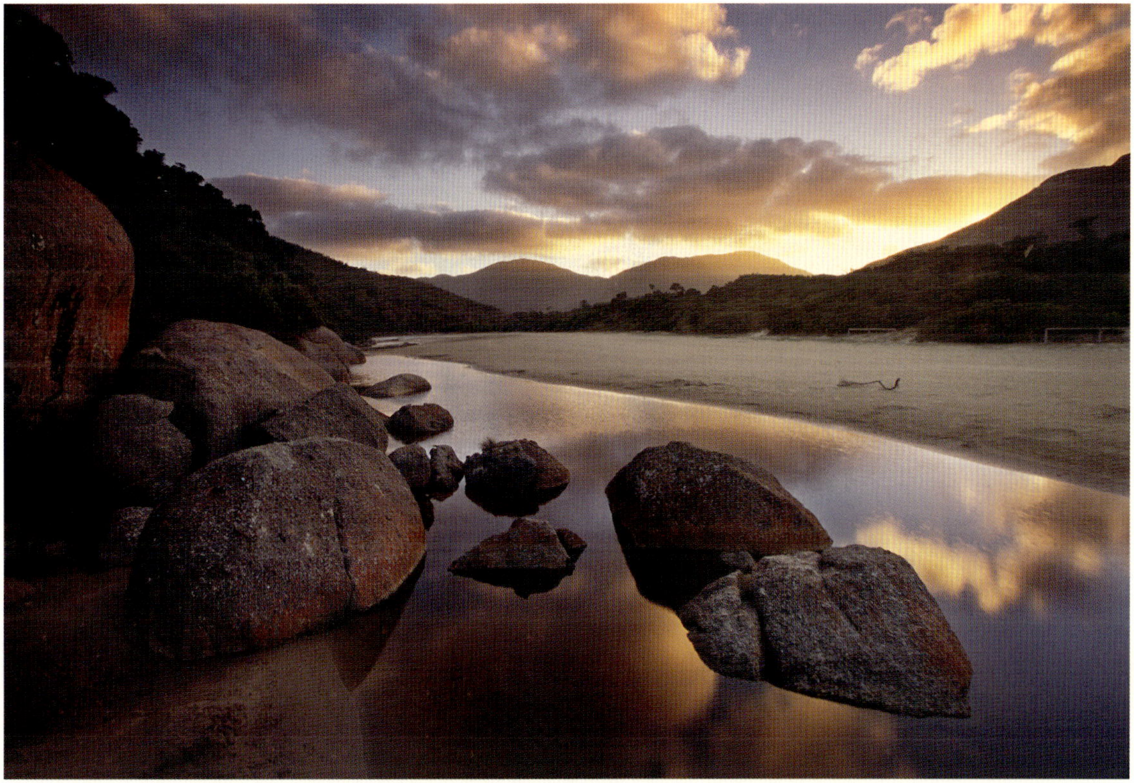

Andrew Teakle

TIDAL RIVER AT DAWN

Wilsons Promontory National Park, VIC

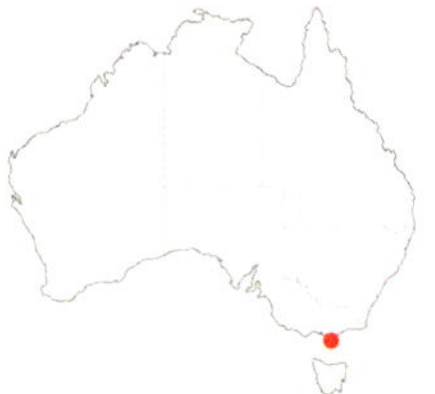

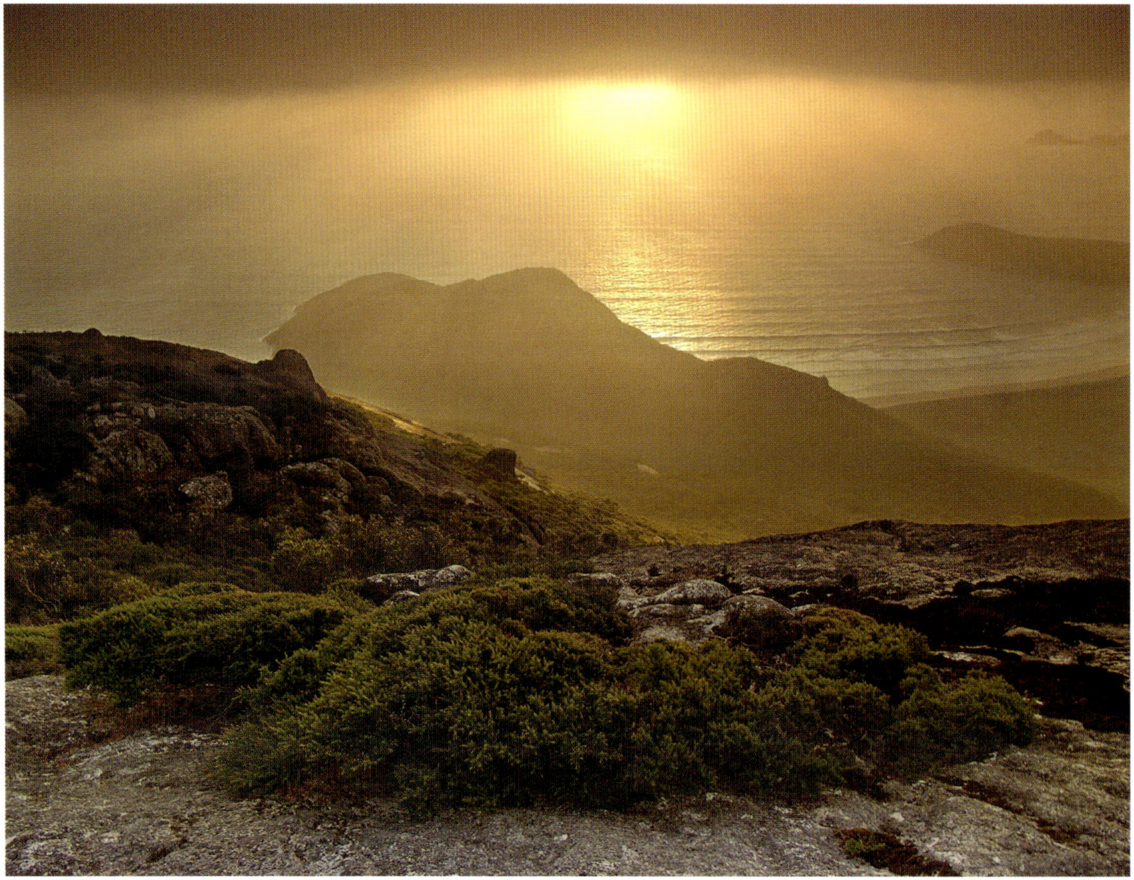

MT OBERON LOOKOUT

Wilsons Promontory National Park, VIC

Andrew Teakle & Debra Doenges

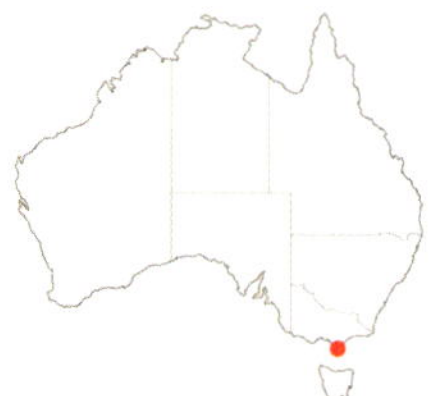

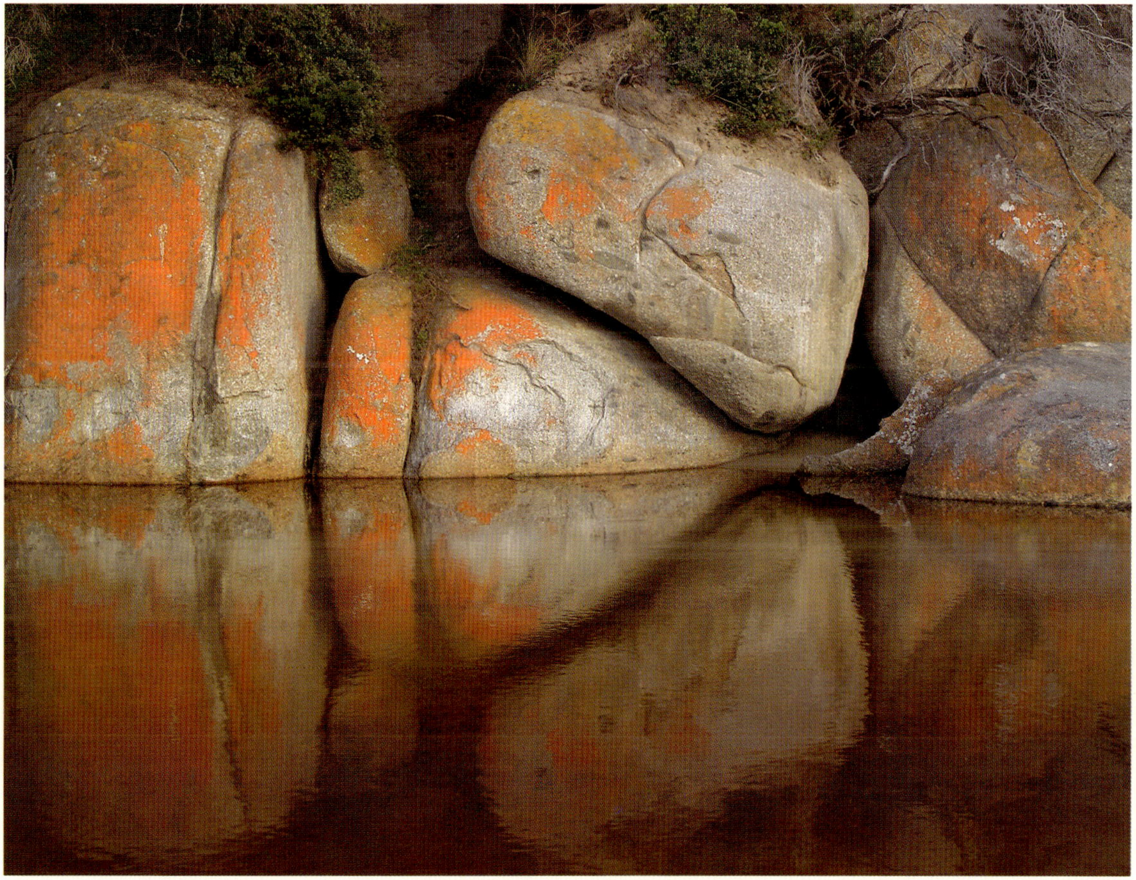

Debra Doenger

GRANITE BOULDERS REFLECTION

Tidal River, Wilsons Promontory National Park, VIC

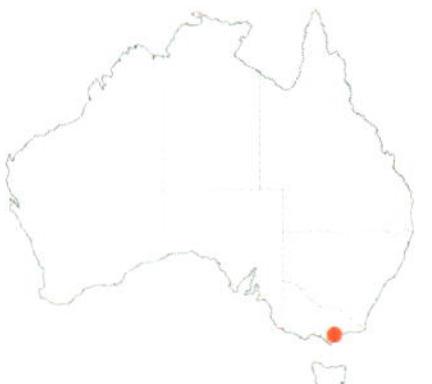

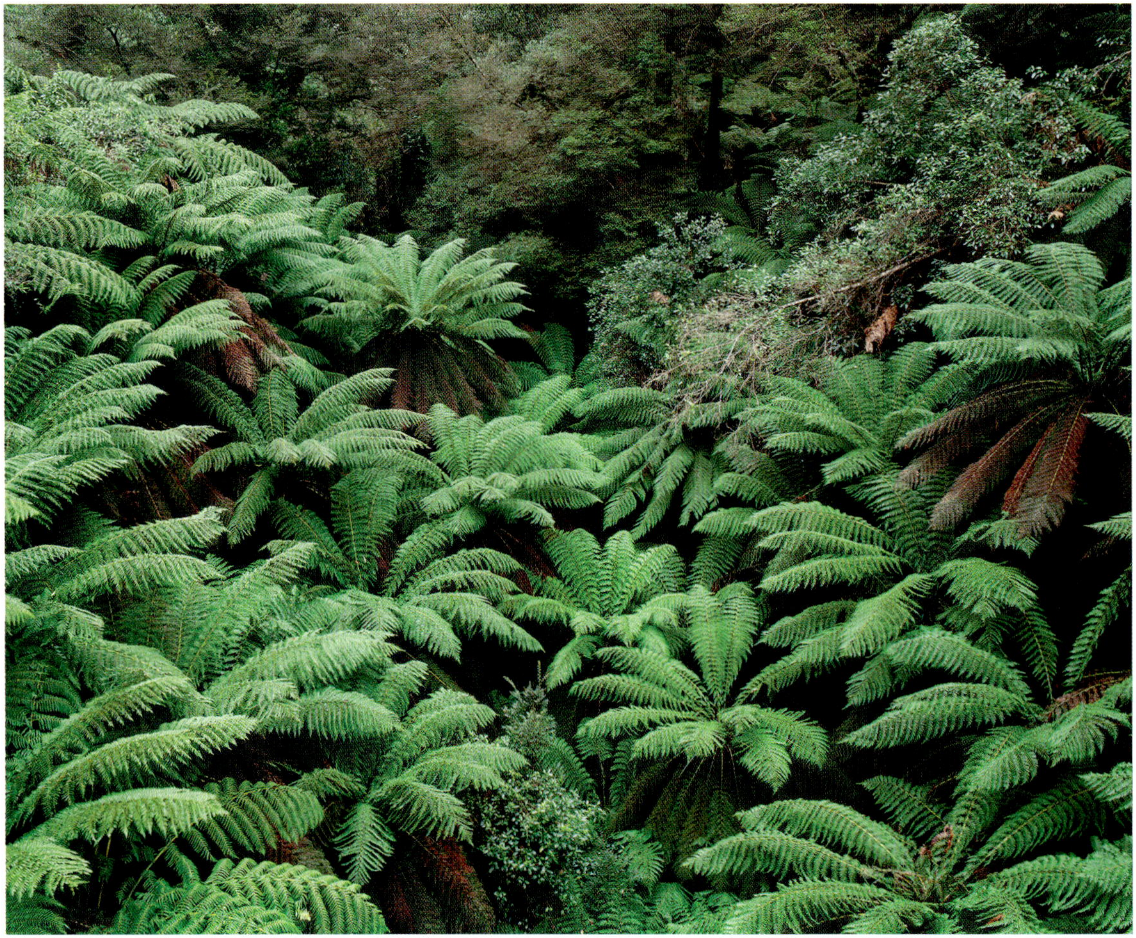

TREE FERN GULLY

Tarra-Bulga National Park, VIC

Debra Doenges

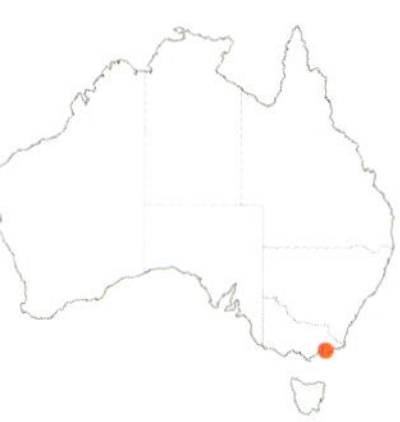

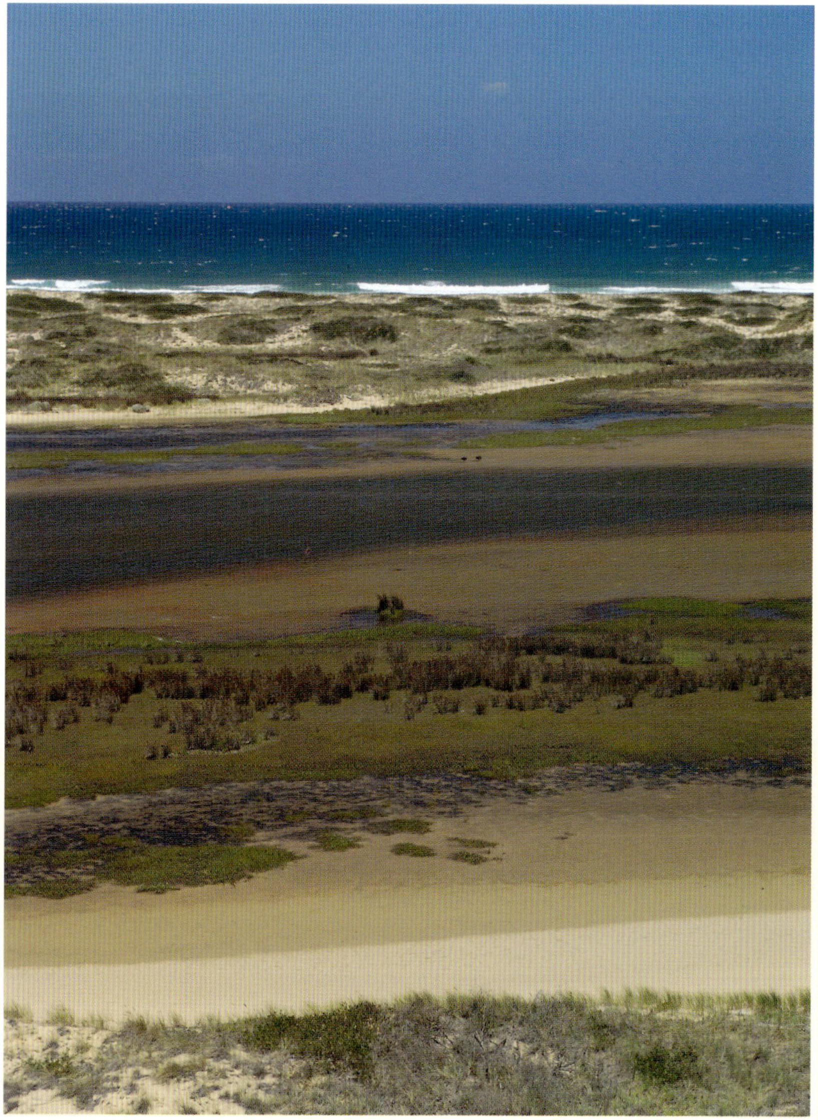

Debra Doenges

SAND BAR PATTERNS
Snowy River Mouth, VIC

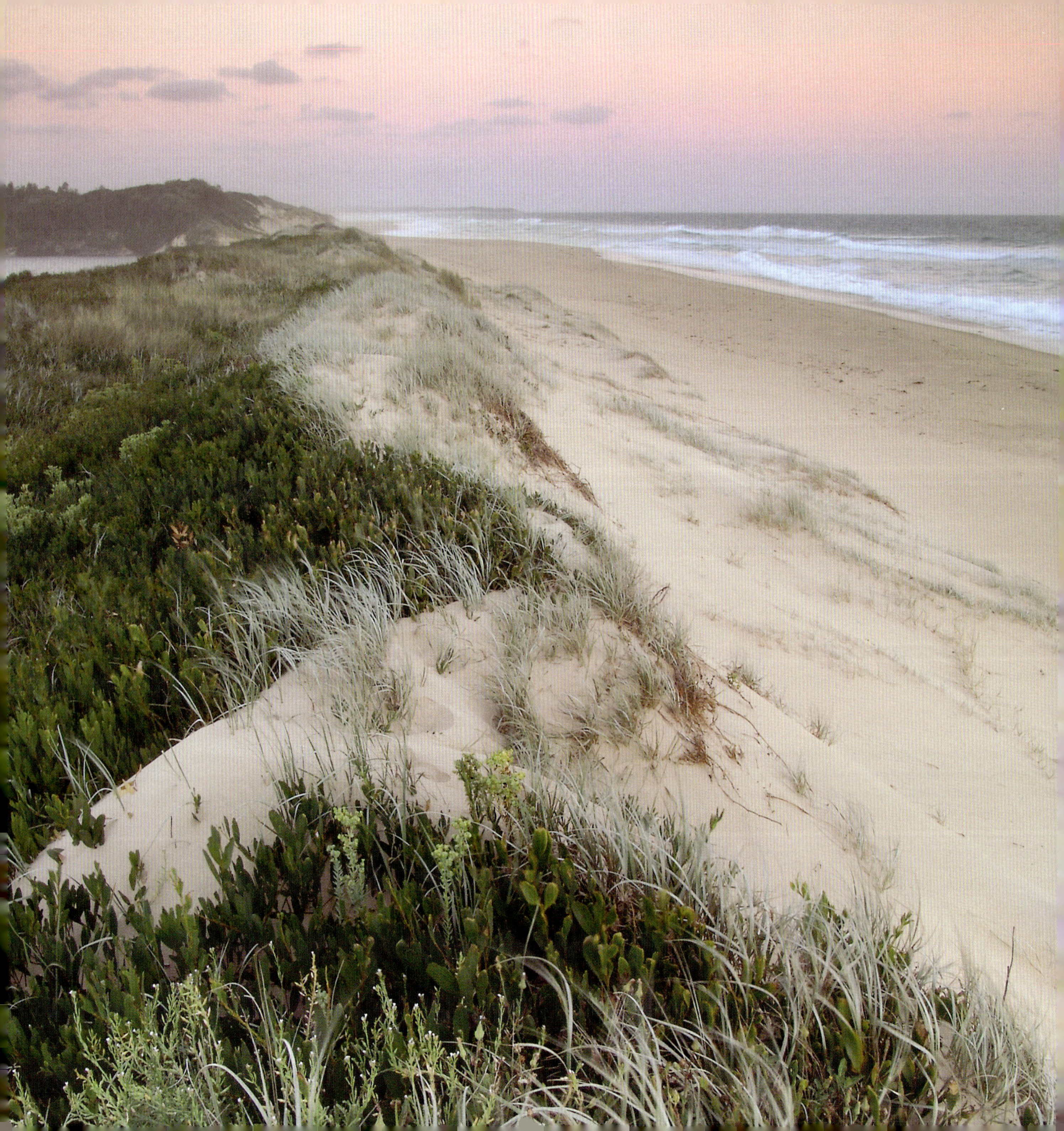

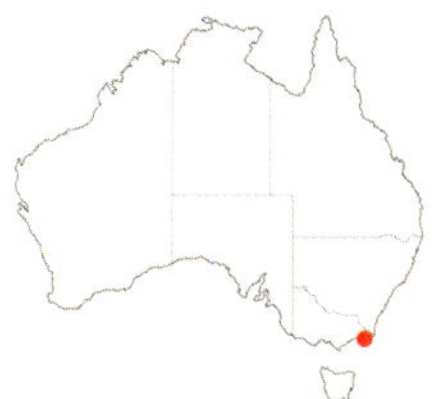

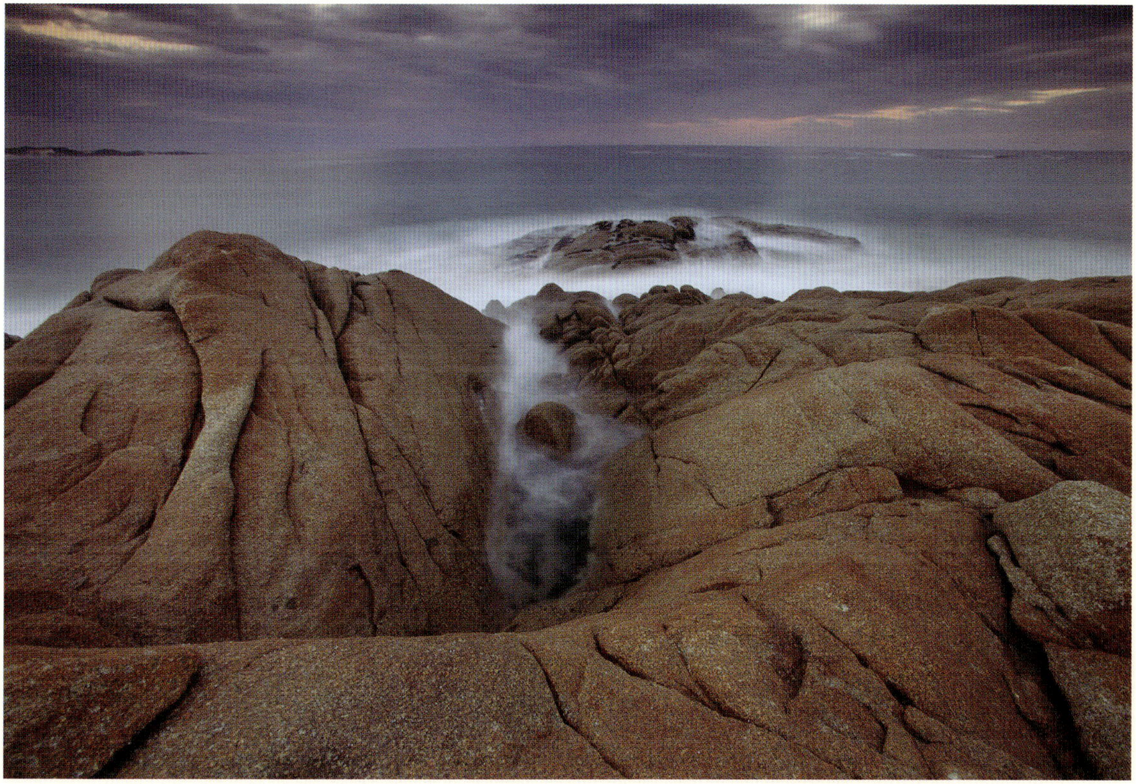

Andrew Teakle

POINT HICKS

Croajingolong National Park, VIC

YEERUNG BEACH

◀ Cape Conran Coastal Park, VIC

Debra Doenges

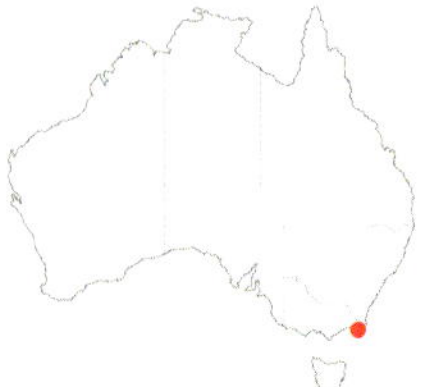

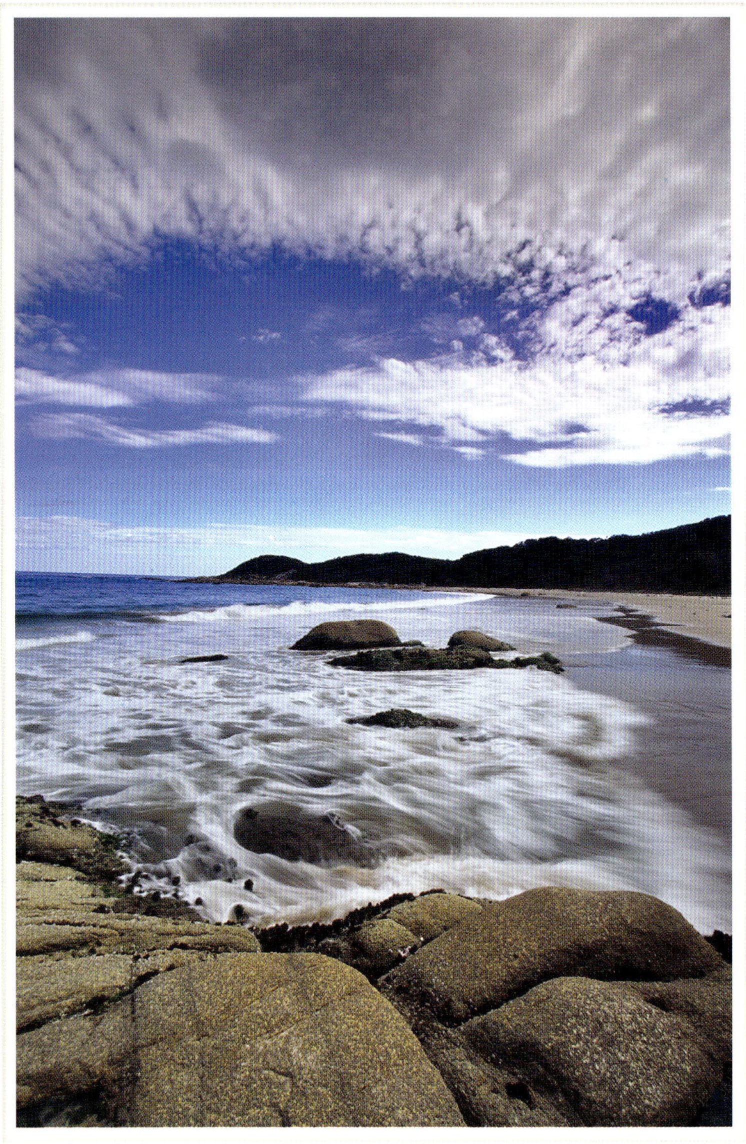

POINT HICKS

Croajingolong National Park, VIC

Andrew Teakle

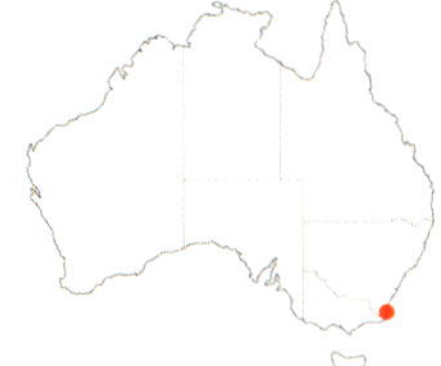

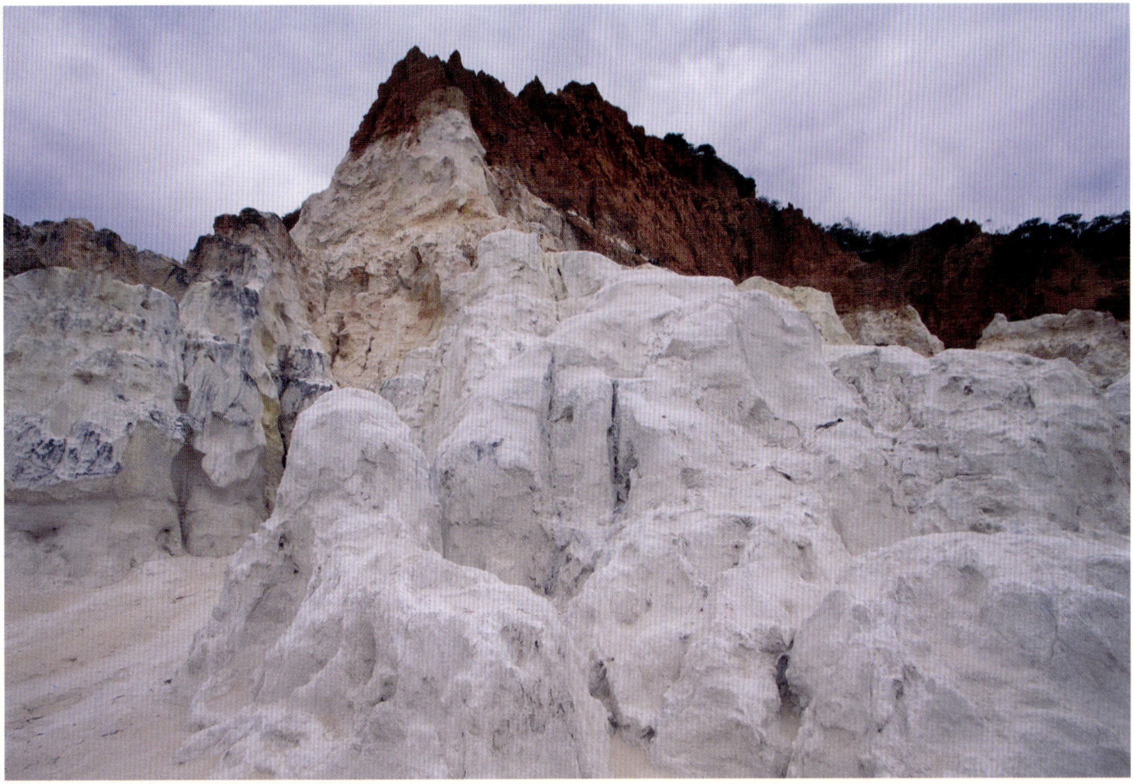

Andrew Teakle & Debra Doenges

PINNACLES

Ben Boyd National Park, NSW

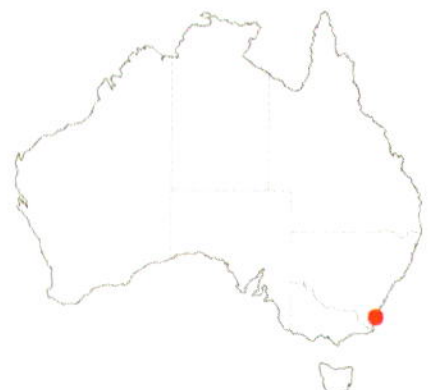

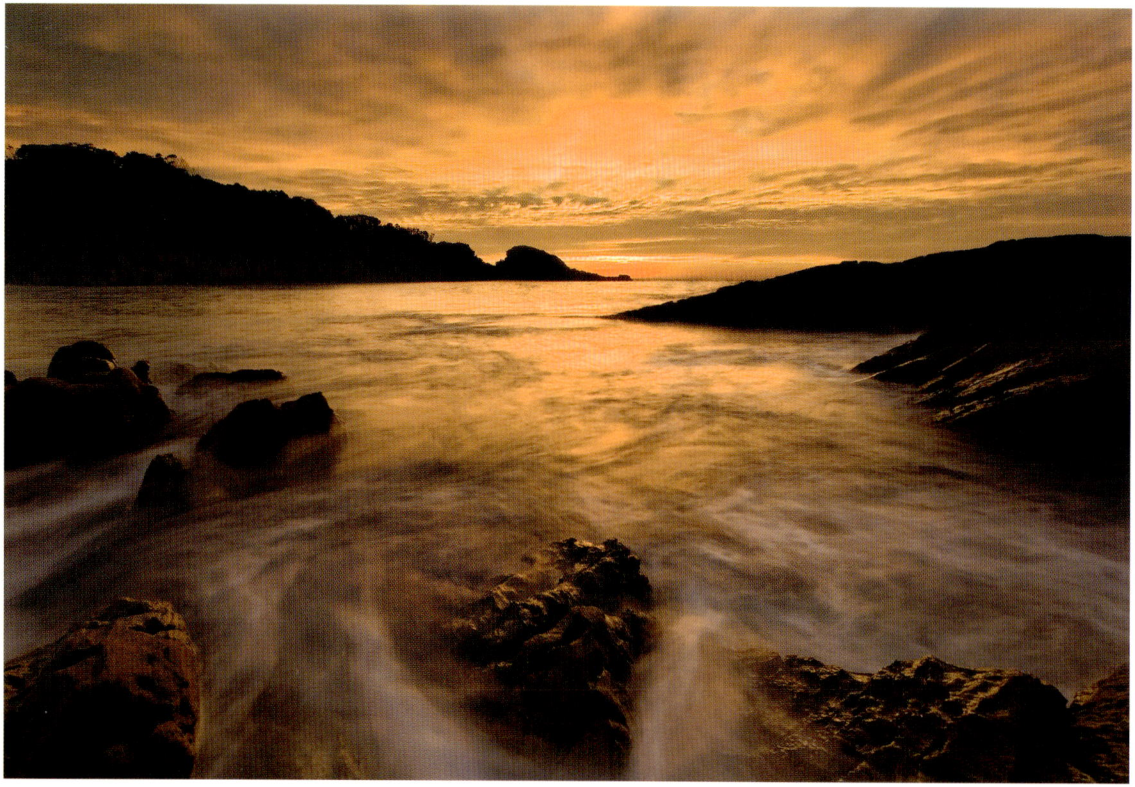

DAWN OVER MOON BAY

Mimosa Rocks National Park, NSW

Andrew Teakle

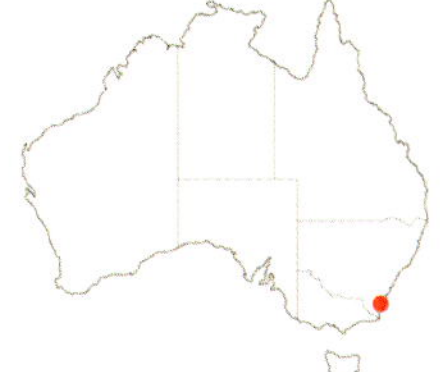

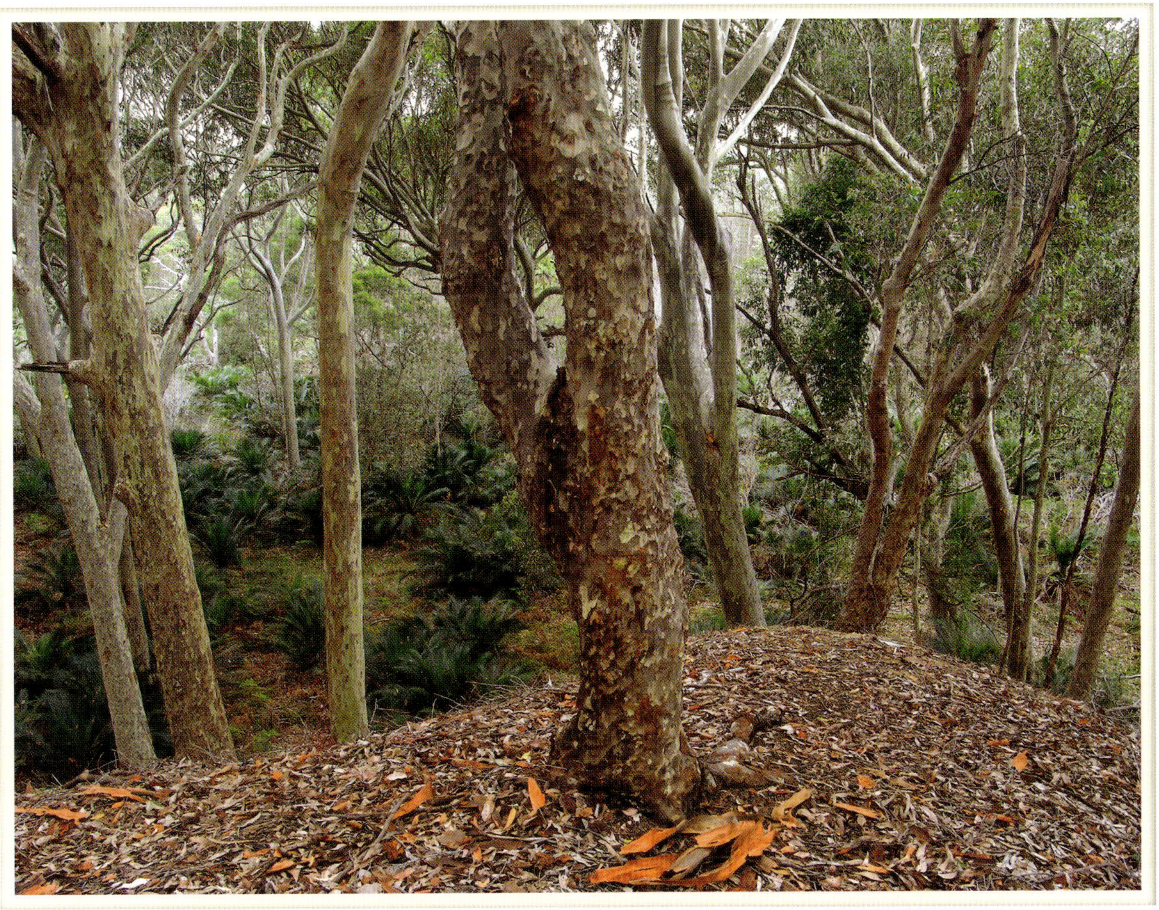

Debra Doenges

SPOTTED GUM FOREST

Mimosa Rocks National Park, NSW

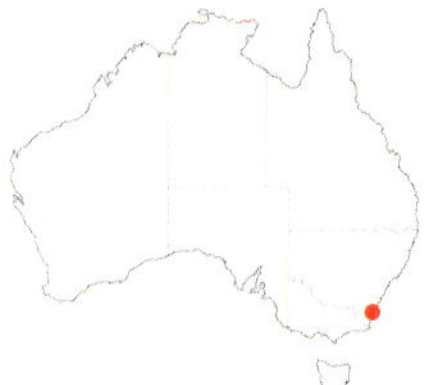

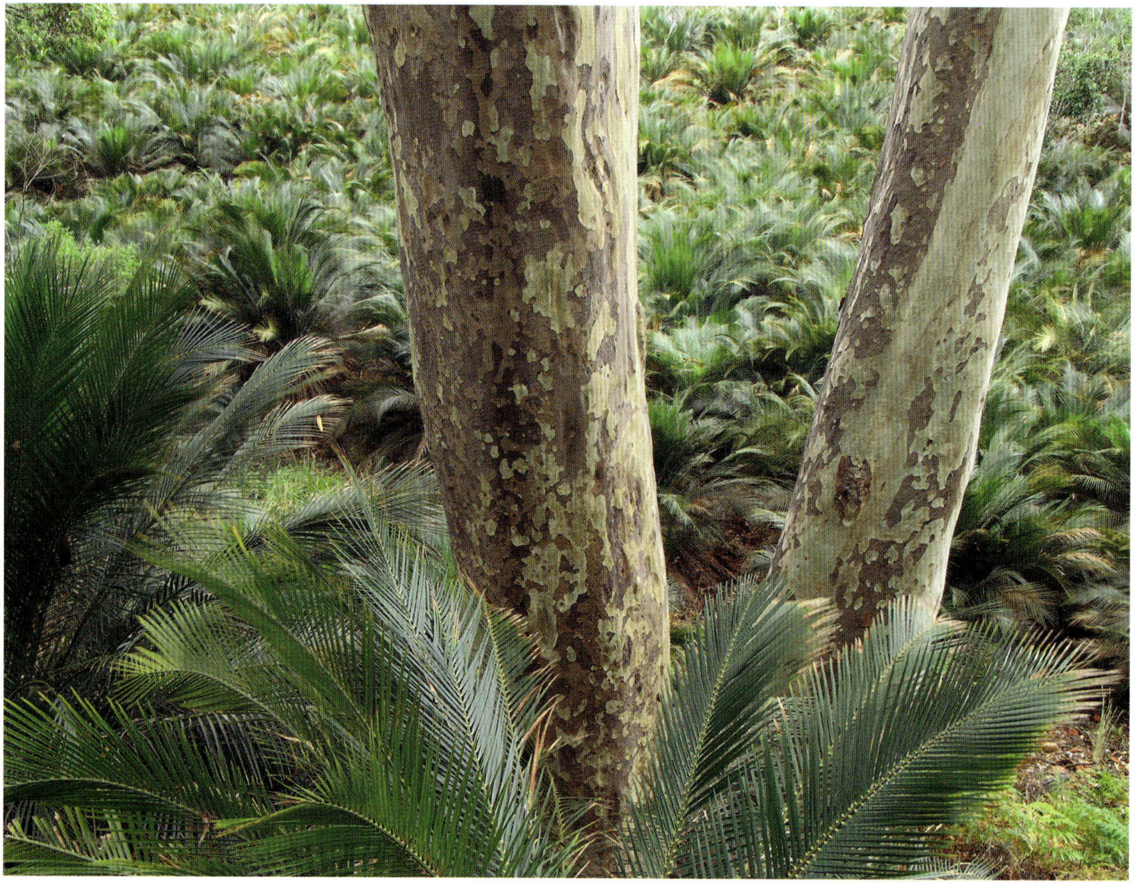

SPOTTED GUMS IN CYCAD FOREST
Mimosa Rocks National Park, NSW

Debra Doenges

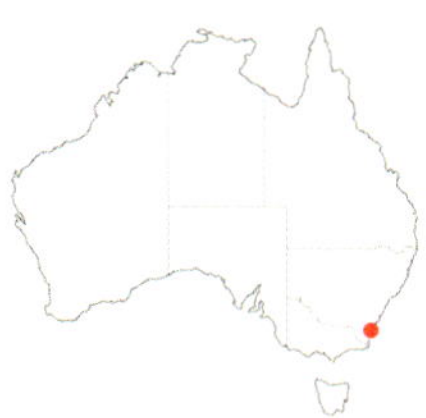

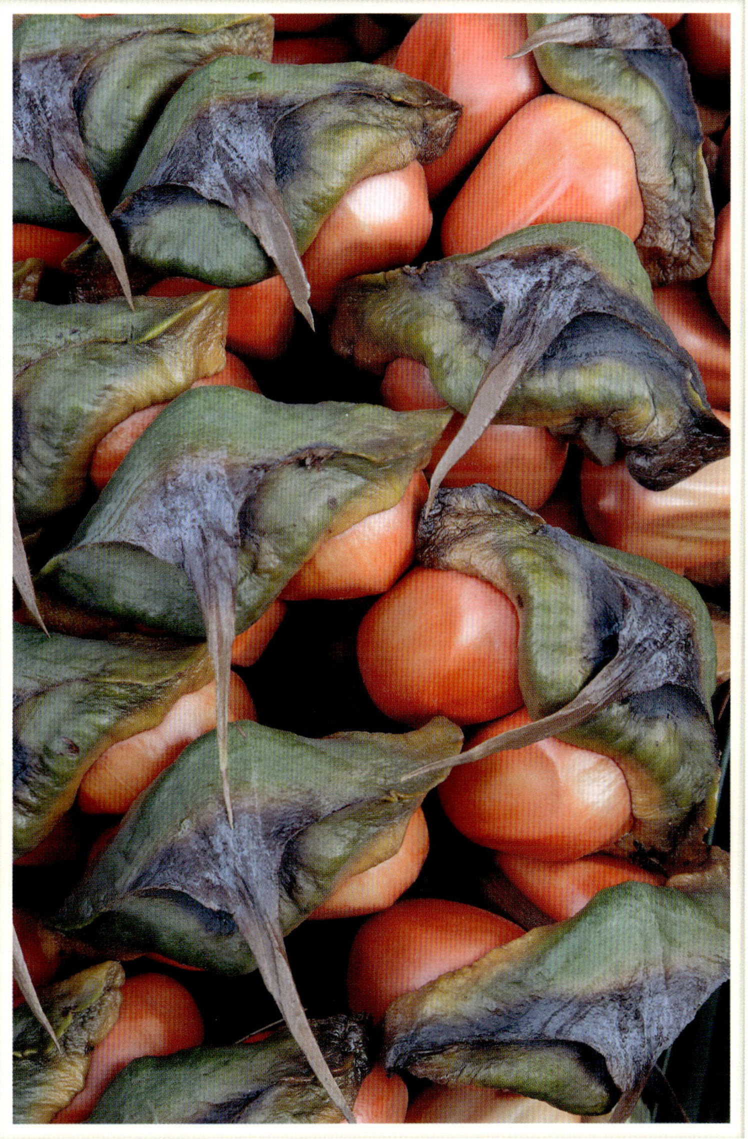

Andrew Teakle

CYCAD FRUIT

Mimosa Rocks National Park, NSW

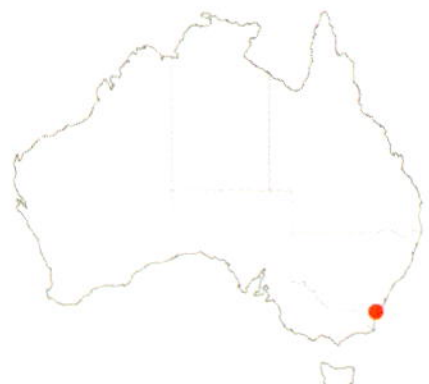

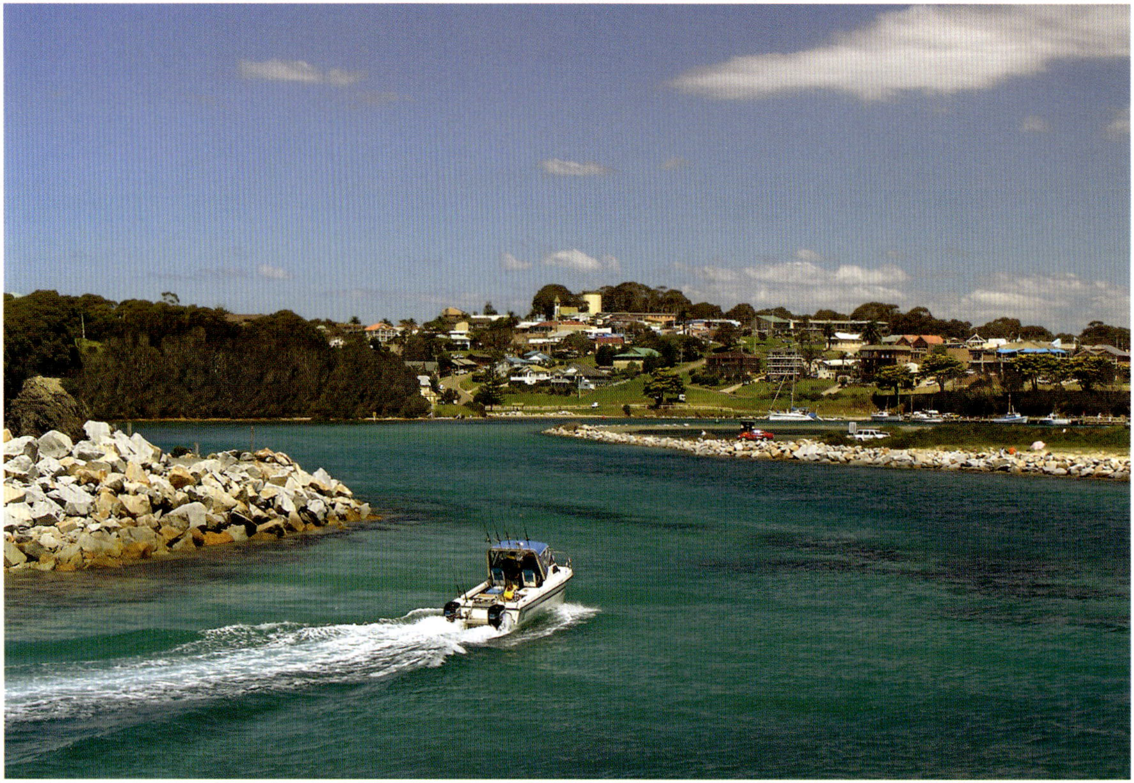

WARGONGA INLET
Narooma, NSW

Debra Doenges & Andrew Teakle

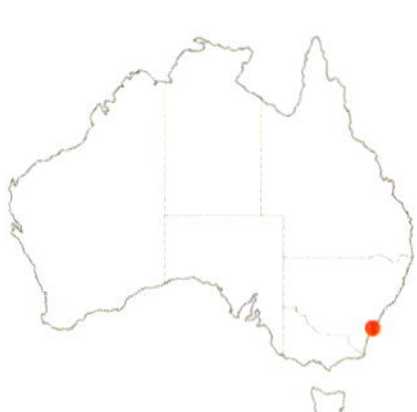

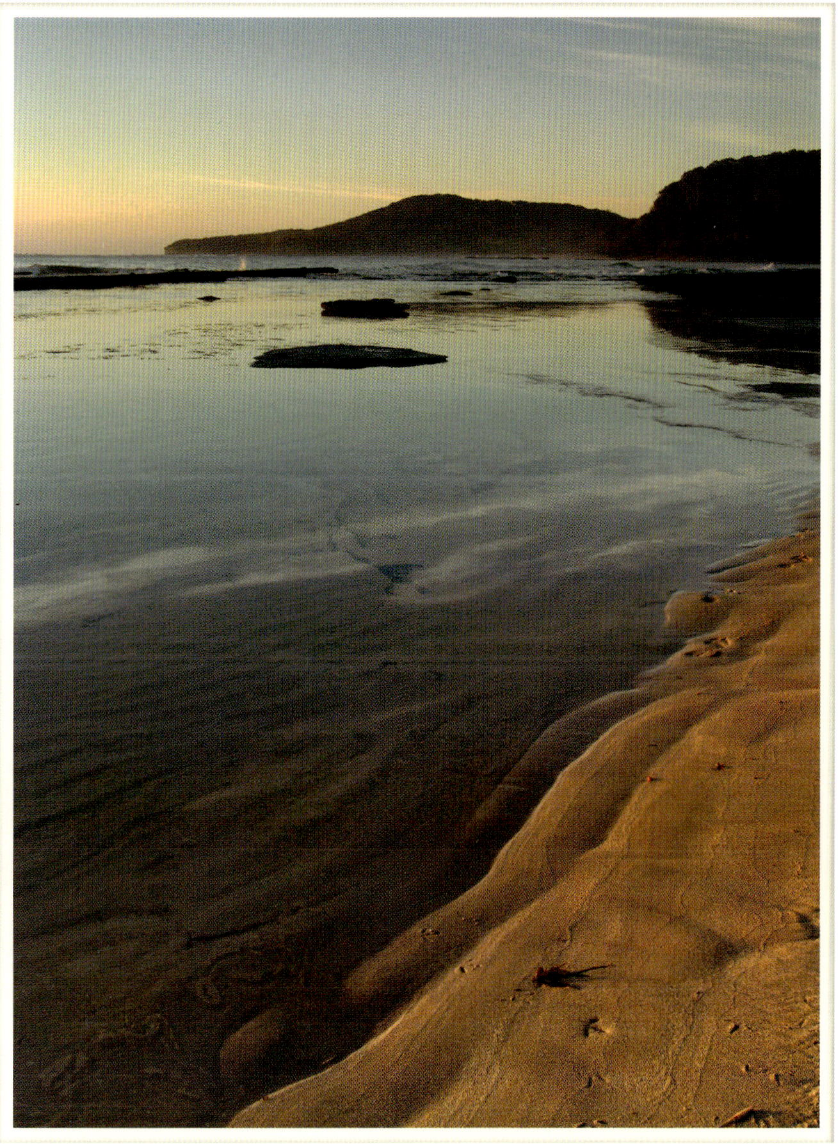

Debra Doenges

PEBBLY BEACH

Murramarang National Park, NSW

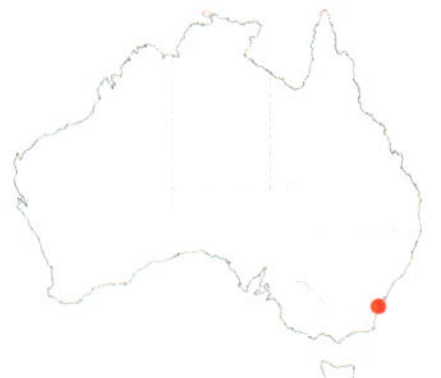

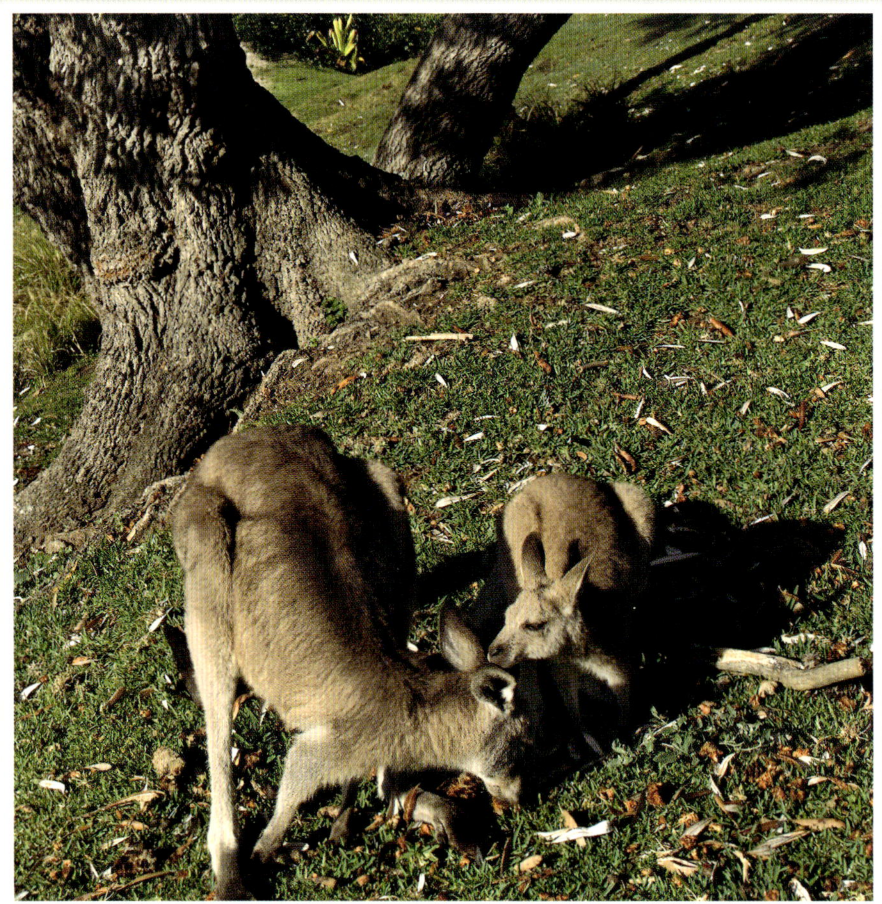

JOEY & MOTHER KANGAROO
Pebbly Beach, Murramarang National Park, NSW

Debra Doenges

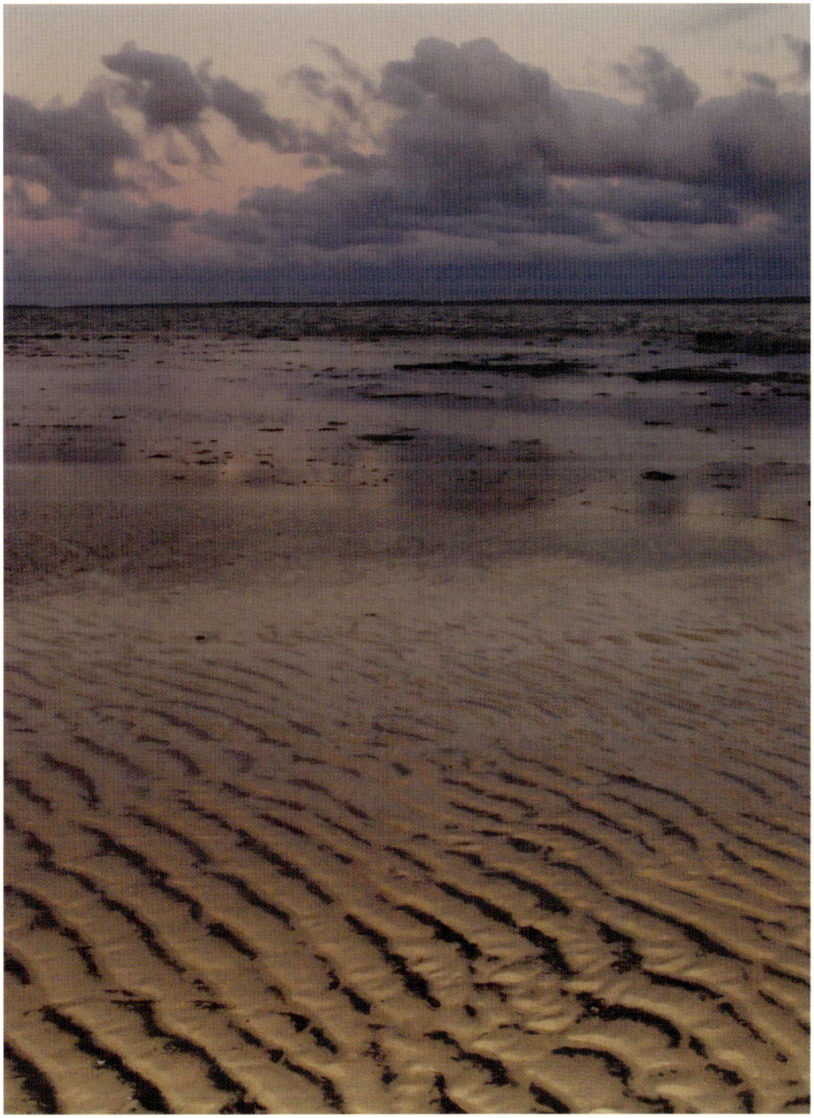

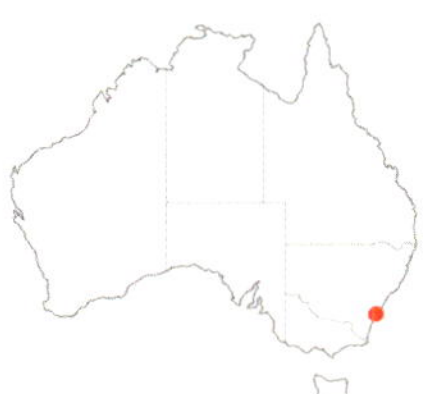

Debra Doenges

TWILIGHT SAND PATTERNS

Jervis Bay, NSW

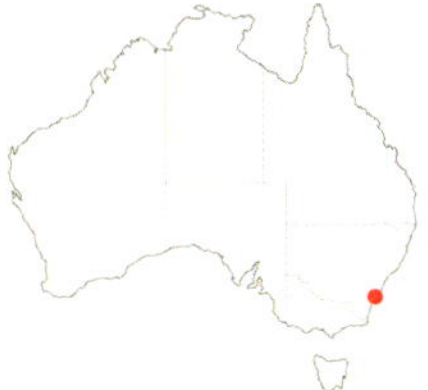

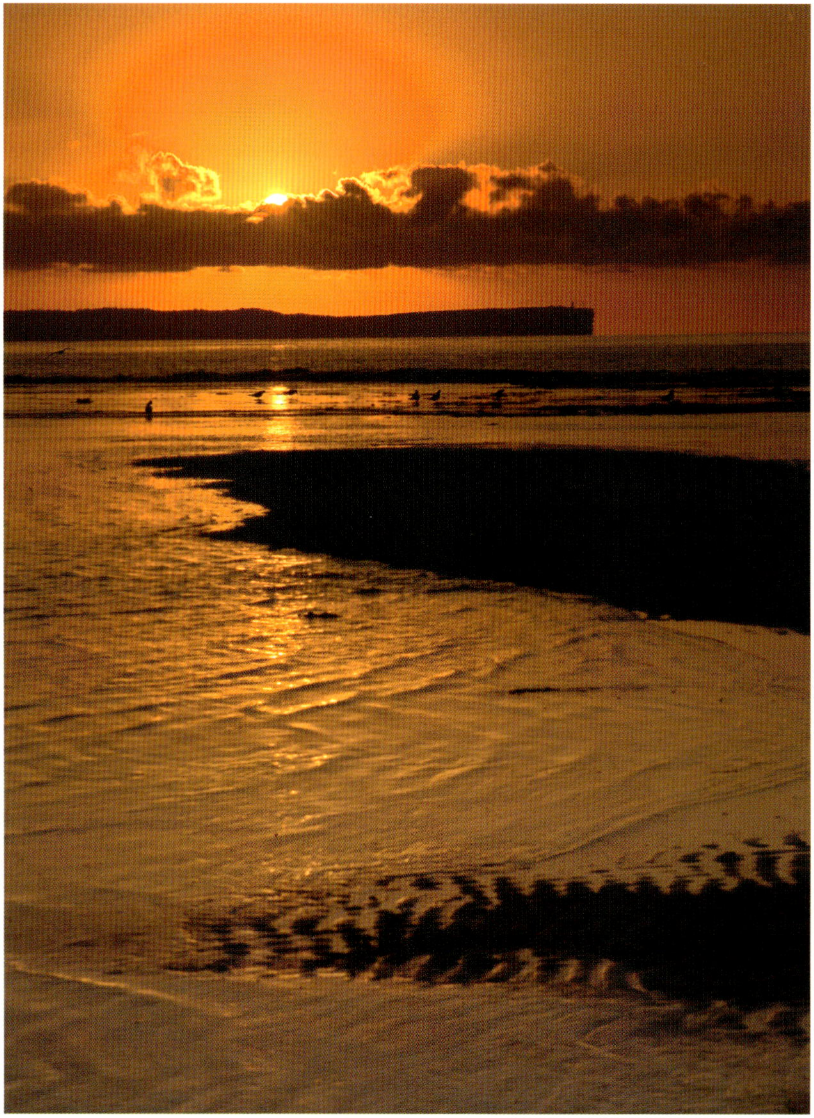

34

DAWN OVER BEECROFT PENINSULA
Jervis Bay, NSW

Debra Doenges

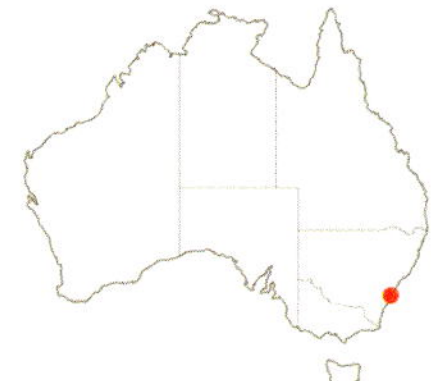

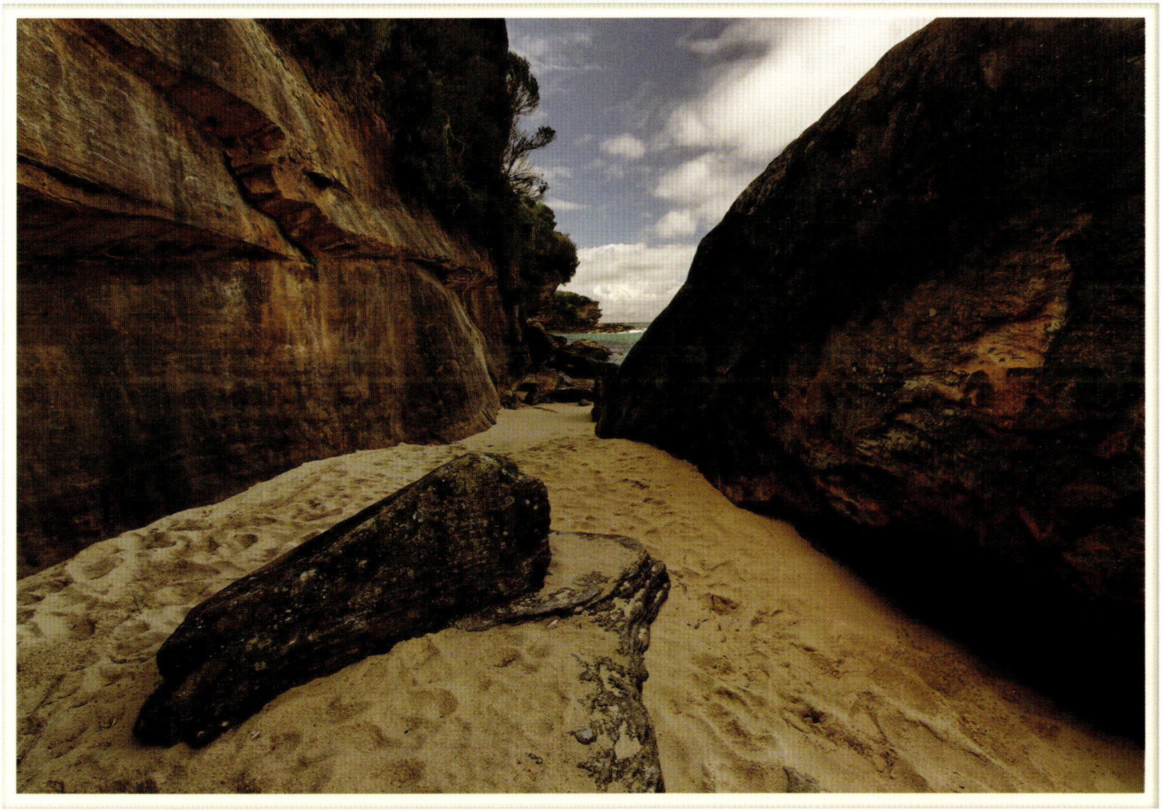

Andrew Teakle

WATTAMOLLA BEACH

Royal National Park, NSW

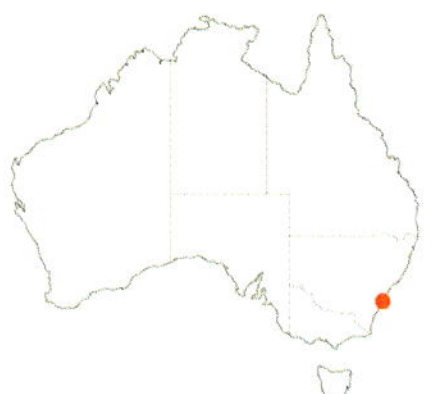

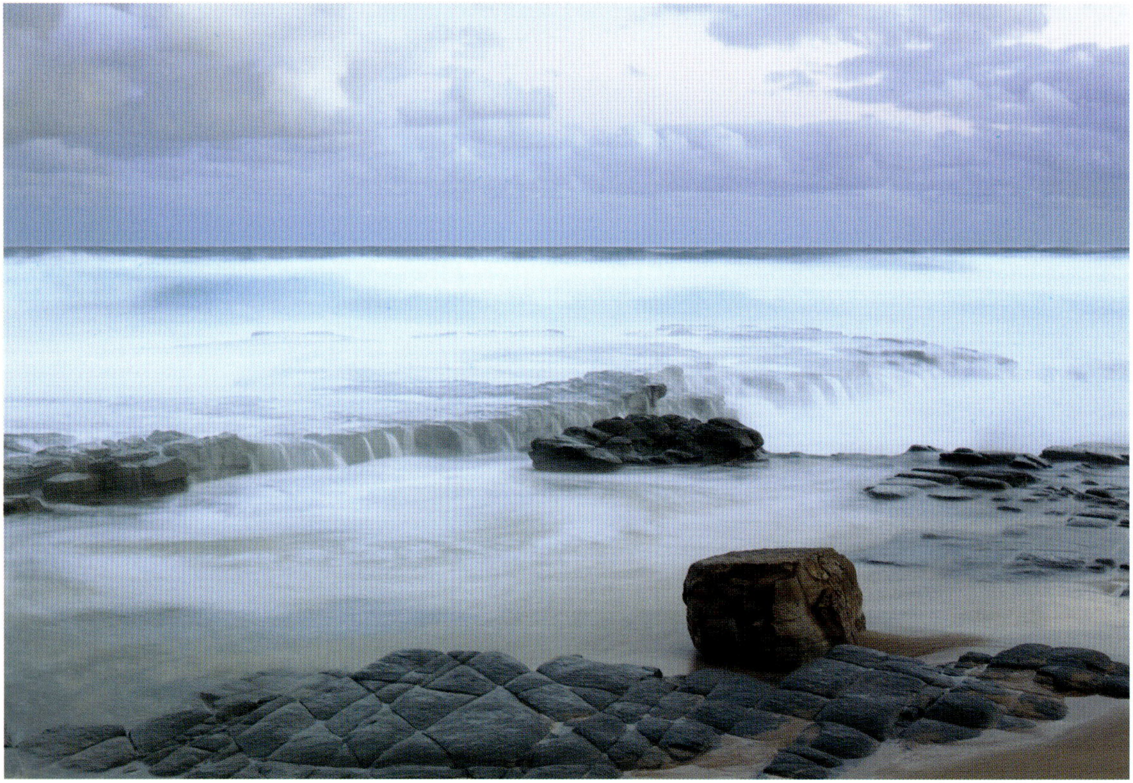

GAIRIE BEACH

Royal National Park, NSW

Debra Doenges

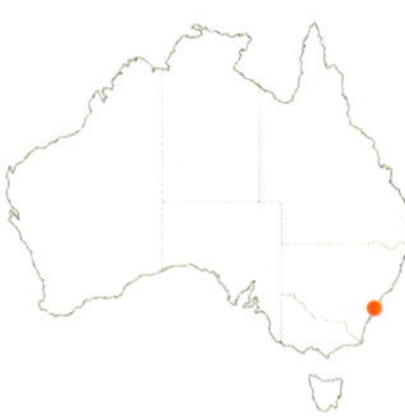

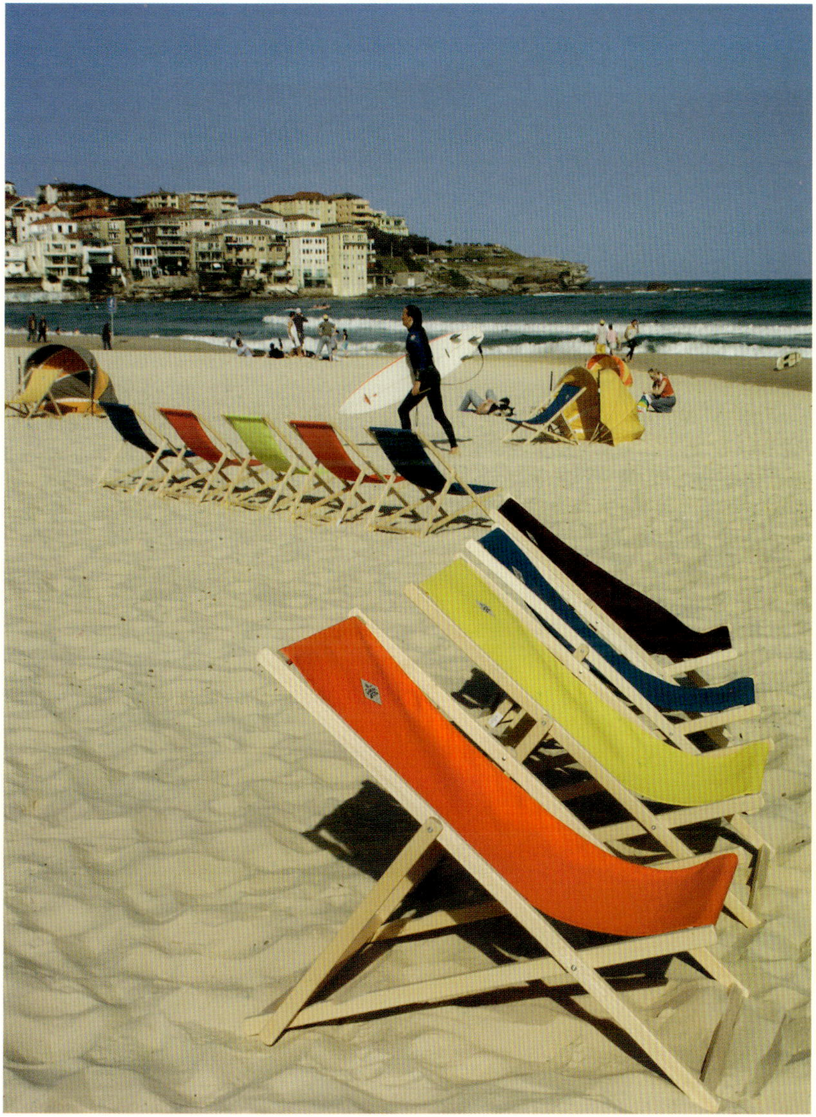

Debra Doenges

BONDI BEACH

Sydney, NSW

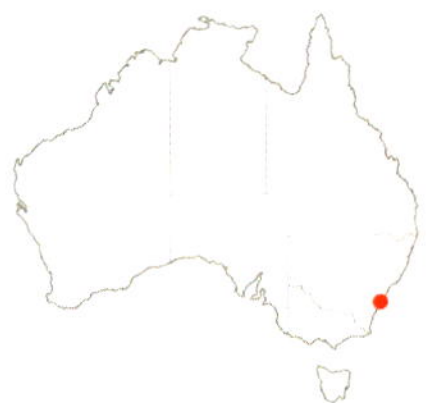

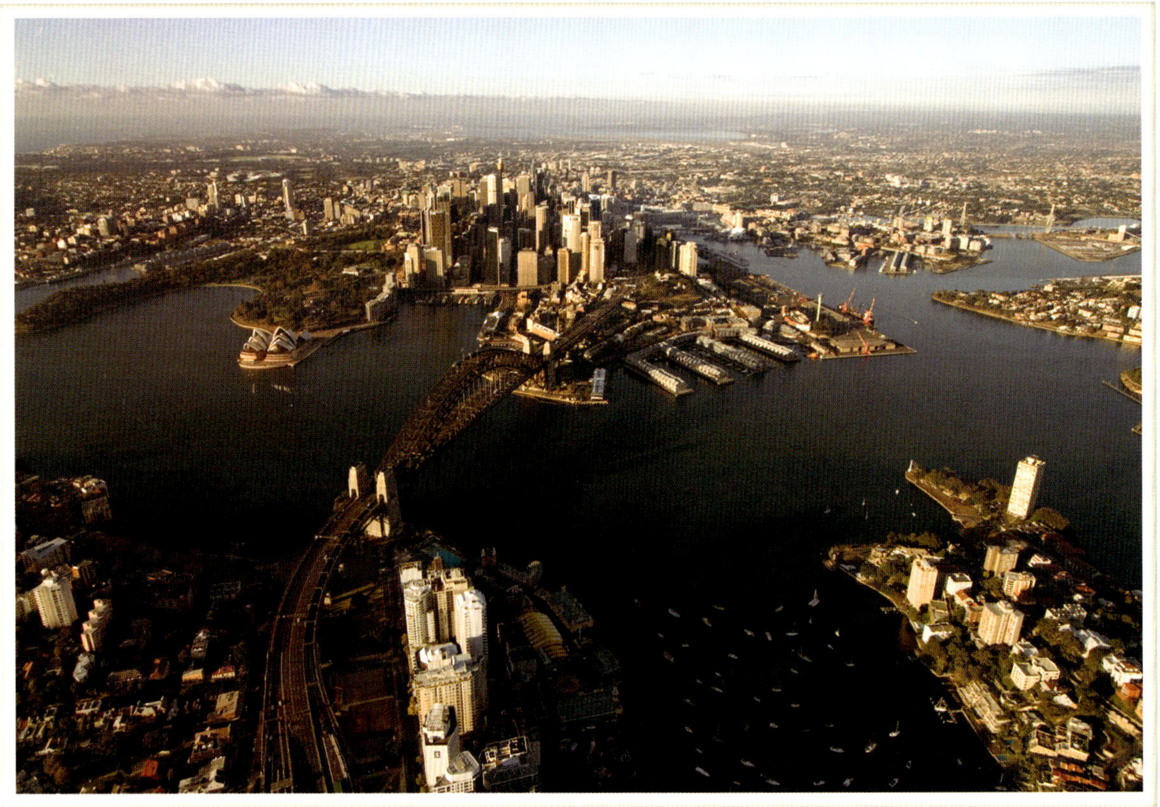

SYDNEY HARBOUR

Sydney, NSW

Andrew Teakle

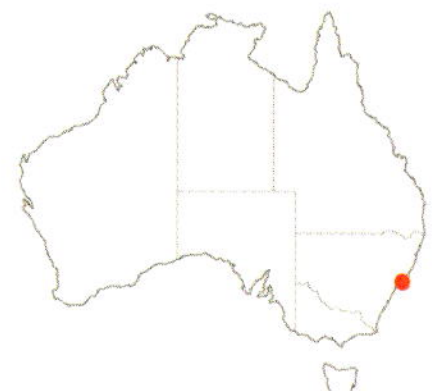

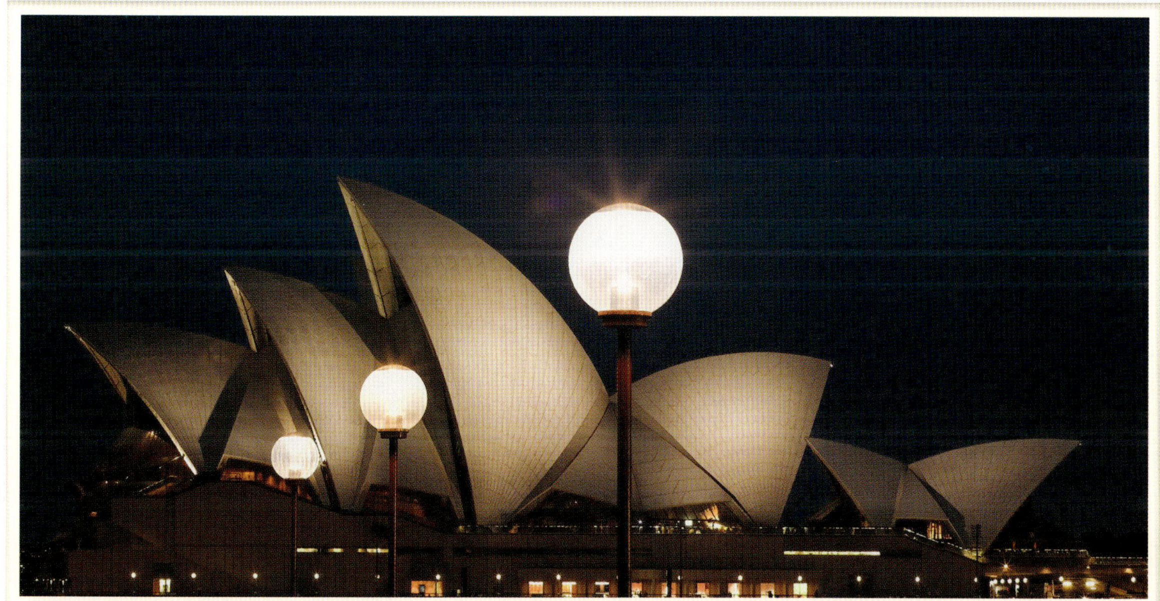

Debra Doenges

OPERA HOUSE AT TWILIGHT

Sydney, NSW

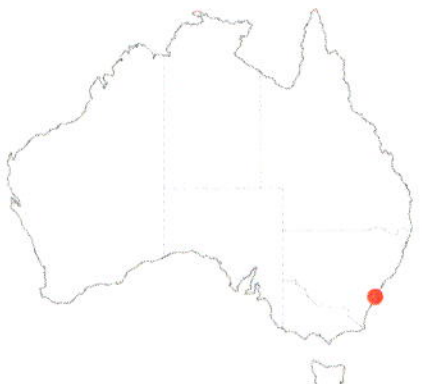

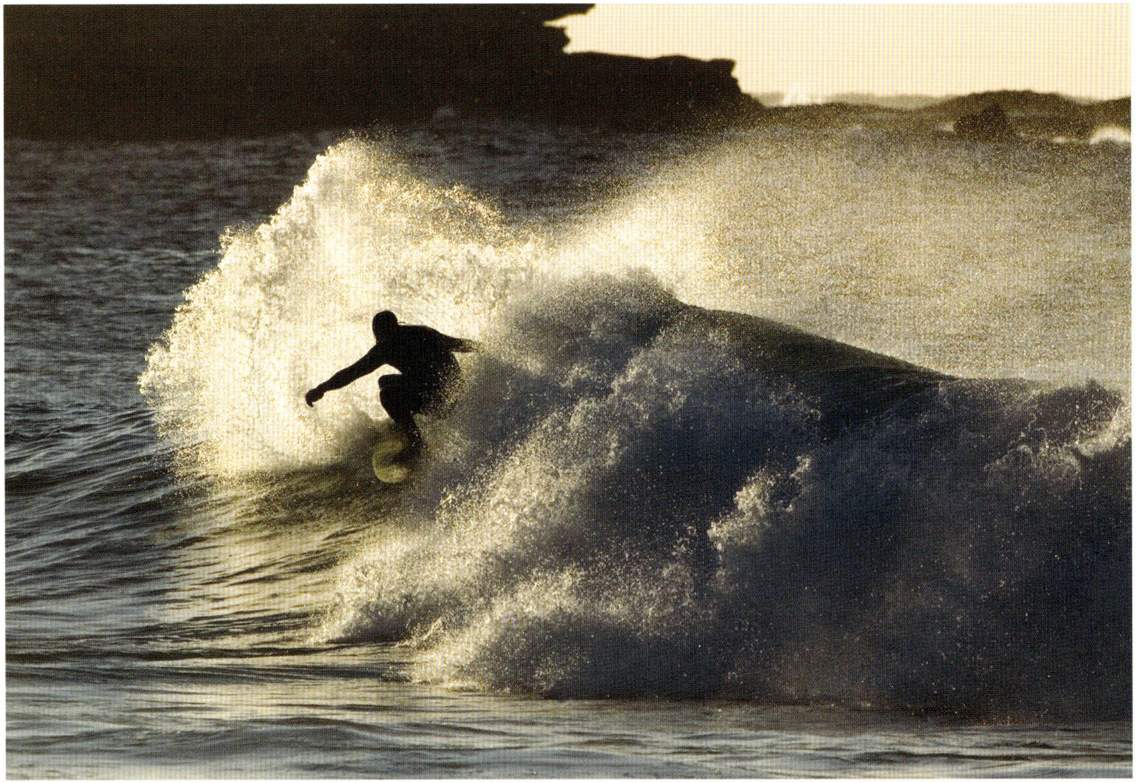

10

DAWN SURFER AT BONDI BEACH

Sydney, NSW

Andrew Teakle

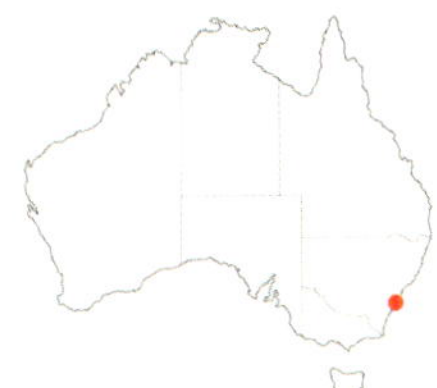

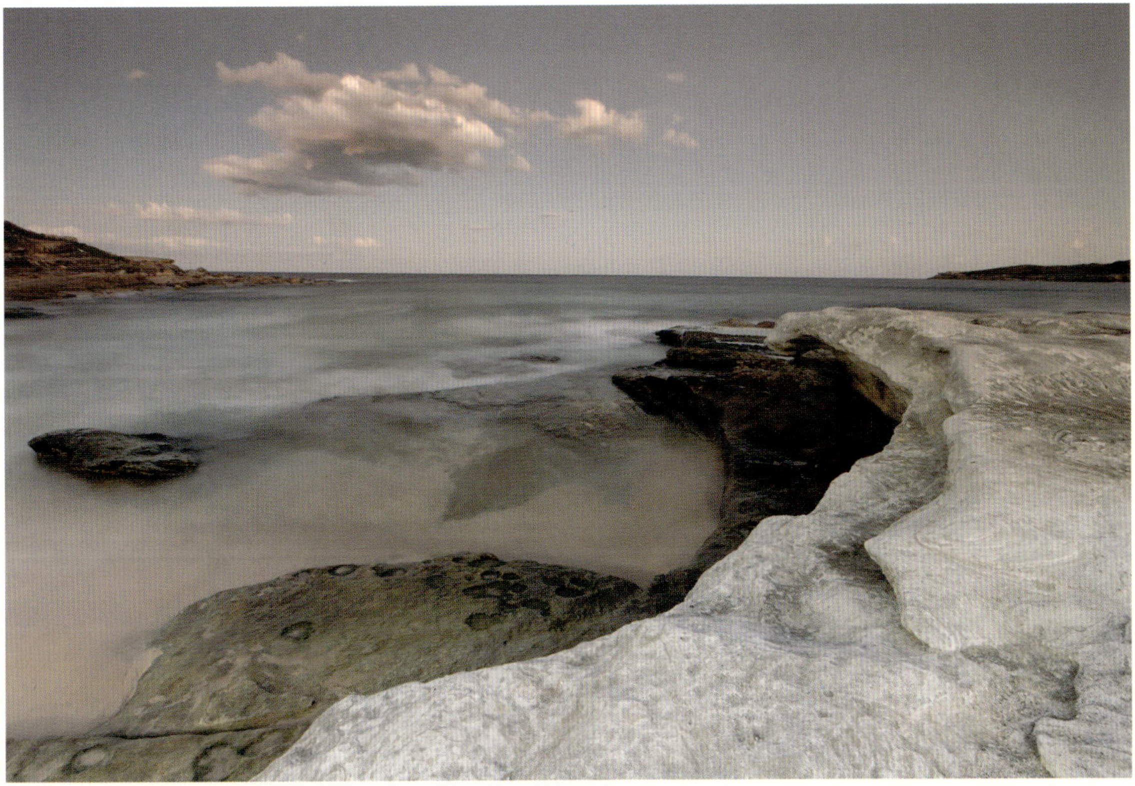

41

Andrew Teakle

MAROUBRA BEACH

Sydney, NSW

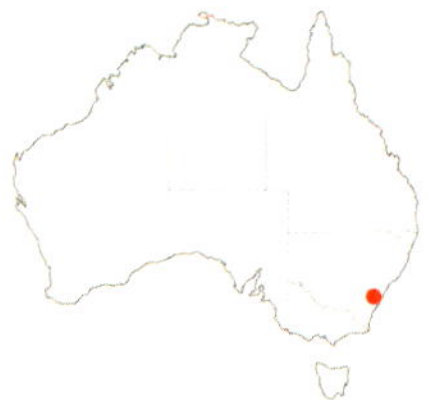

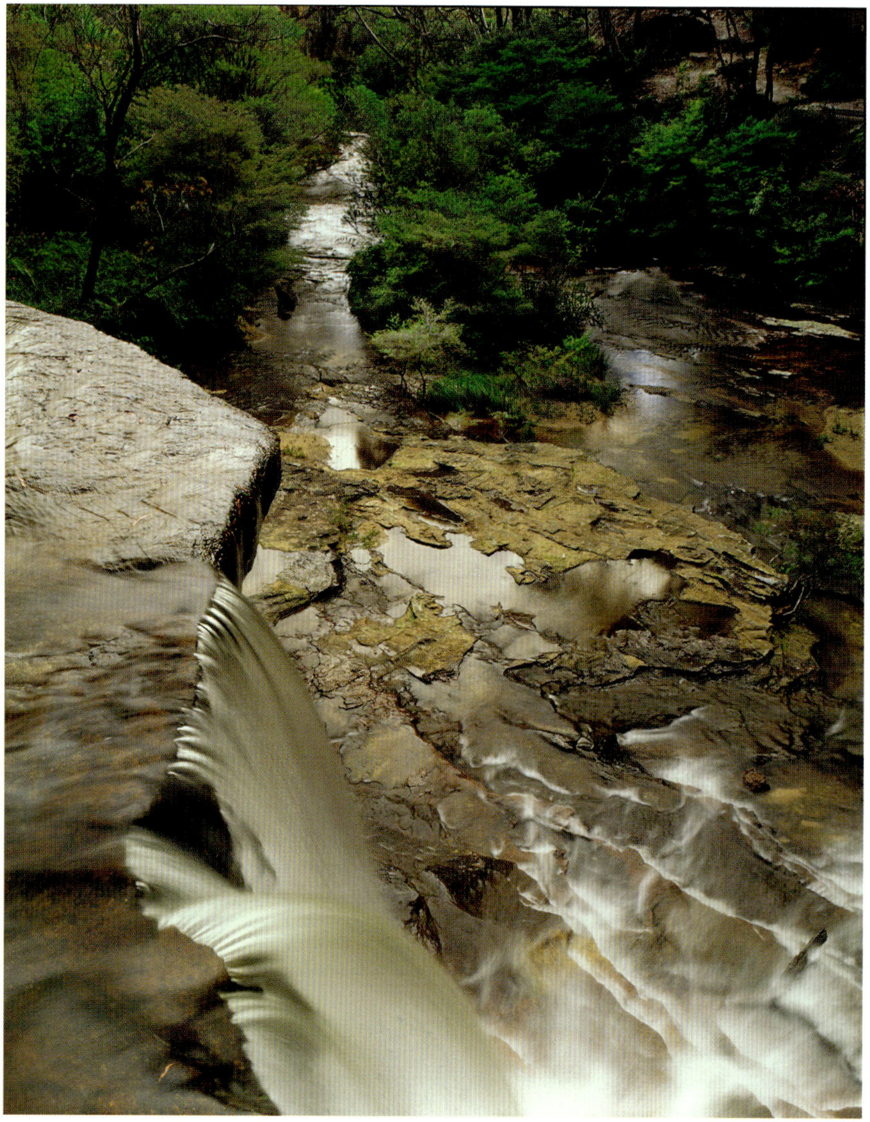

UPPER WENTWORTH FALLS
Blue Mountains National Park, NSW

Debra Doenges

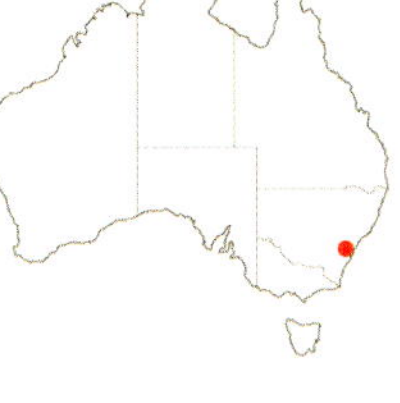

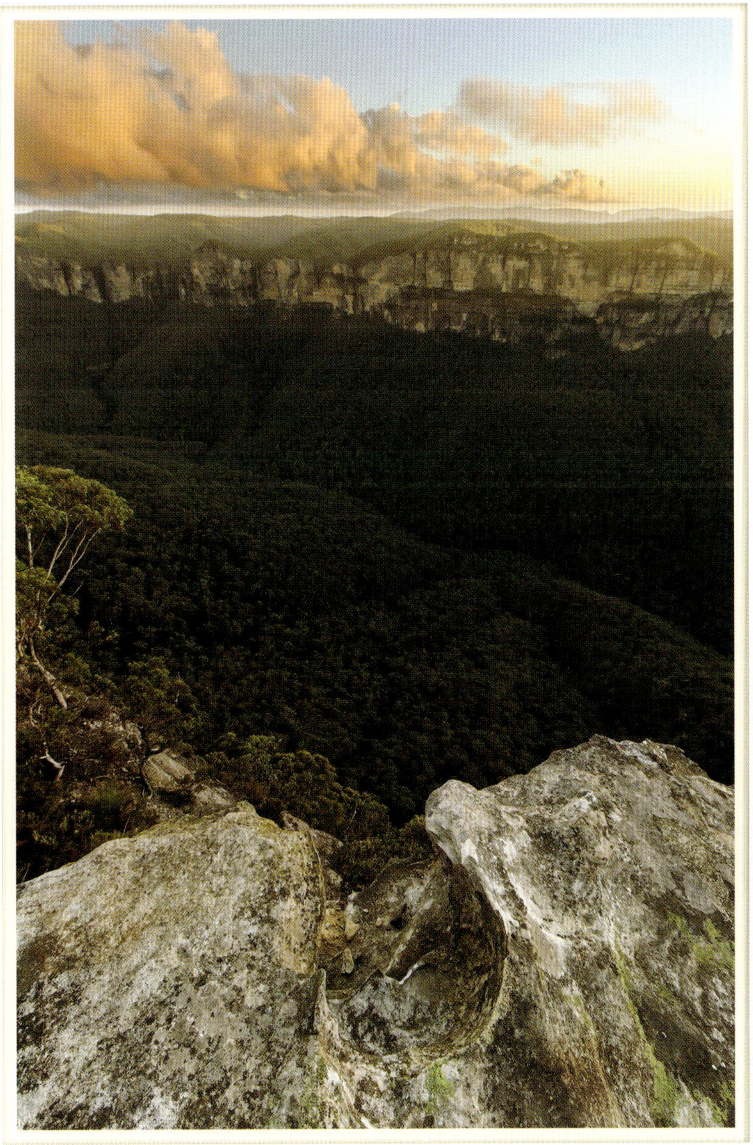

Andrew Teakle

DAWN FROM ANVIL ROCK

Blue Mountains National Park, NSW

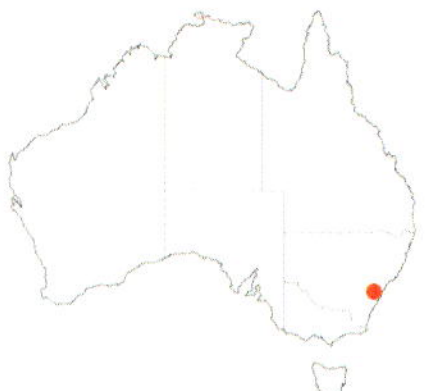

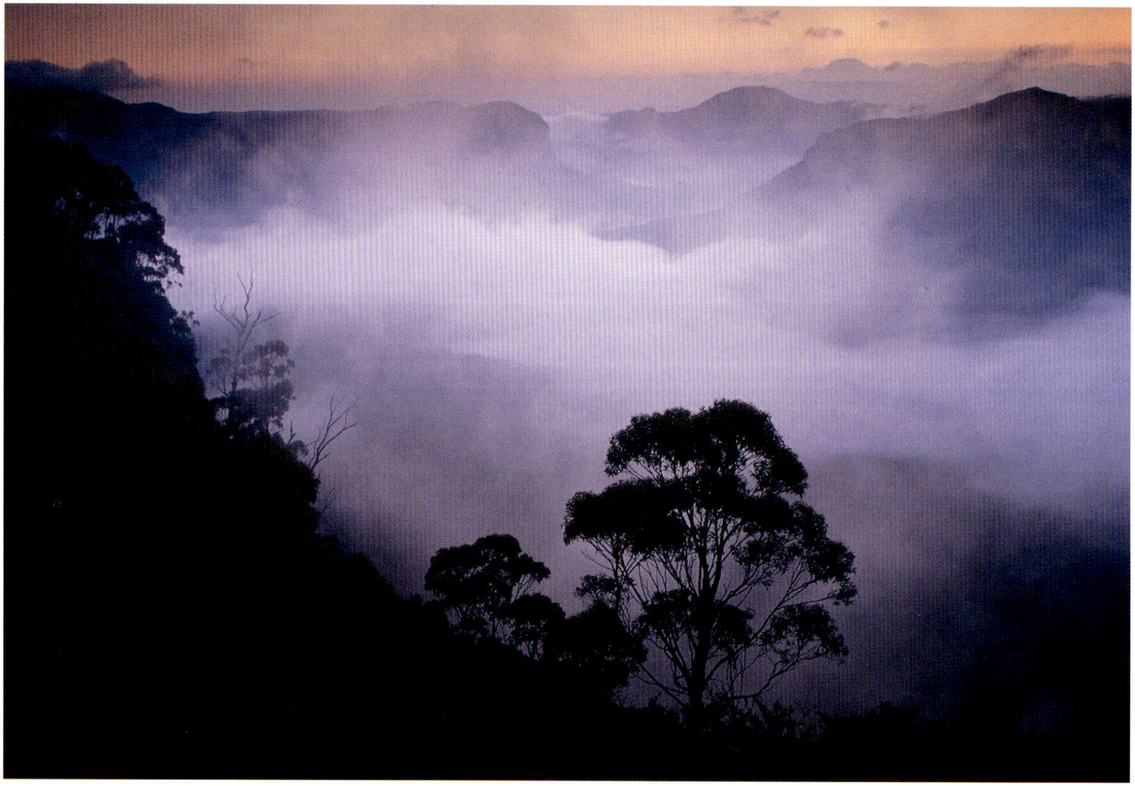

DAWN MIST

Pulpit Rock, Blue Mountains National Park, NSW

Andrew Teakle

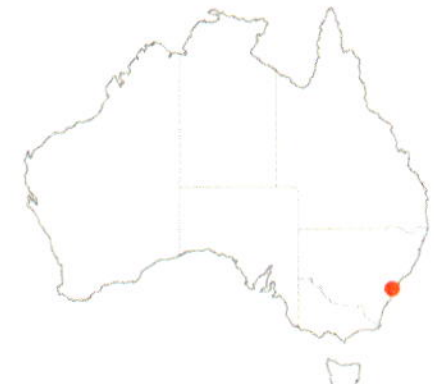

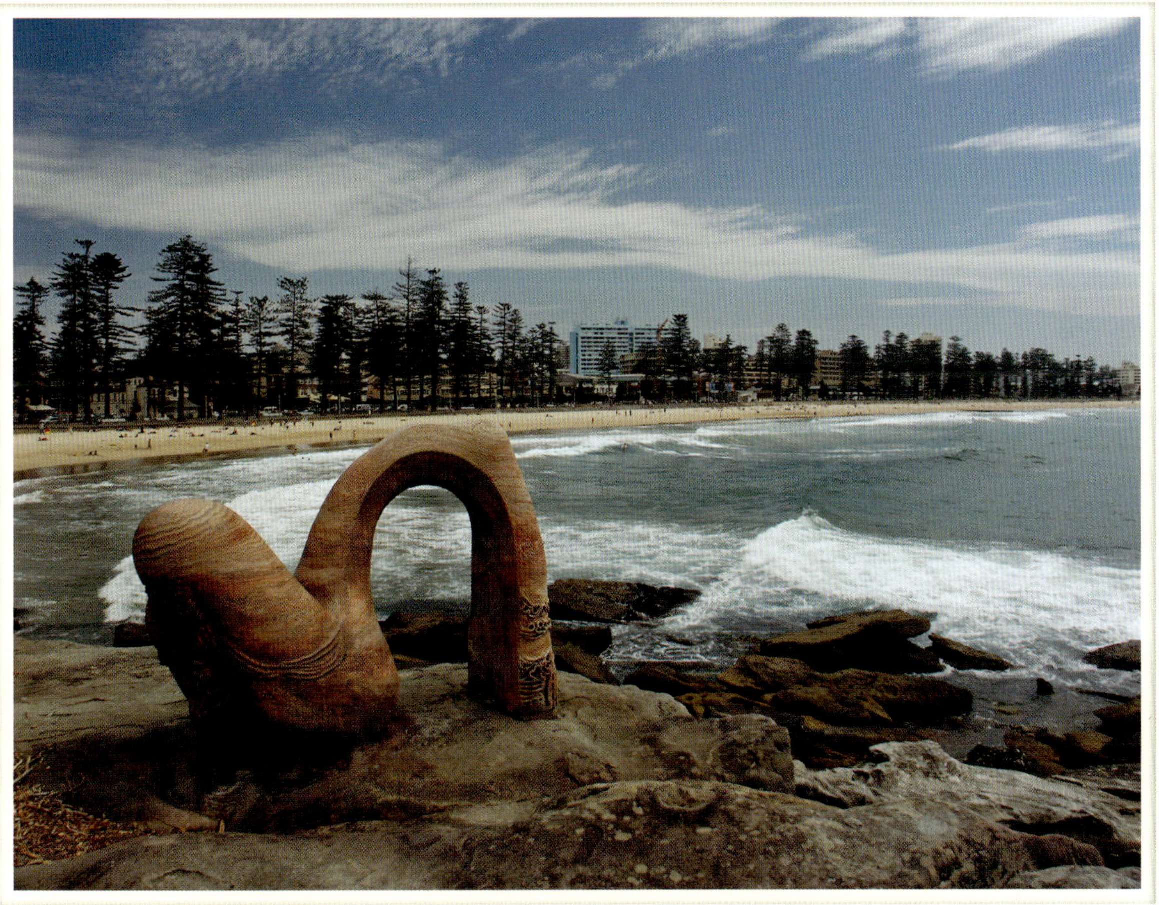

Debra Doenges & Andrew Teakle

MANLY BEACH

Manly, Sydney, NSW

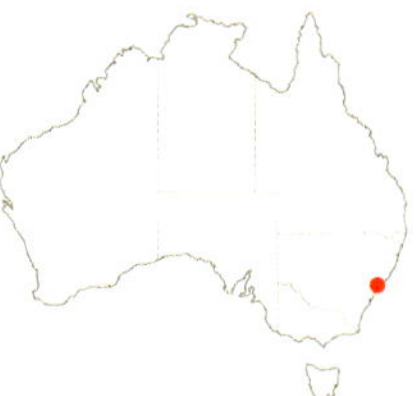

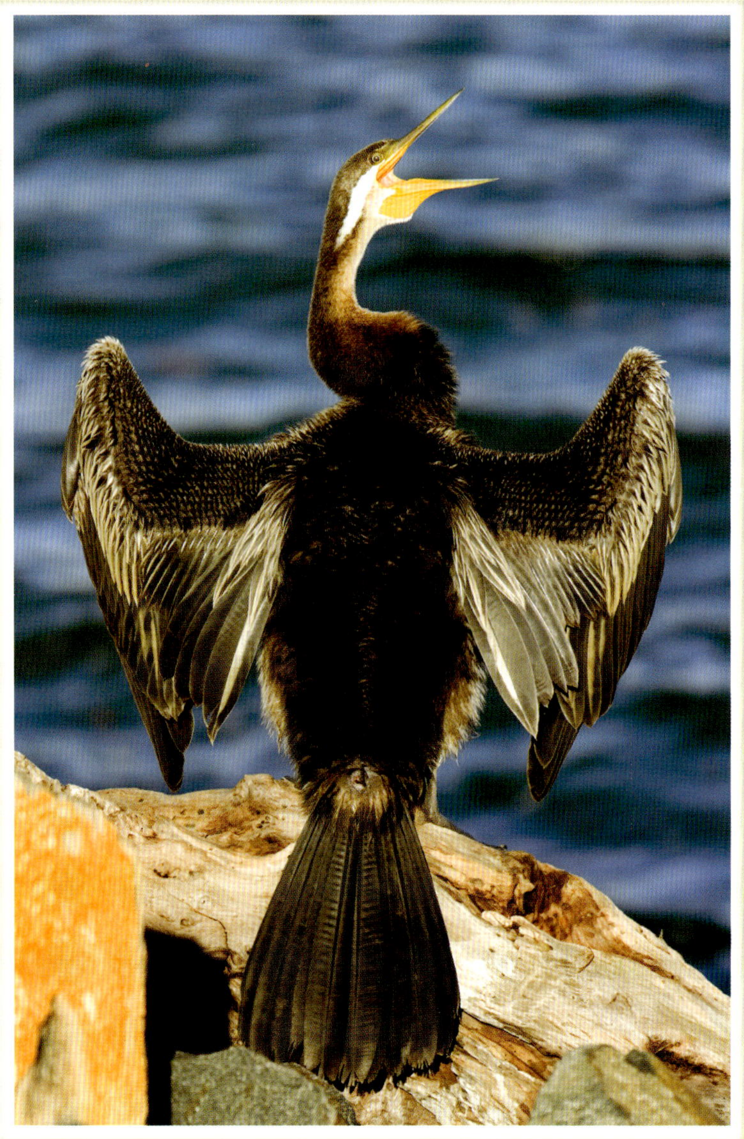

DARTER

Newcastle, NSW

Andrew Teakle

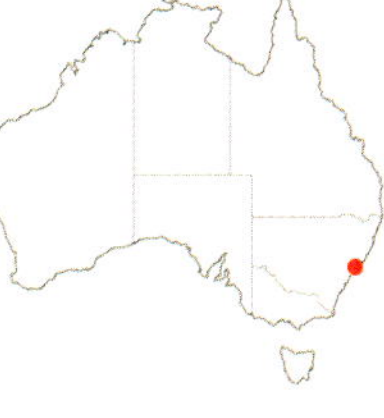

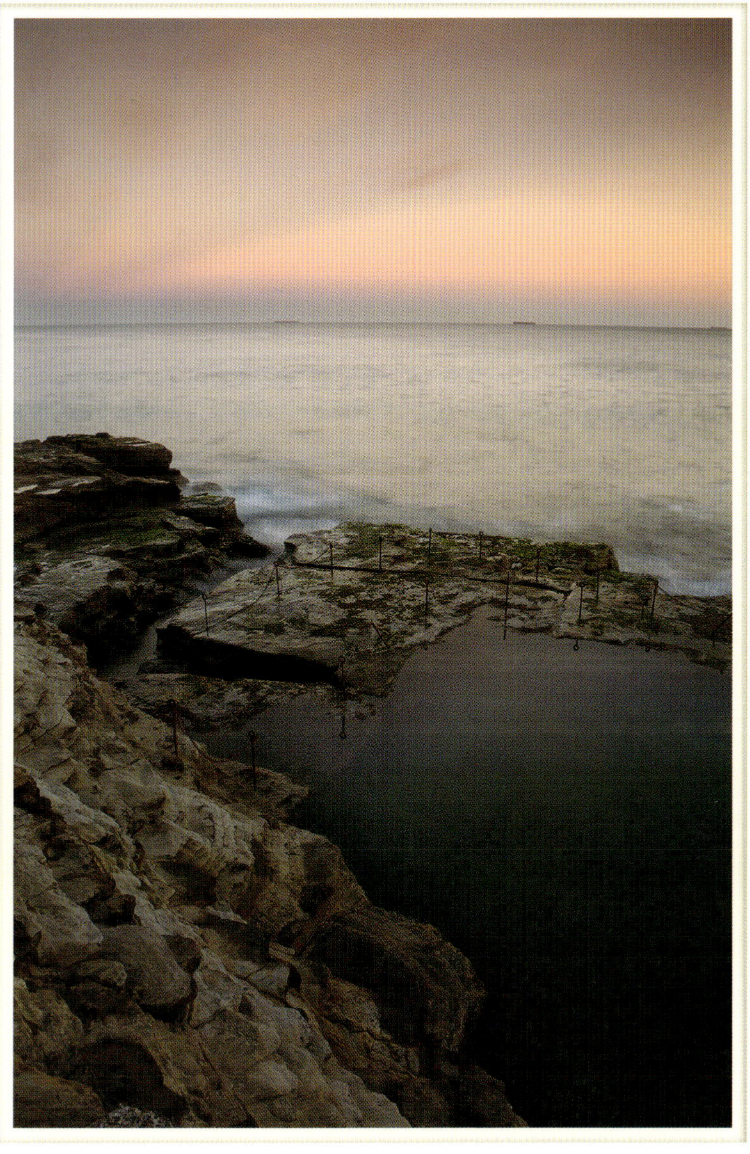

Debra Doenges

SUNSET OVER BOGEY HOLE
Newcastle, NSW

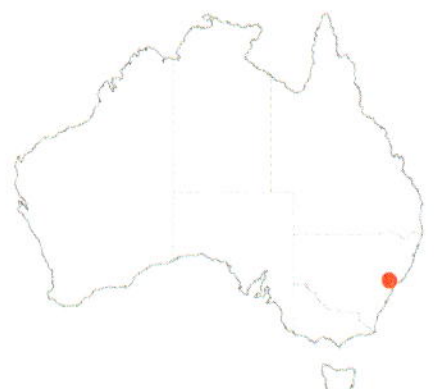

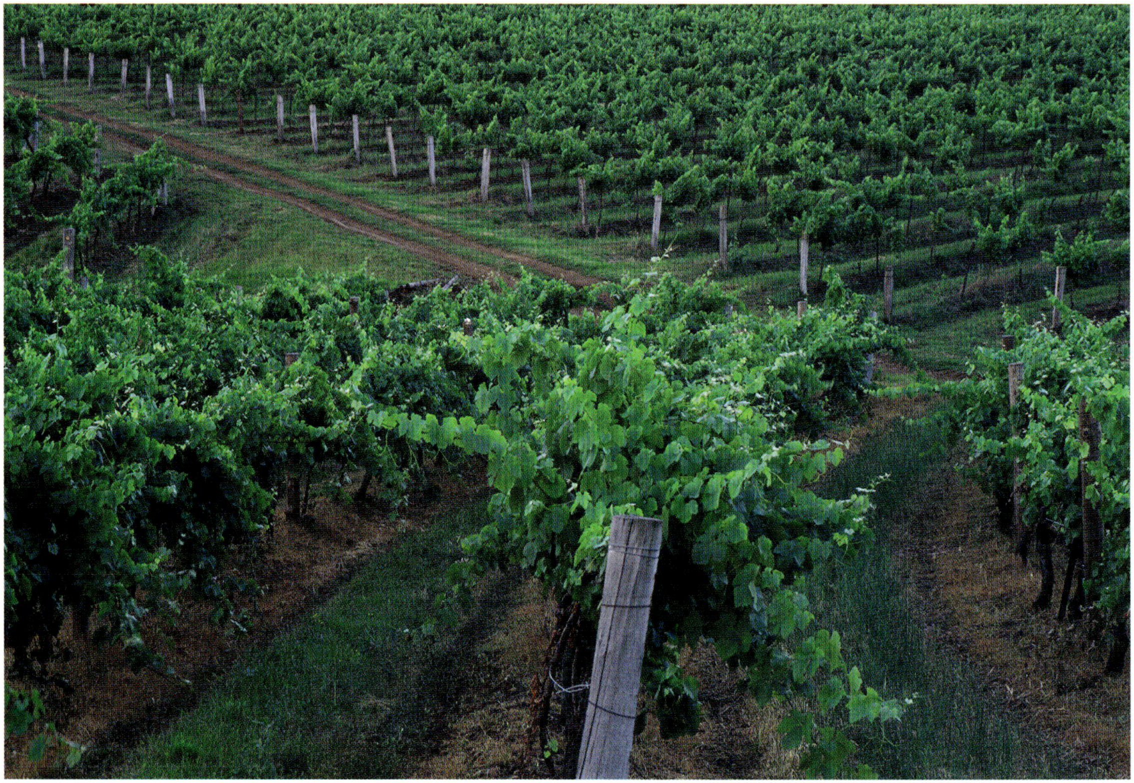

VINEYARD
Hunter Valley, NSW

Andrew Teakle

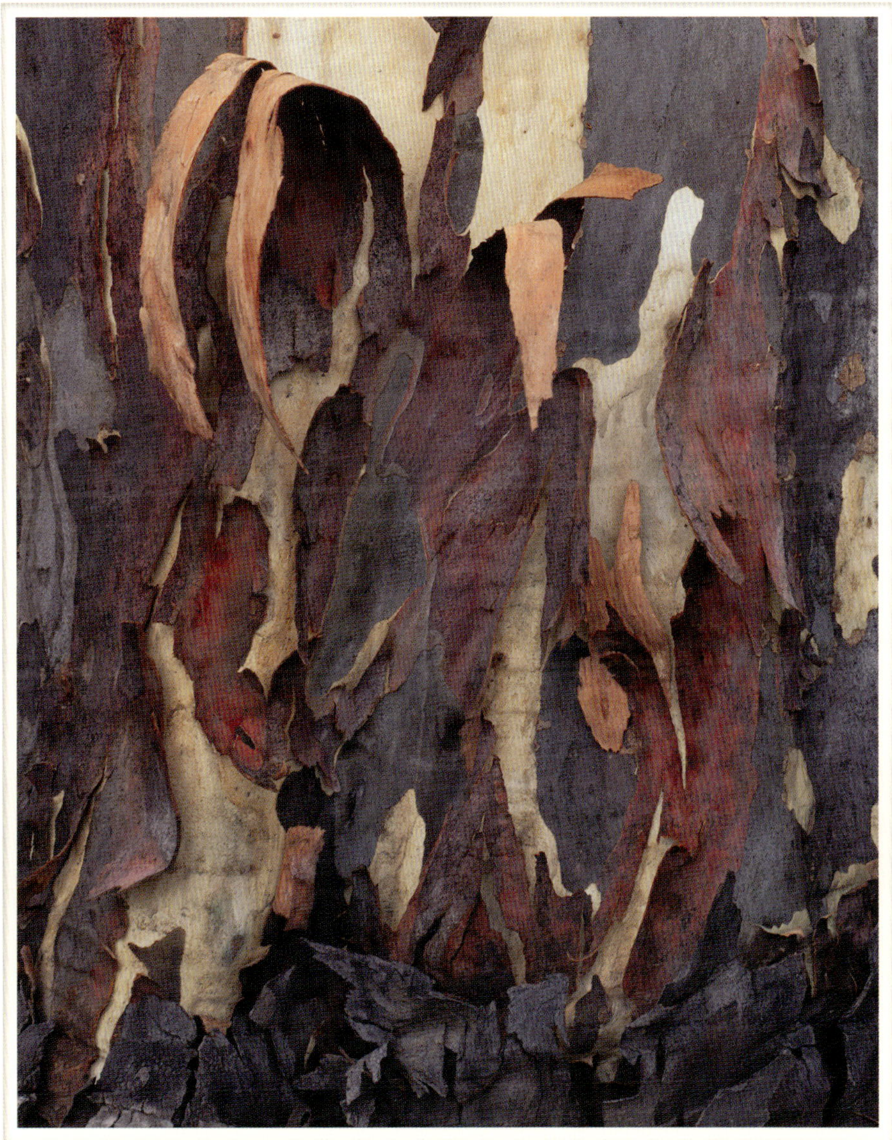

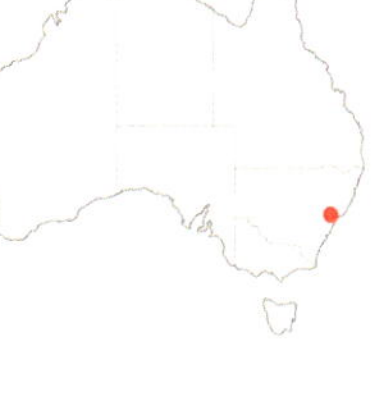

Debra Doenges

STRINGY GUM BARK

Hunter Valley, NSW

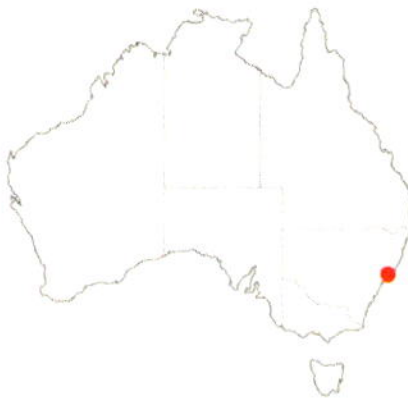

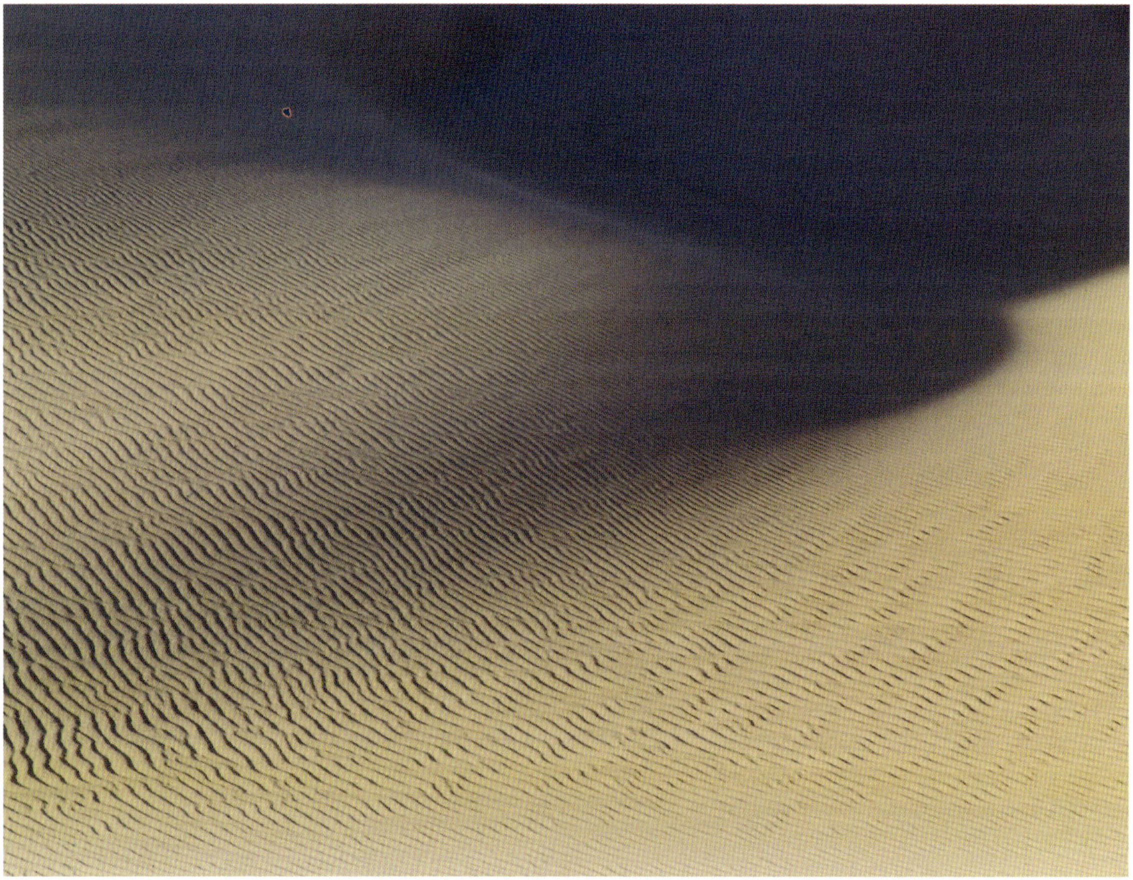

DUNE SHADOWS

Dark Point, Myall Lakes National Park, NSW

Debra Doenges

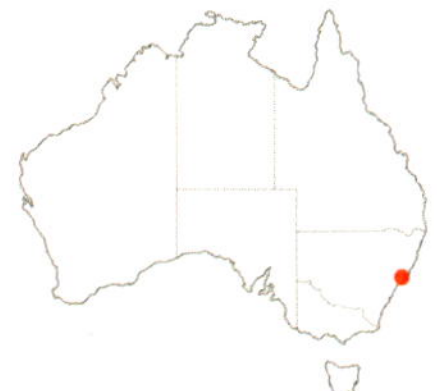

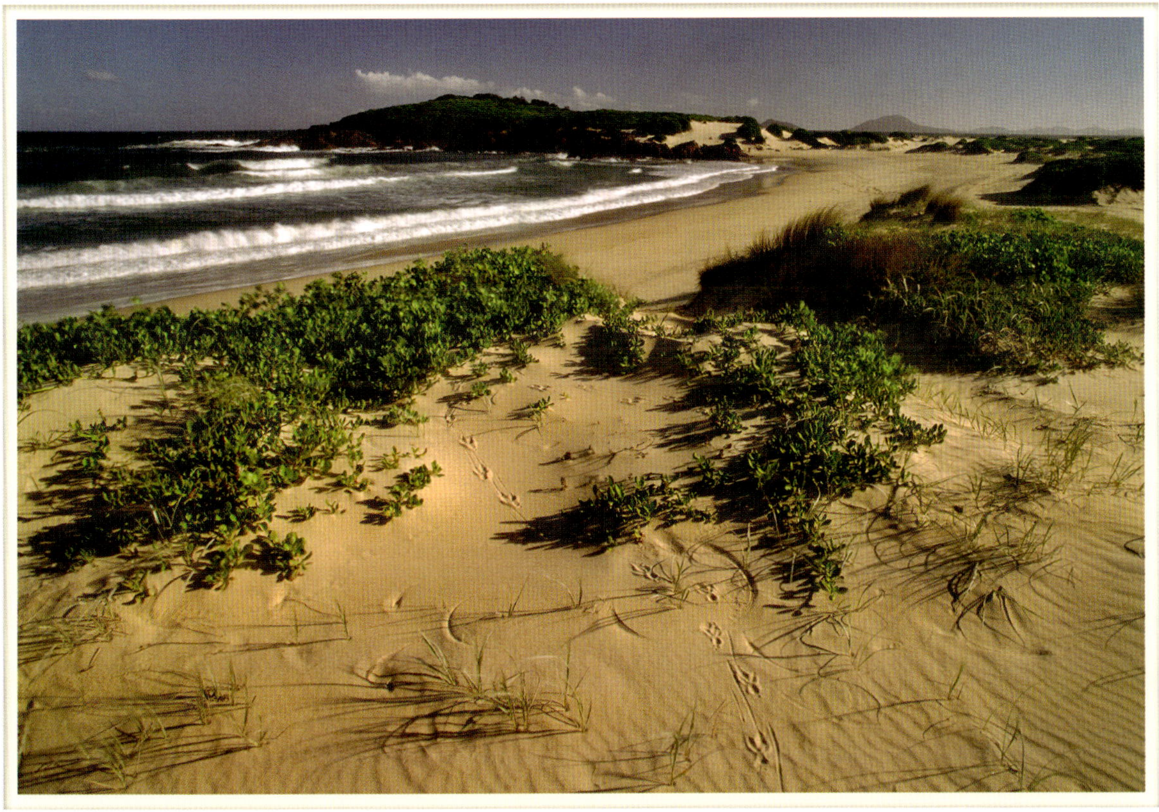

Andrew Teakle

DARK POINT

Myall Lakes National Park, NSW

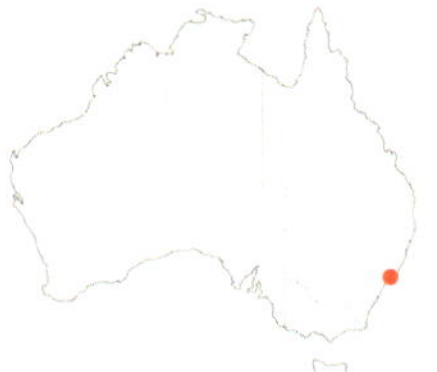

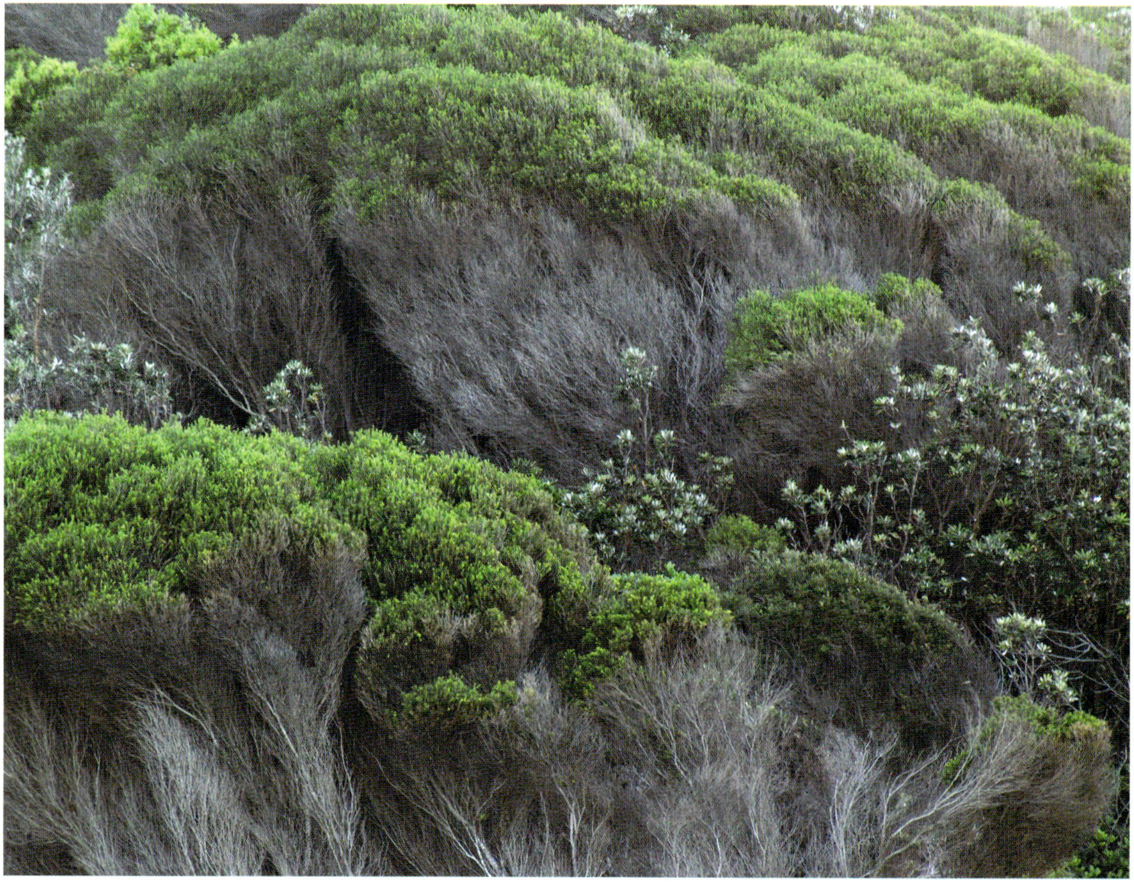

COASTAL MELALEUCA TREES
Seal Rocks, The Great Lakes, NSW

Debra Doenges

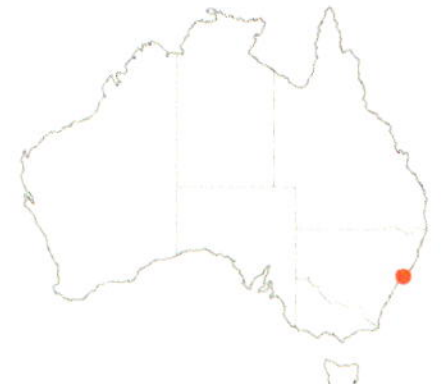

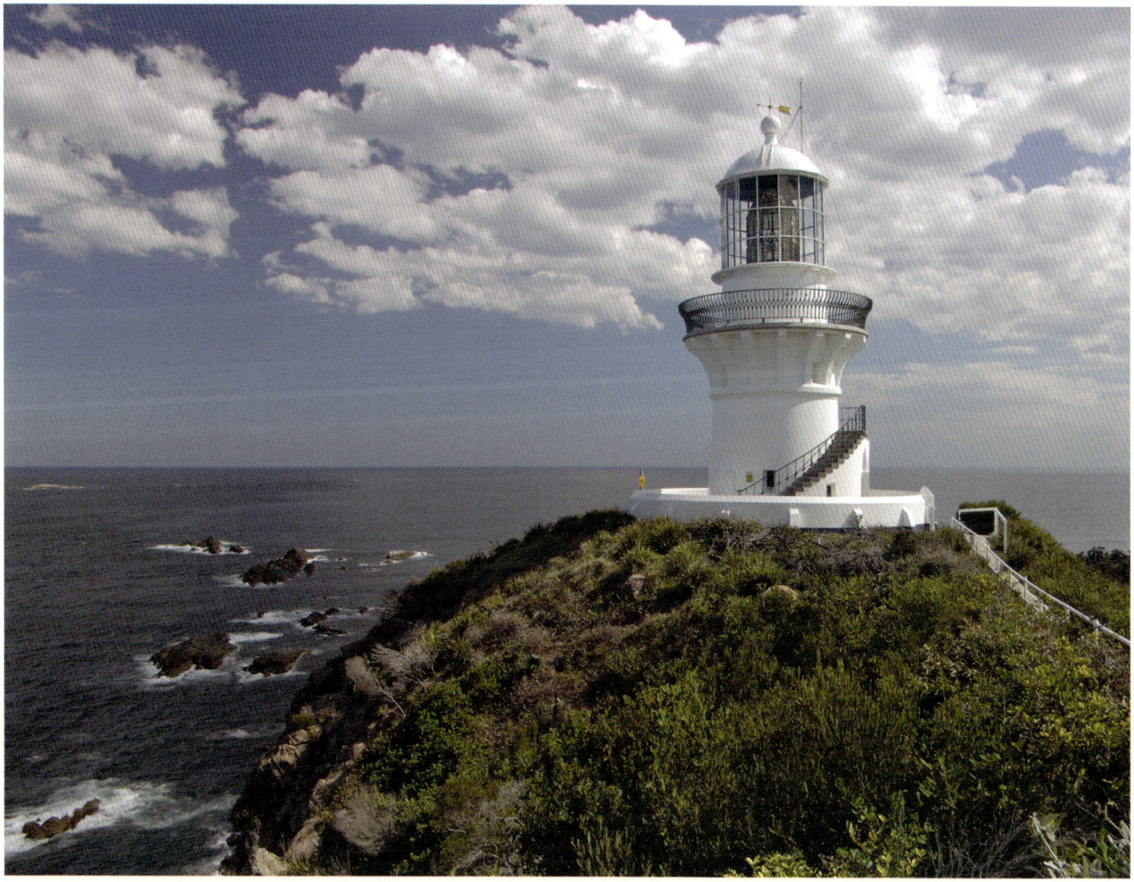

Debra Doenges

SUGARLOAF POINT LIGHTHOUSE

Seal Rocks, The Great Lakes, NSW

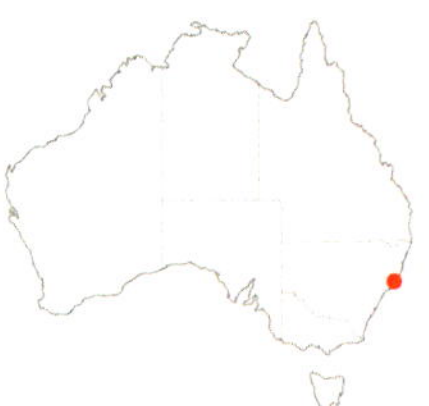

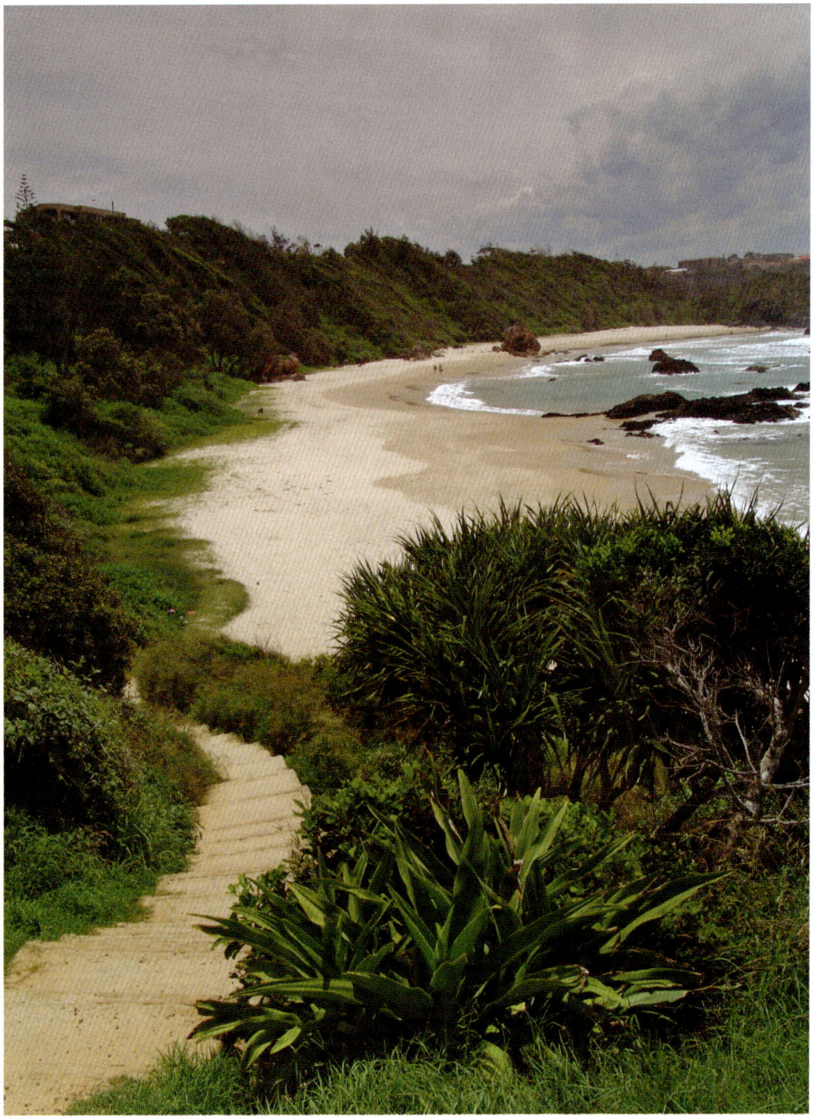

54

NOBBYS BEACH
Port Macquarie, NSW

Debra Doenges

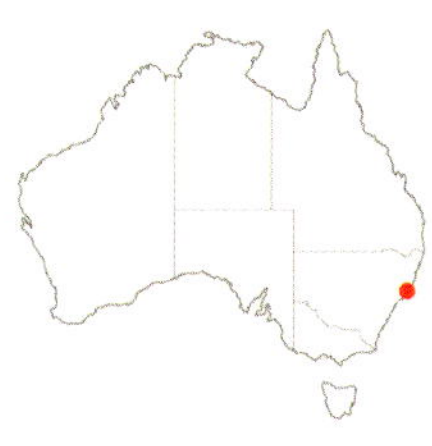

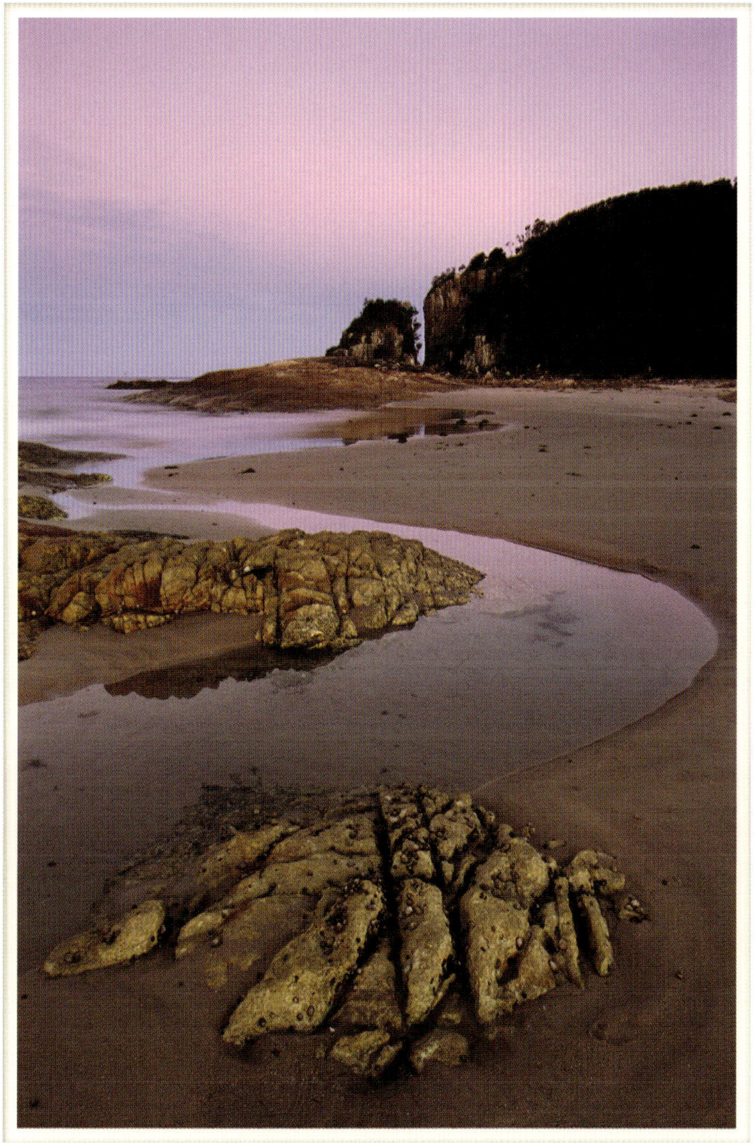

Debra Doenges

DIAMOND HEAD SUNSET

Crowdy Bay National Park, NSW

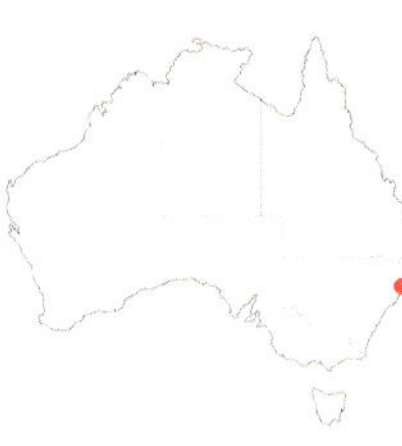

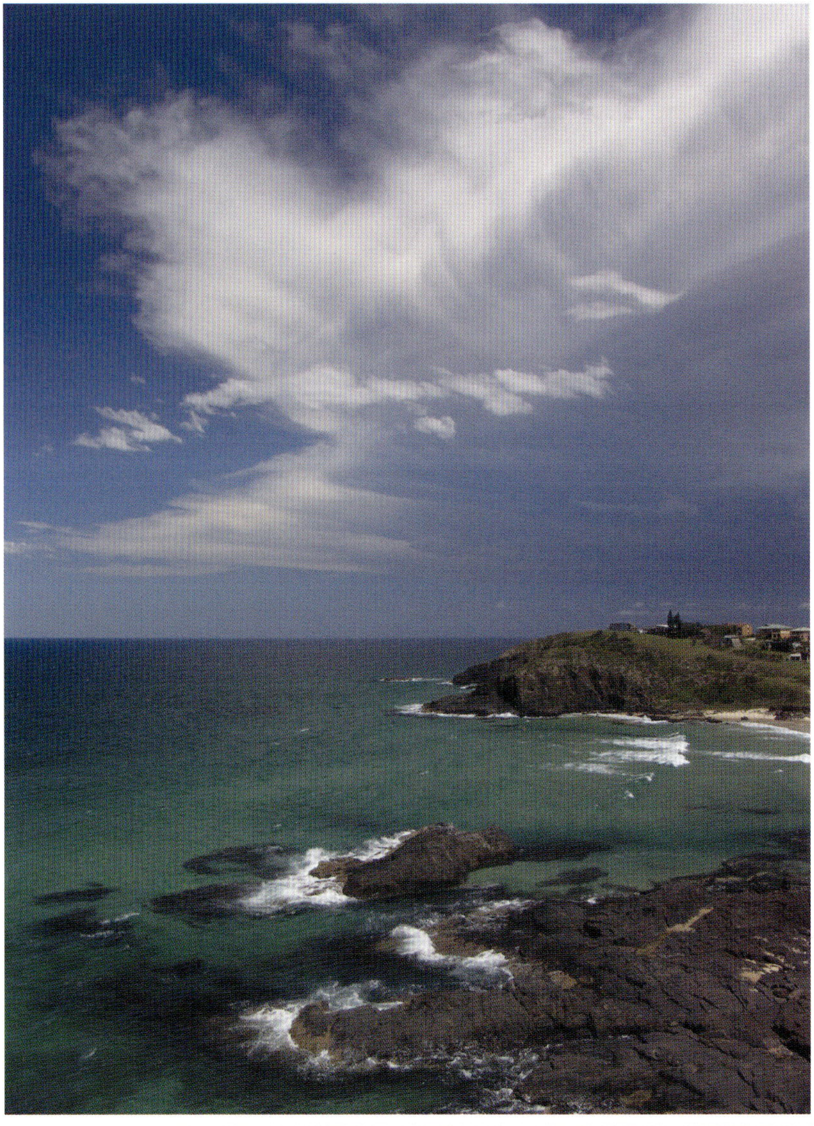

SUMMER STORM

Scotts Head, NSW

Debra Doenges

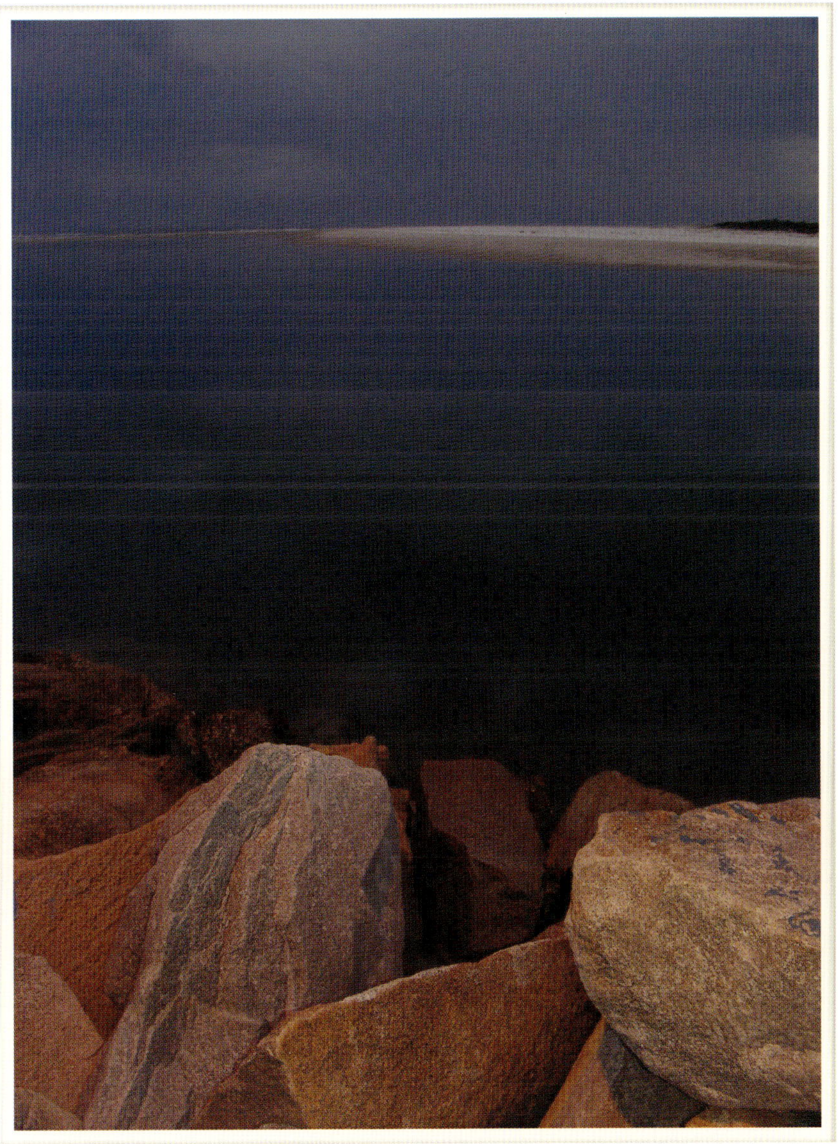

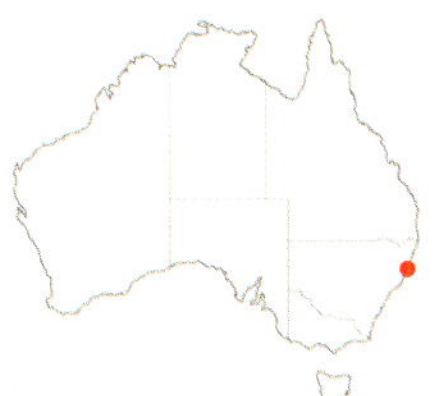

Debra Doenges

DUSK OVER NAMBUCCA RIVER

Nambucca Heads, NSW

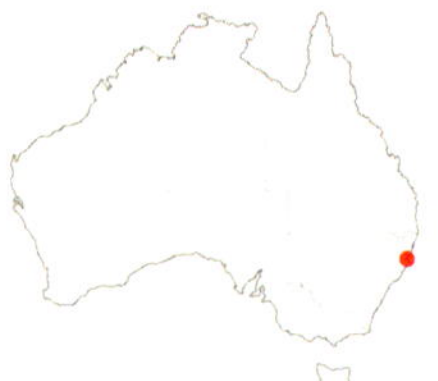

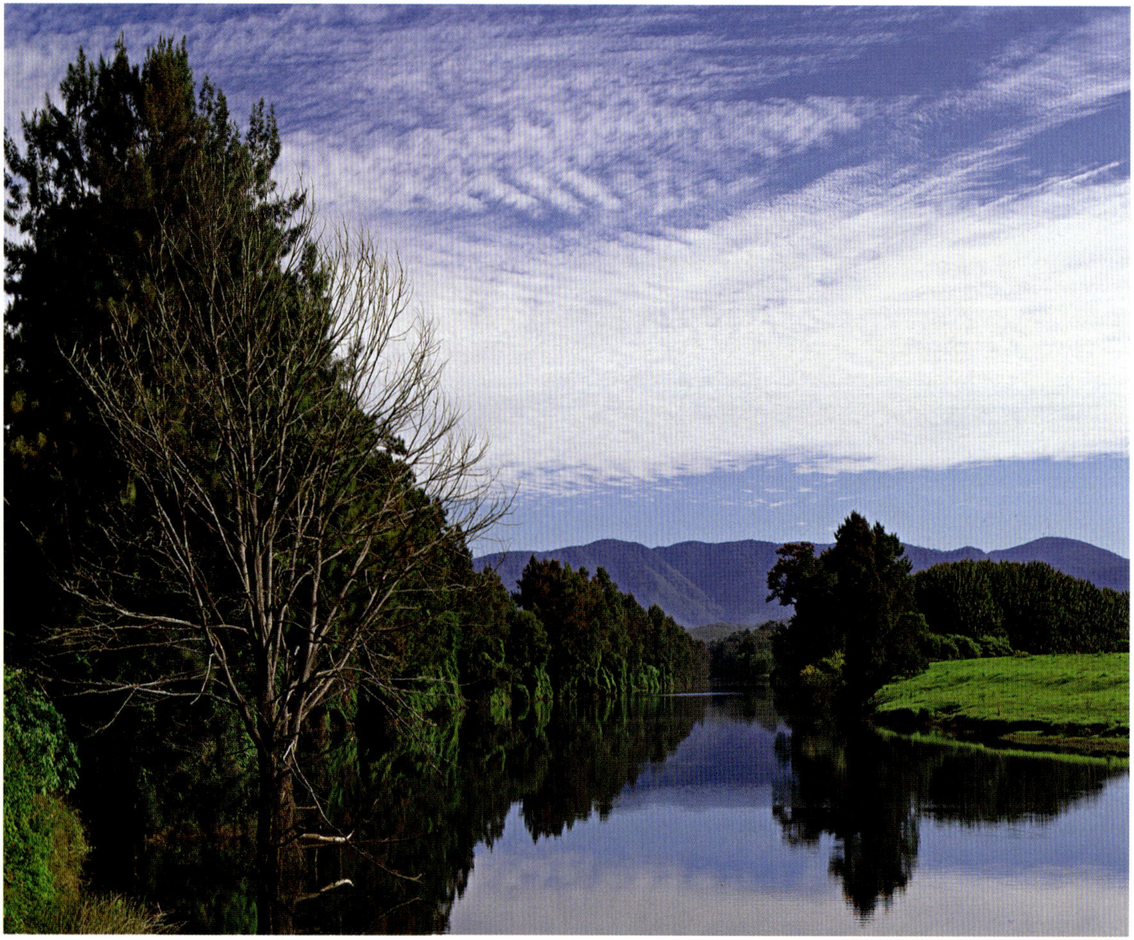

BELLINGER RIVER
Dorrigo, NSW

Debra Doenges

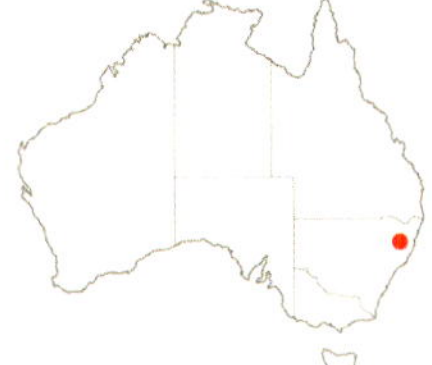

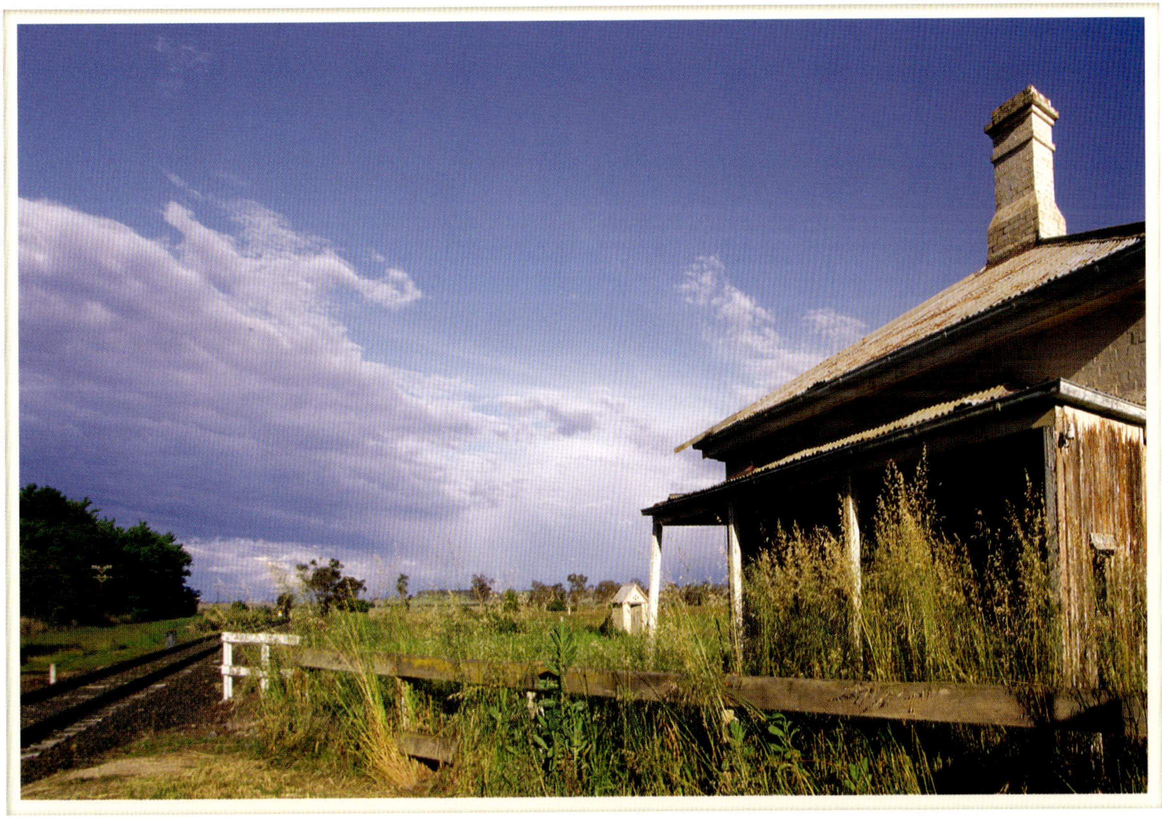

Andrew Teakle

OLD RAILWAY STATION
New England Highway, NSW

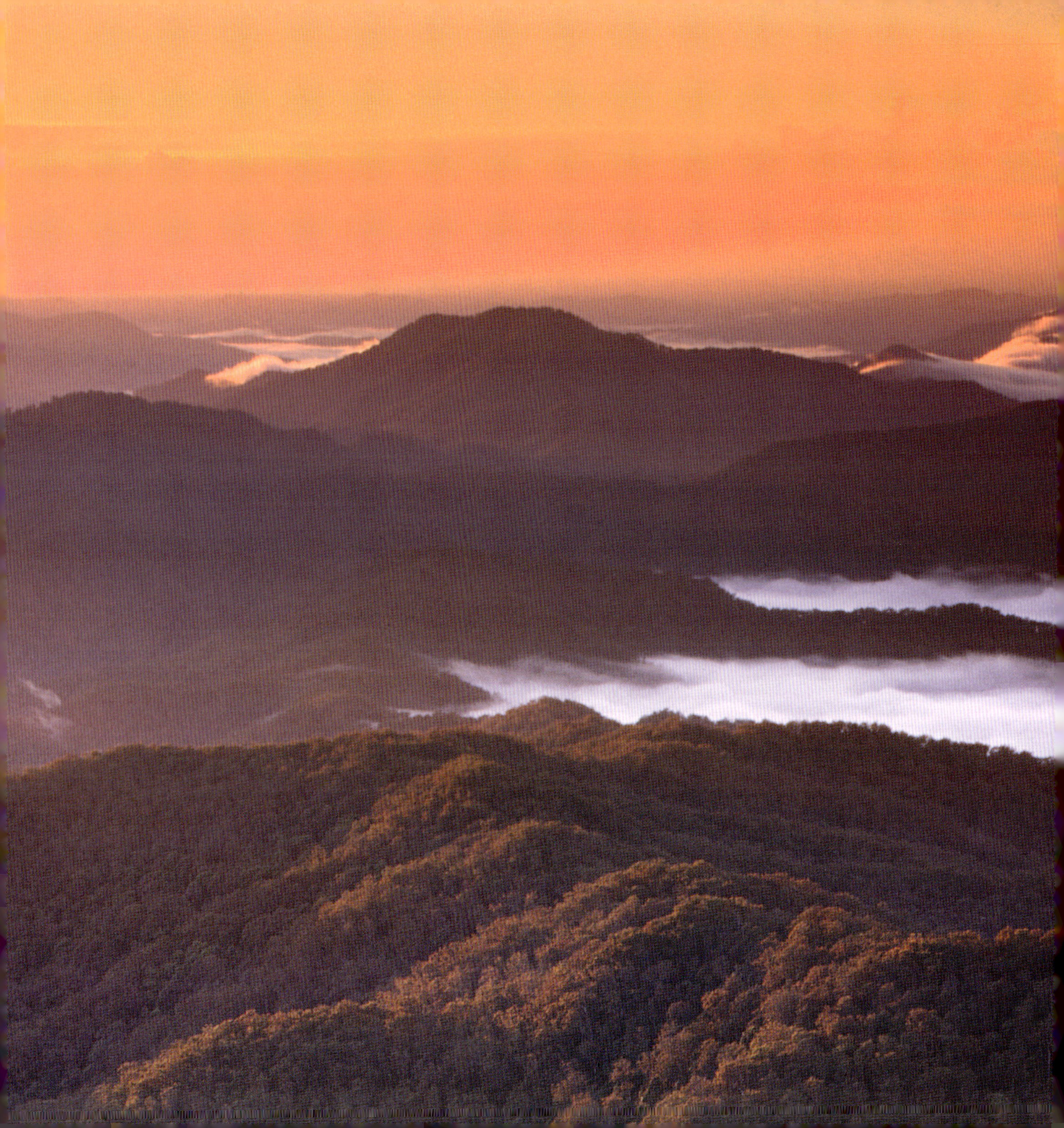

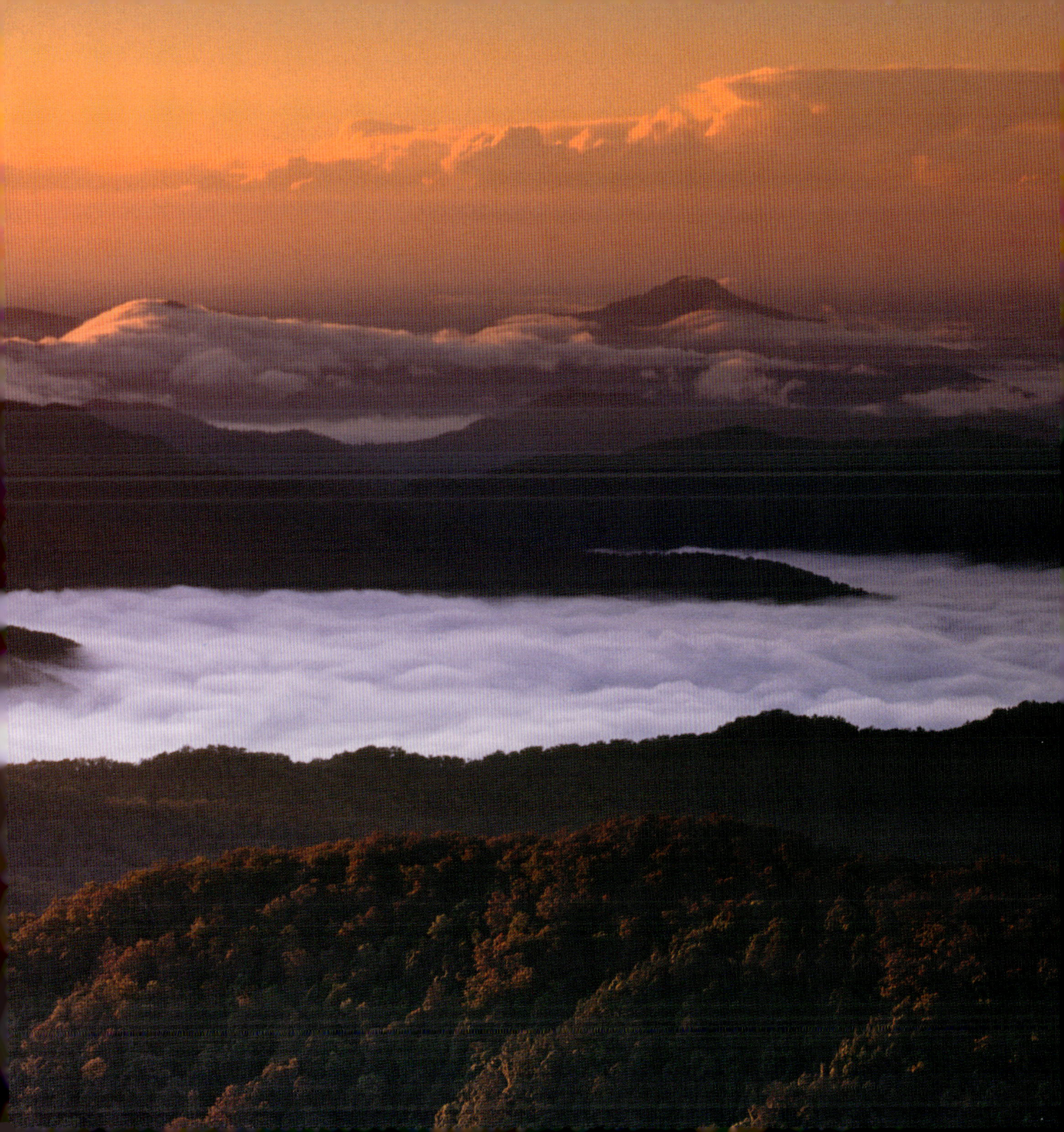

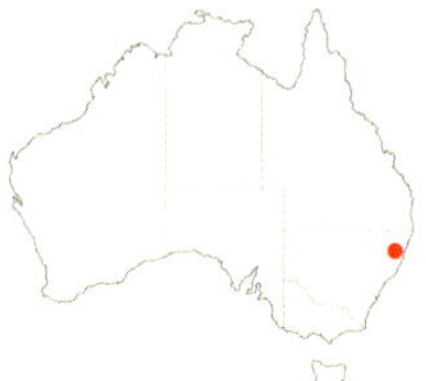

GRASSTREES

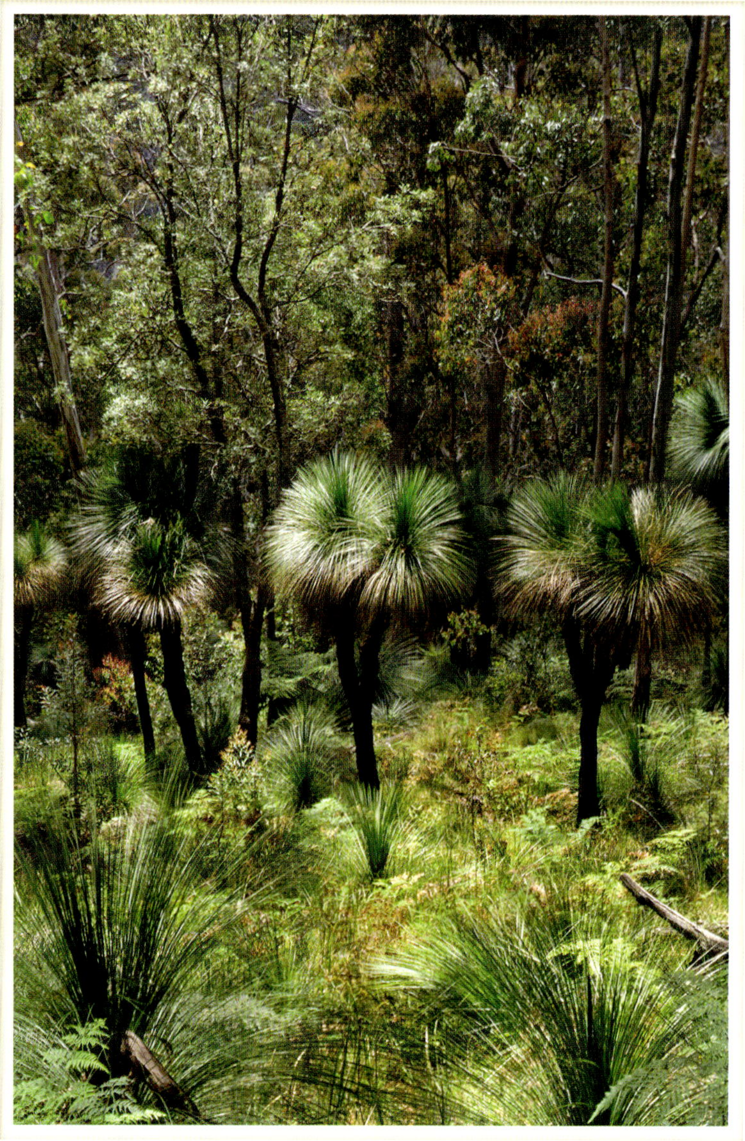

Andrew Teakle

Guy Fawkes River National Park, NSW

POINT LOOKOUT DAWN

◀ Bellinger Valley, NSW

Andrew Teakle

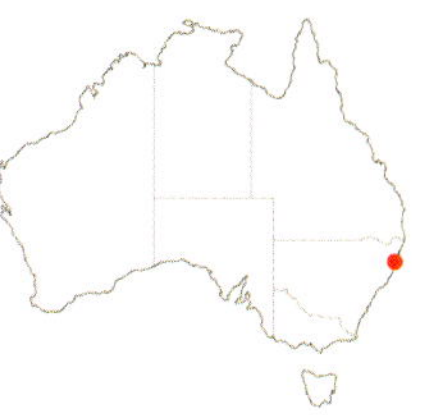

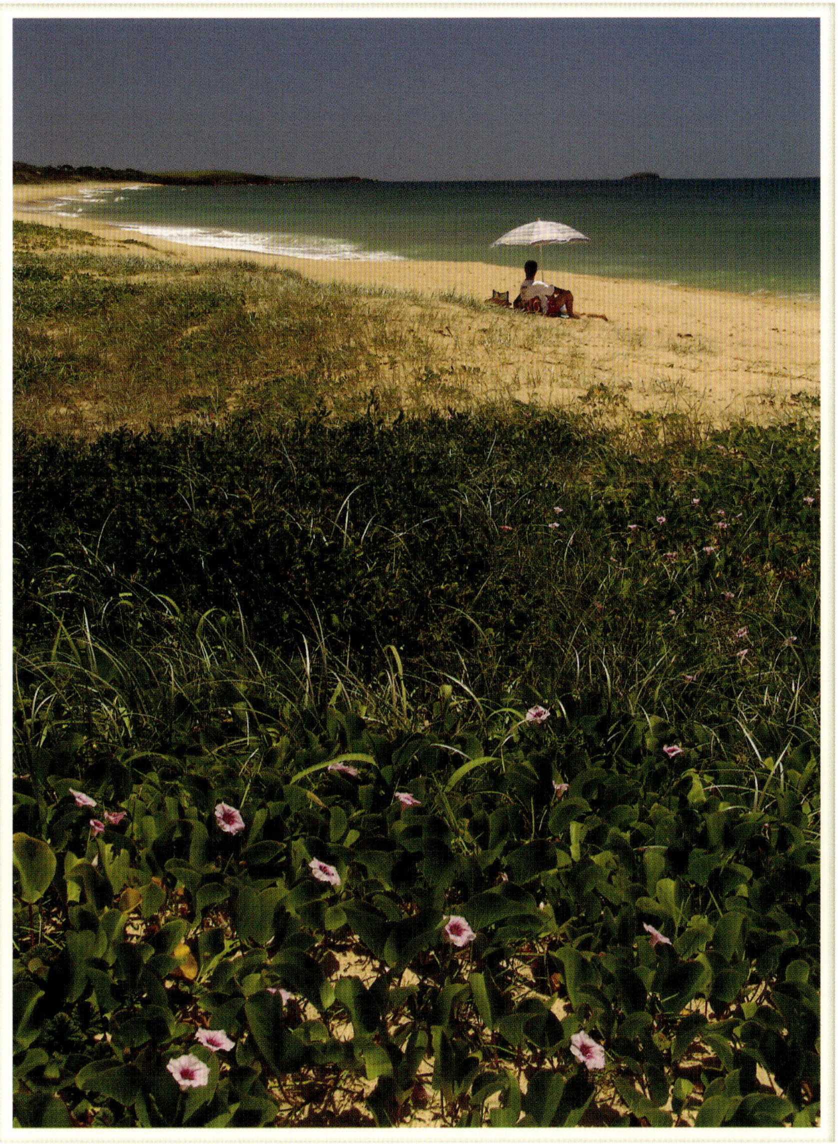

Debra Doenges

SAPPHIRE BEACH

Coffs Coast, NSW

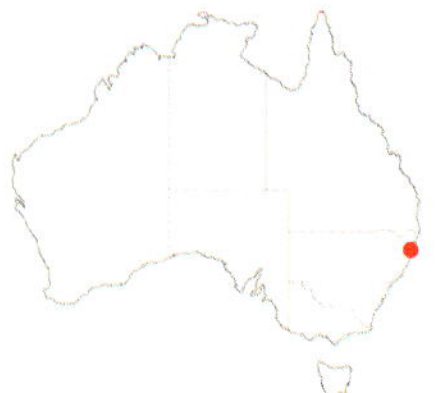

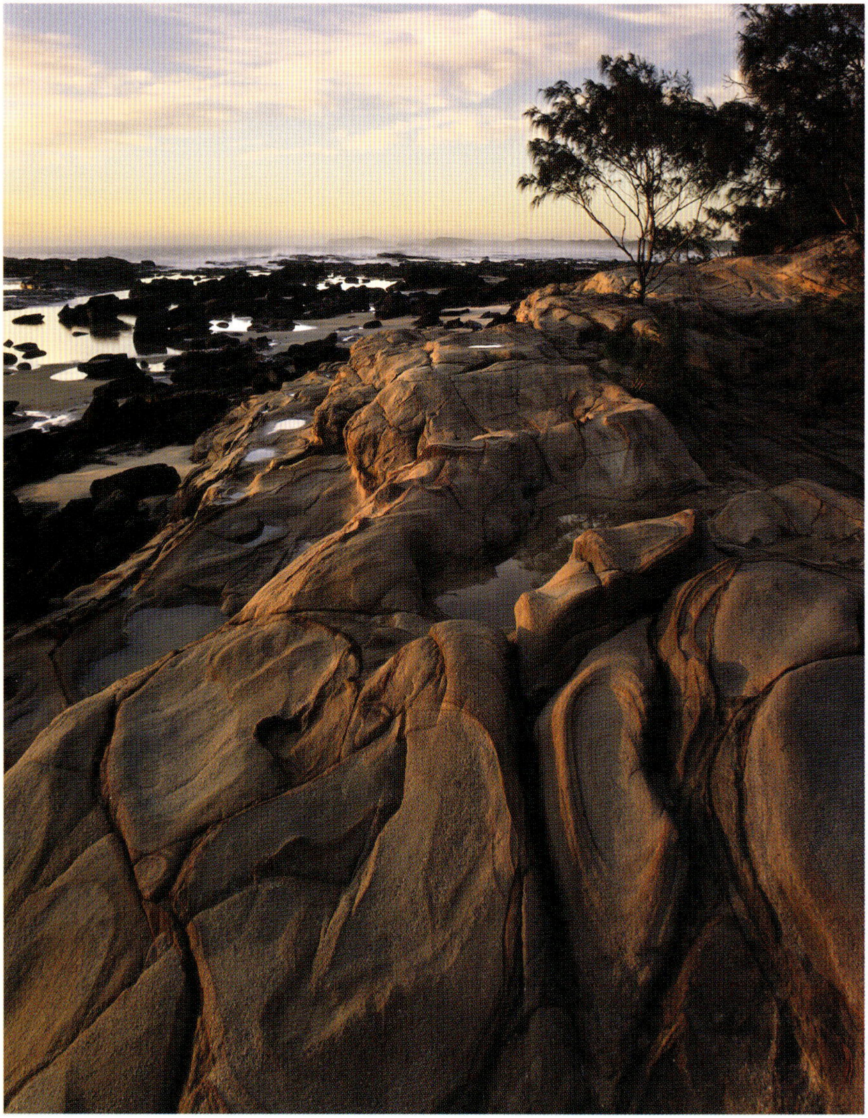

WOODY HEAD
Bundjalung National Park, NSW

Andrew Teakle

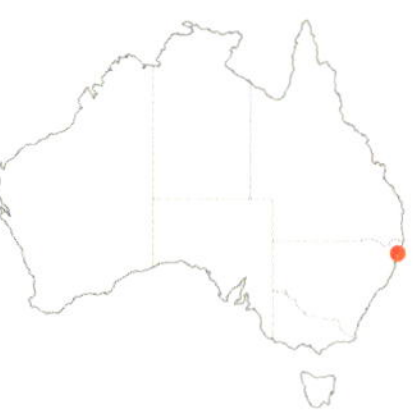

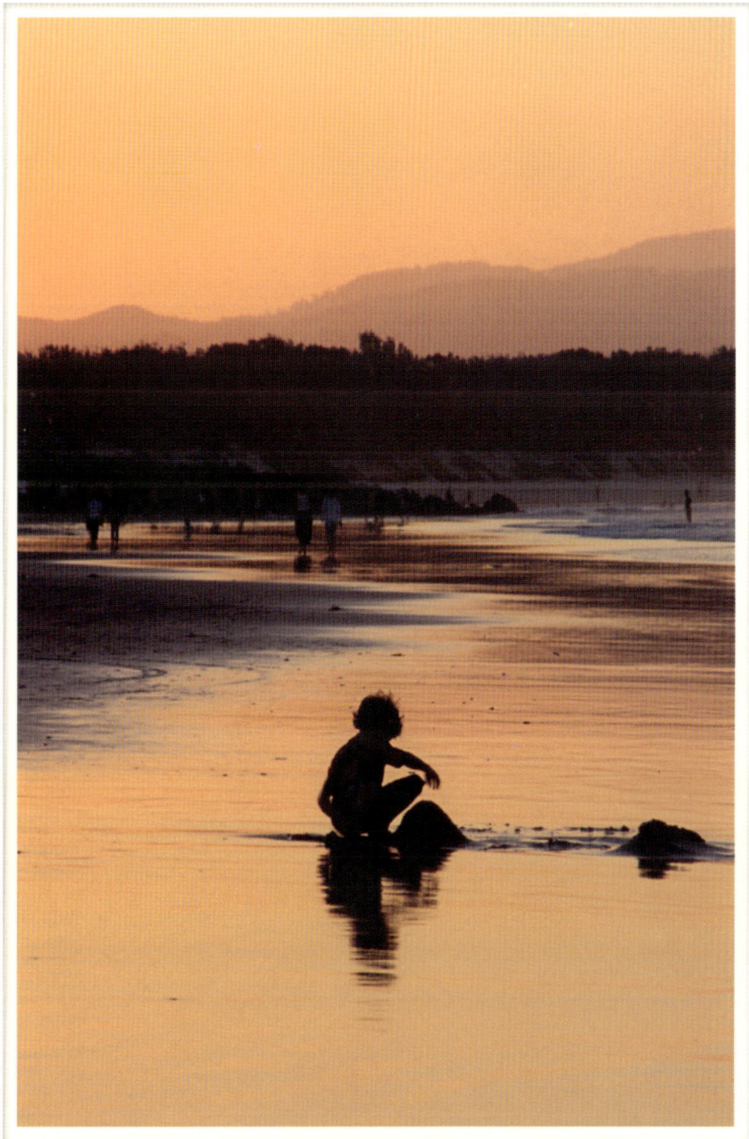

Andrew Teakle

MAIN BEACH SUNSET

Byron Bay, NSW

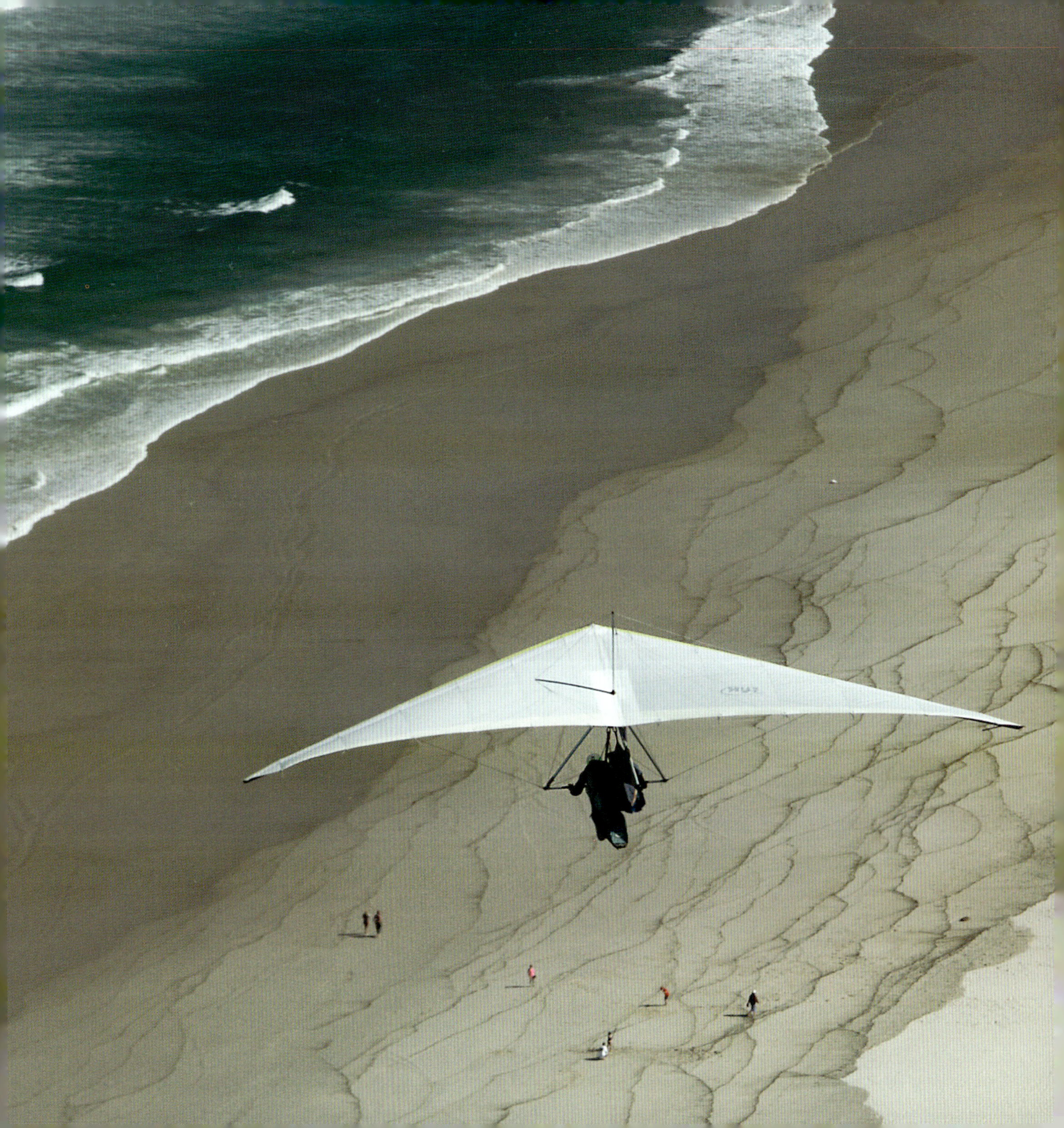

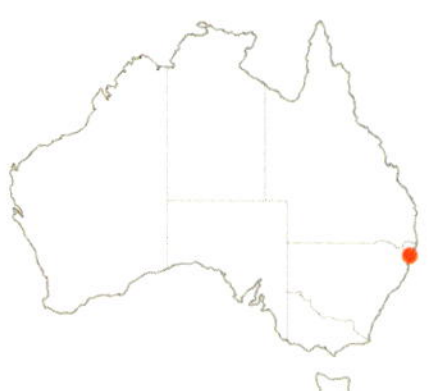

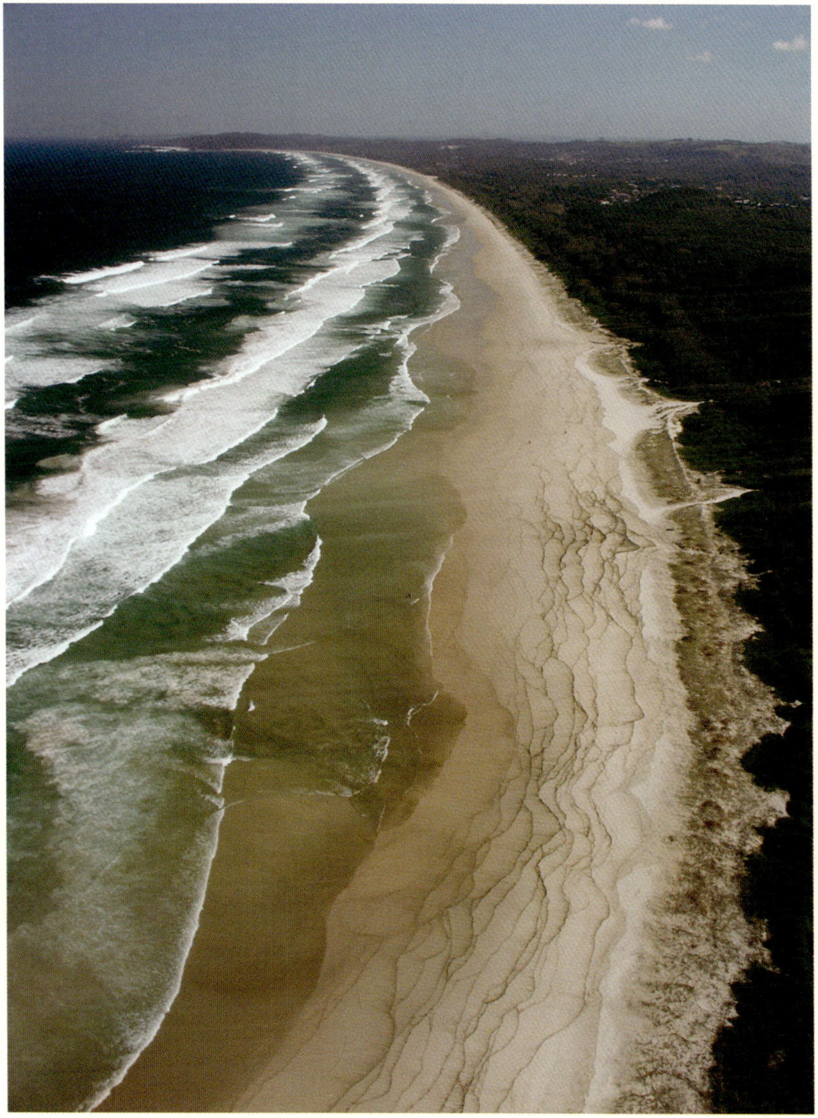

Debra Doenges

TALLOW BEACH

Byron Bay, NSW

HANG-GLIDER

◀ Tallow Beach, Byron Bay, NSW

Debra Doenges

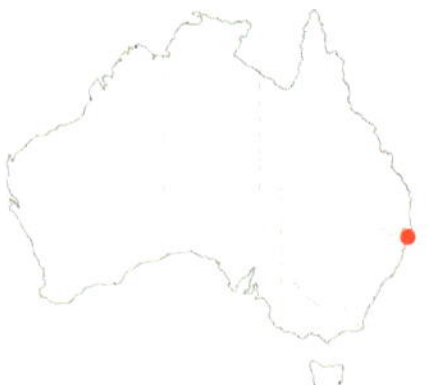

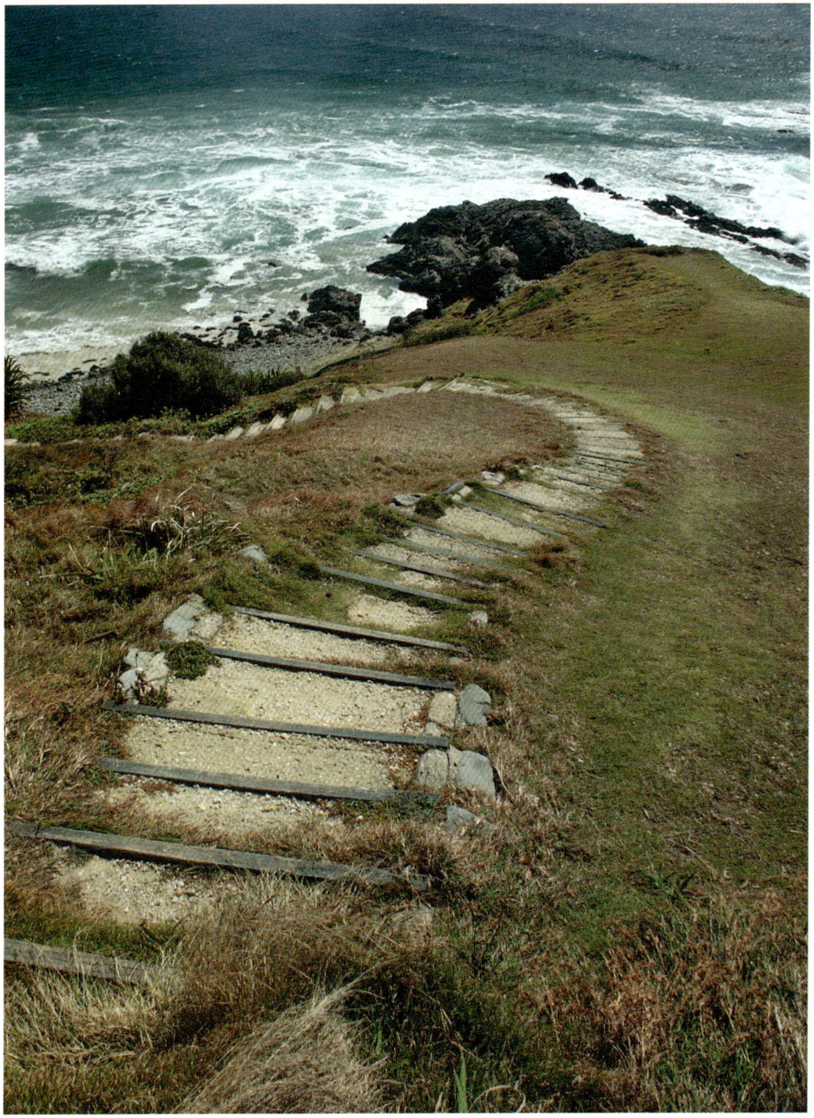

BROKEN HEAD

Far North Coast, NSW

Debra Doenges & Andrew Teakle

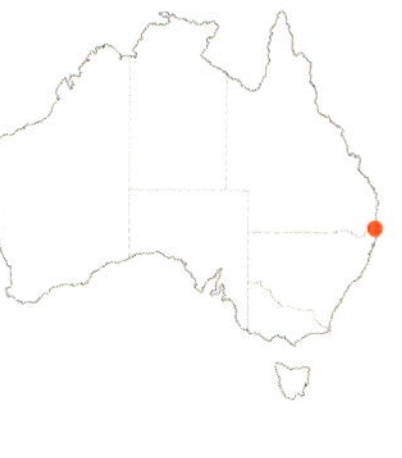

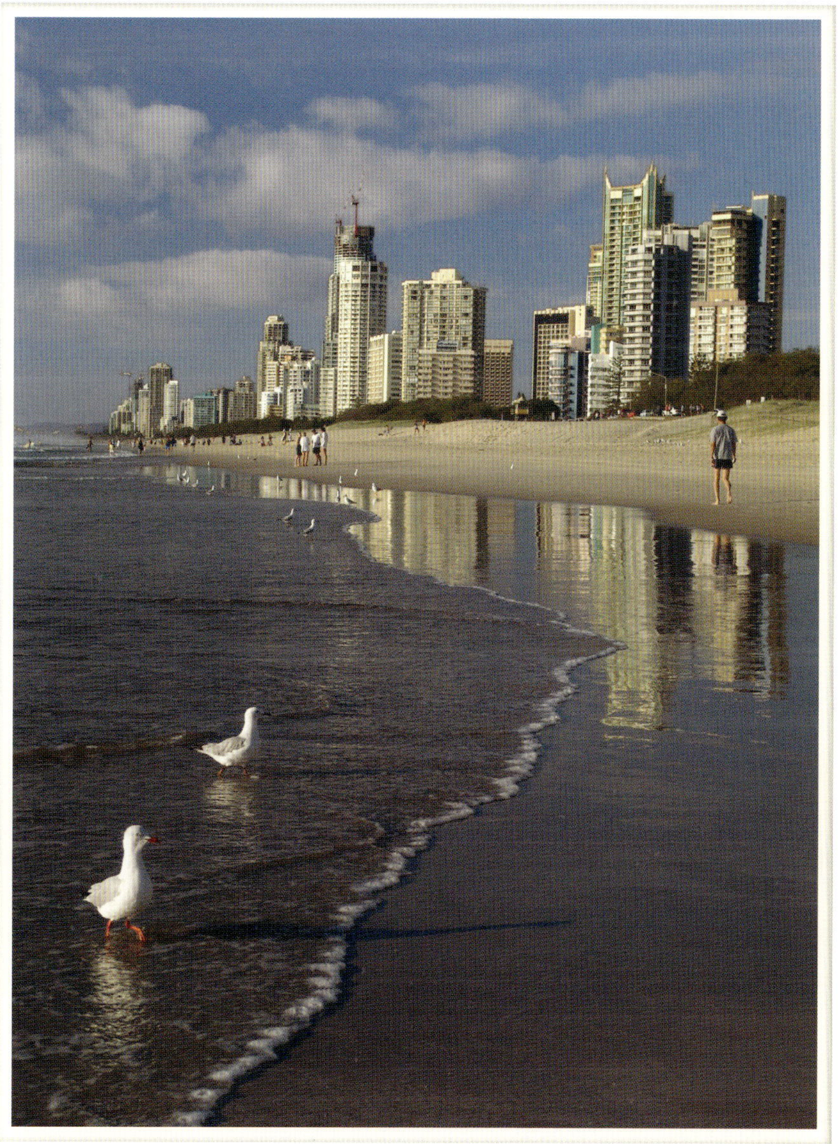

Debra Doenges

SURFERS PARADISE
Gold Coast, QLD

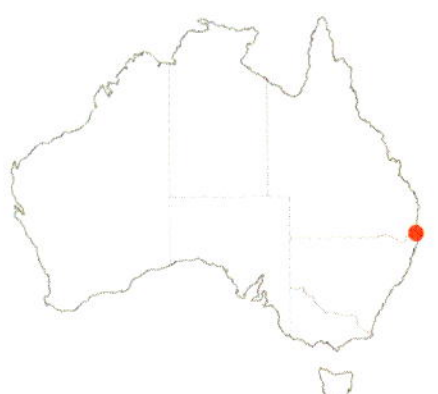

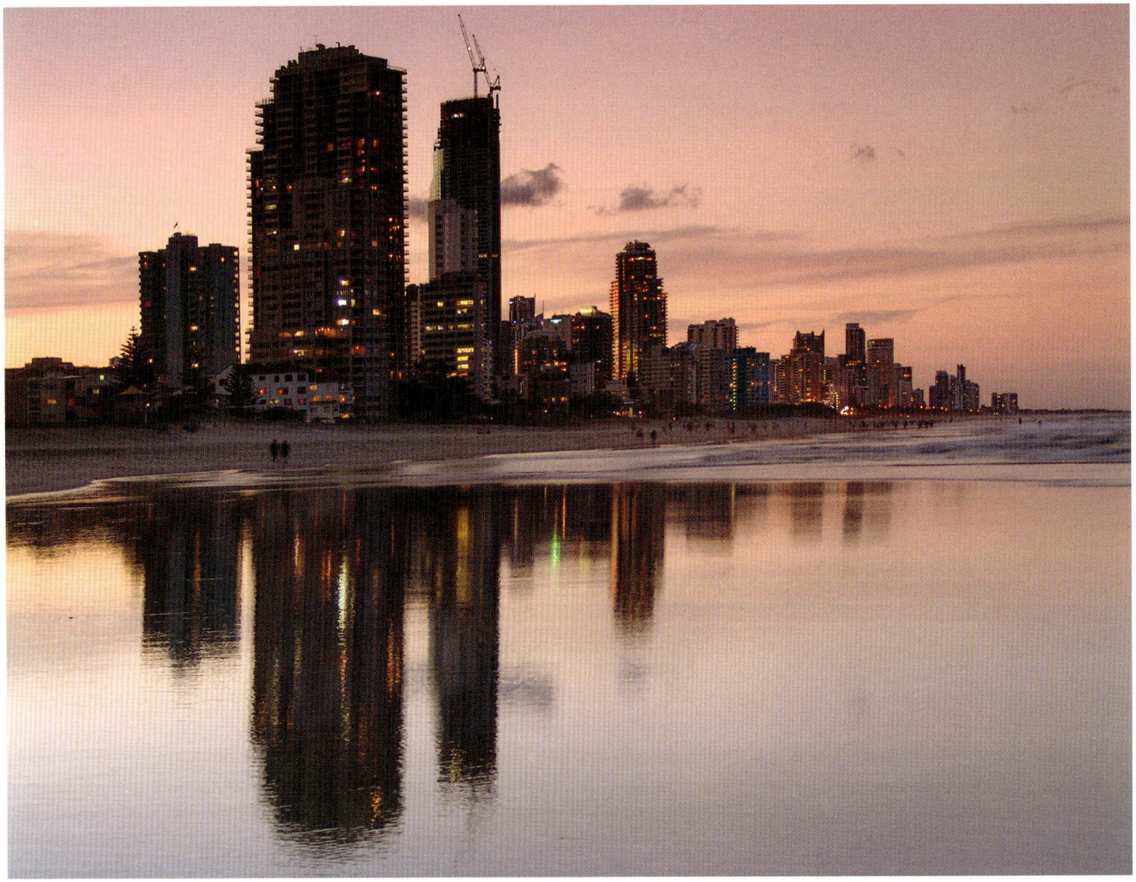

TWILIGHT ON SURFERS PARADISE
Gold Coast, QLD

Debra Doenges

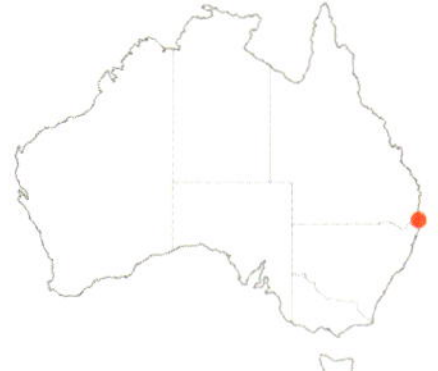

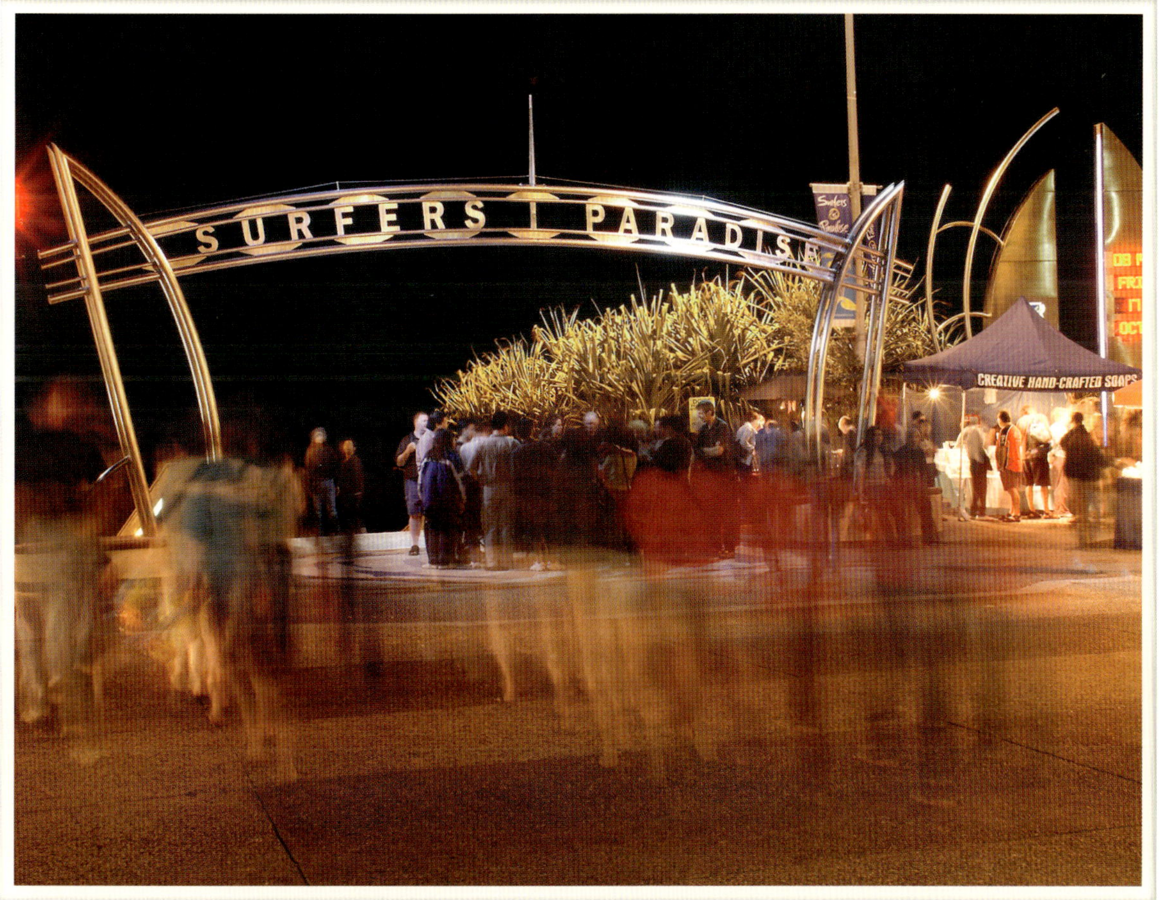

Andrew Teakle & Debra Doenges

SURFERS PARADISE

Gold Coast, QLD

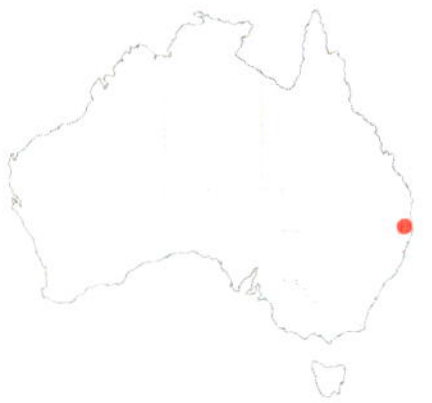

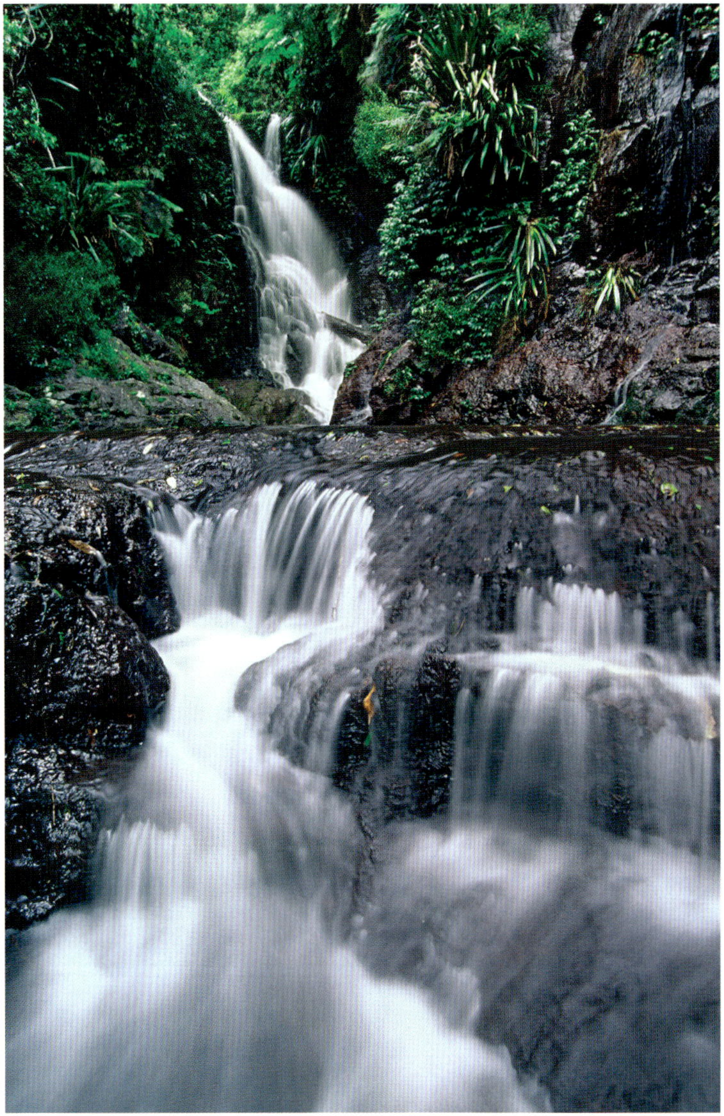

ELABANA FALLS

Lamington National Park, QLD

Andrew Teakle

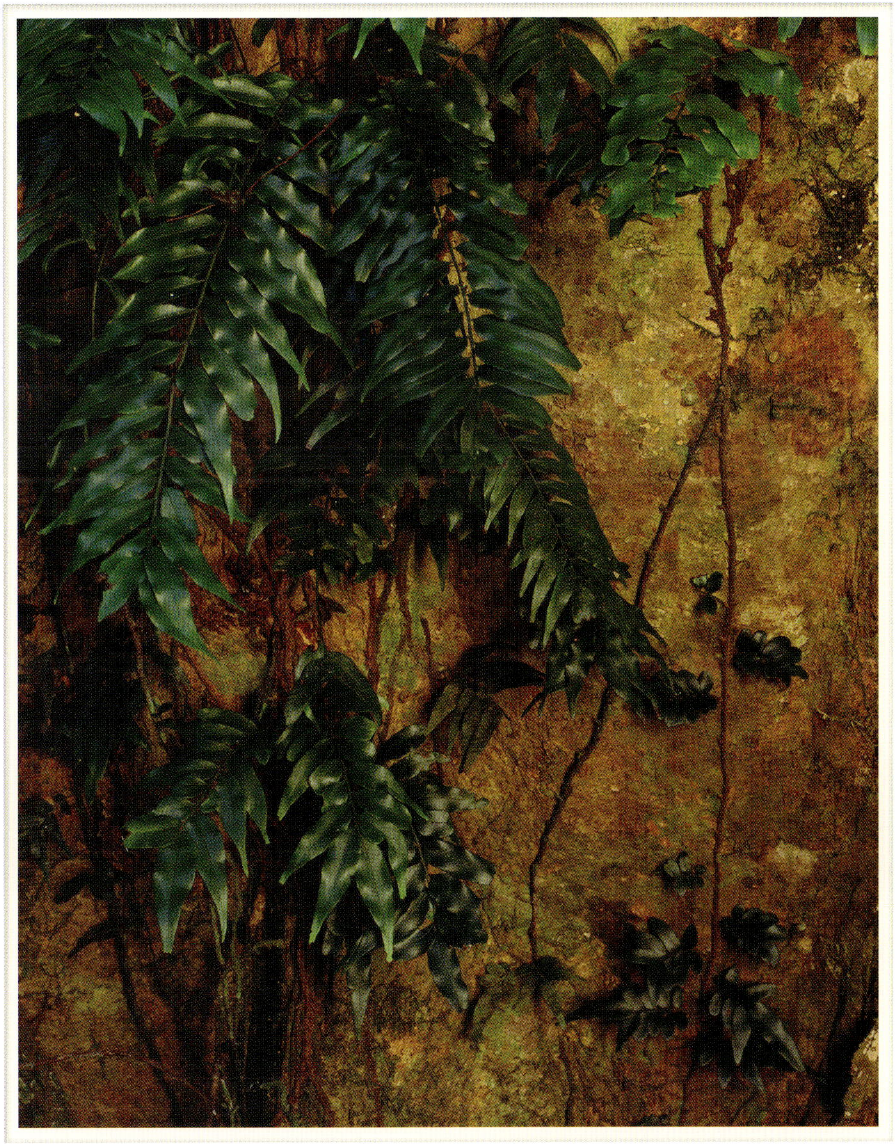

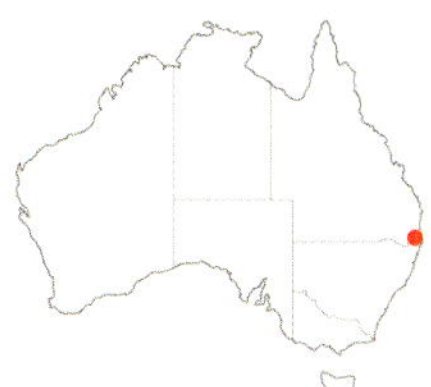

Debra Doenges

FERN VINE & POTHOS VINE

Lamington National Park, QLD

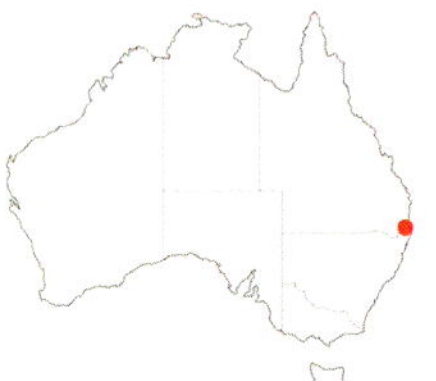

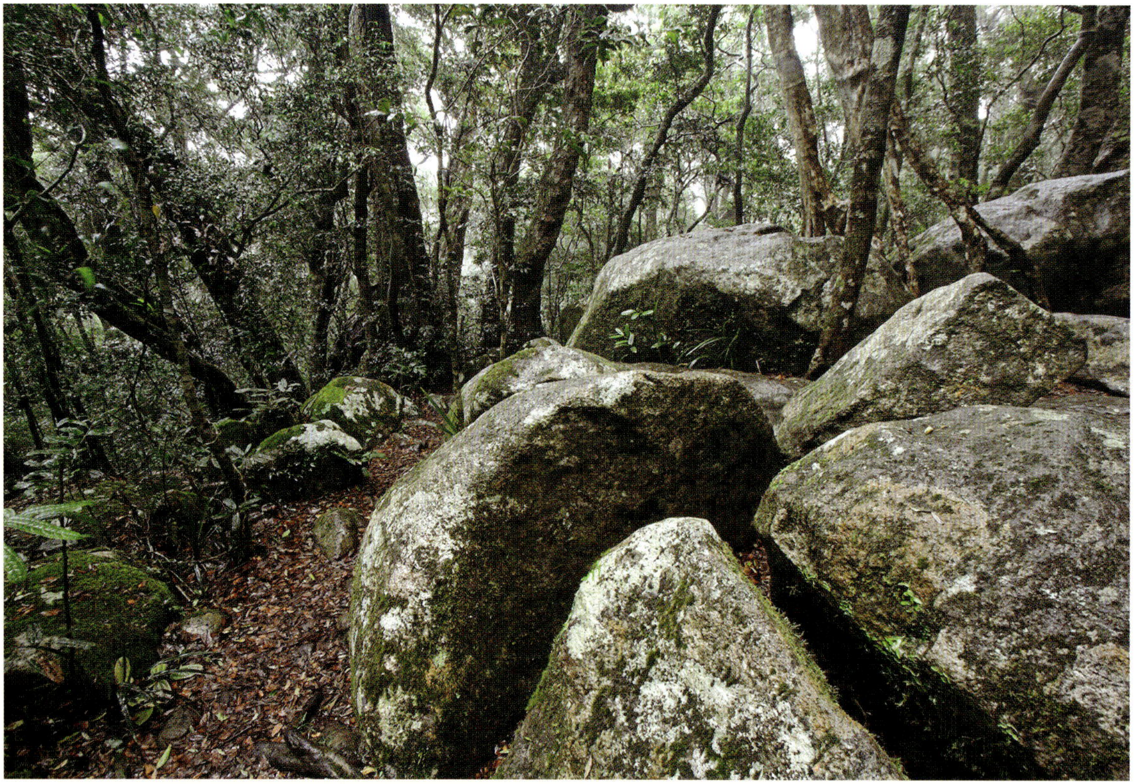

ANTARCTIC BEECH FOREST
Lamington National Park, QLD

Debra Doenges

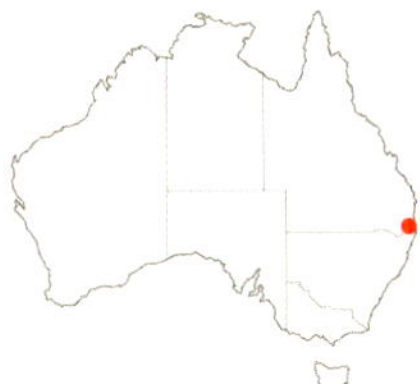

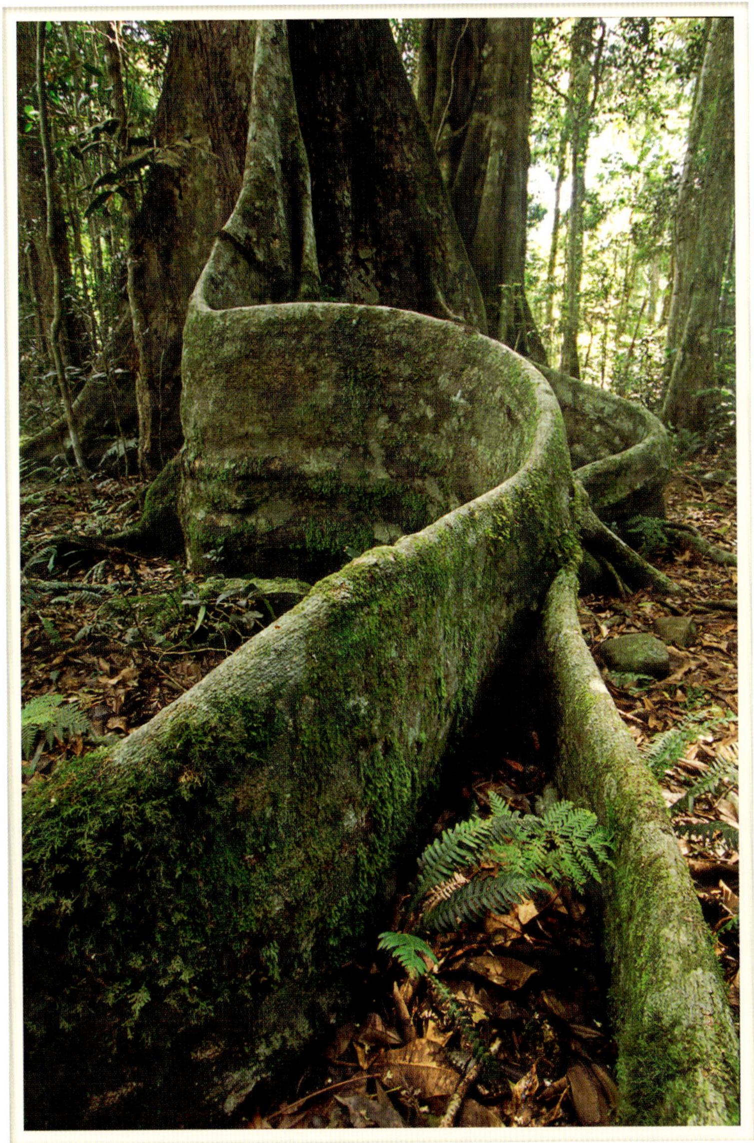

Andrew Teakle & Debra Doenges

BUTTRESS ROOTS

Laminton National Park, QLD

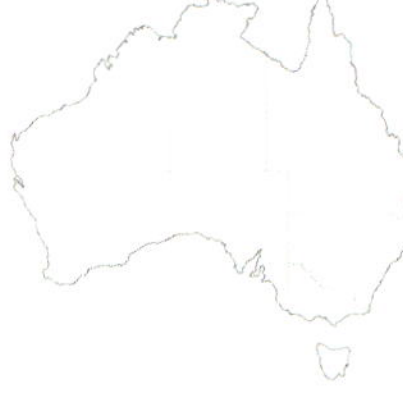

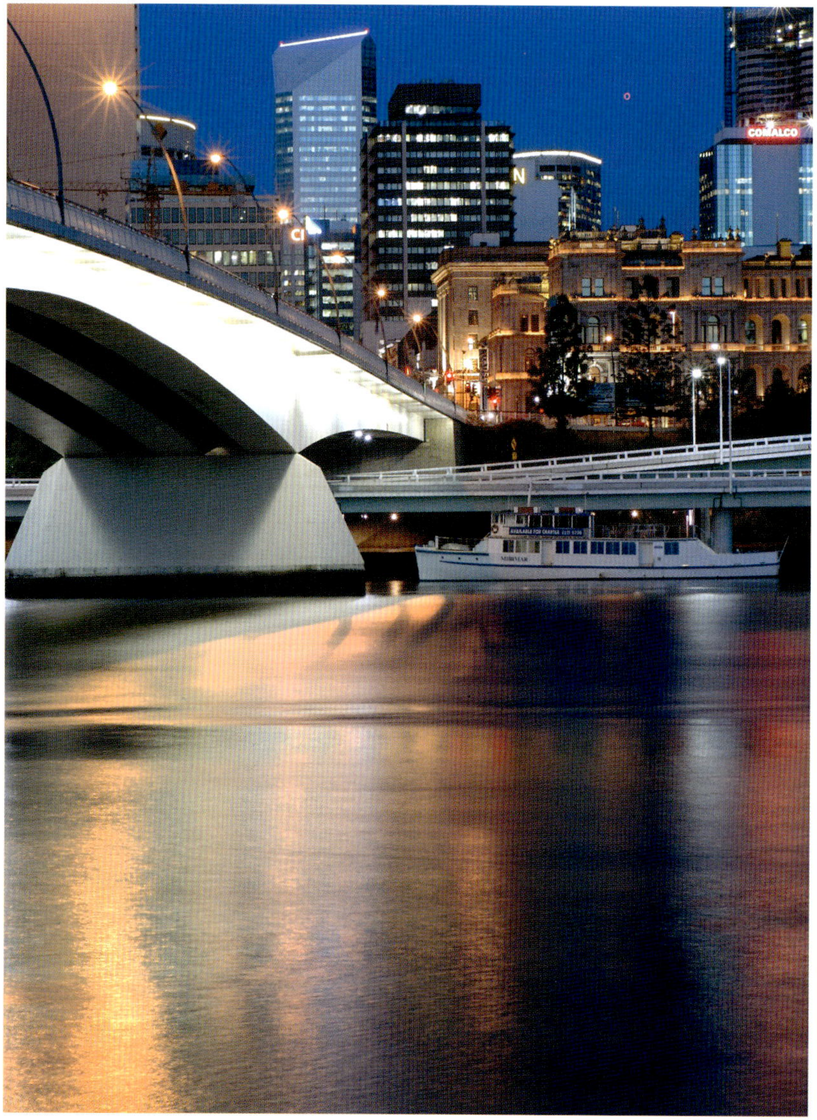

CITY LIGHTS' REFLECTION
Brisbane, QLD

Debra Doenges

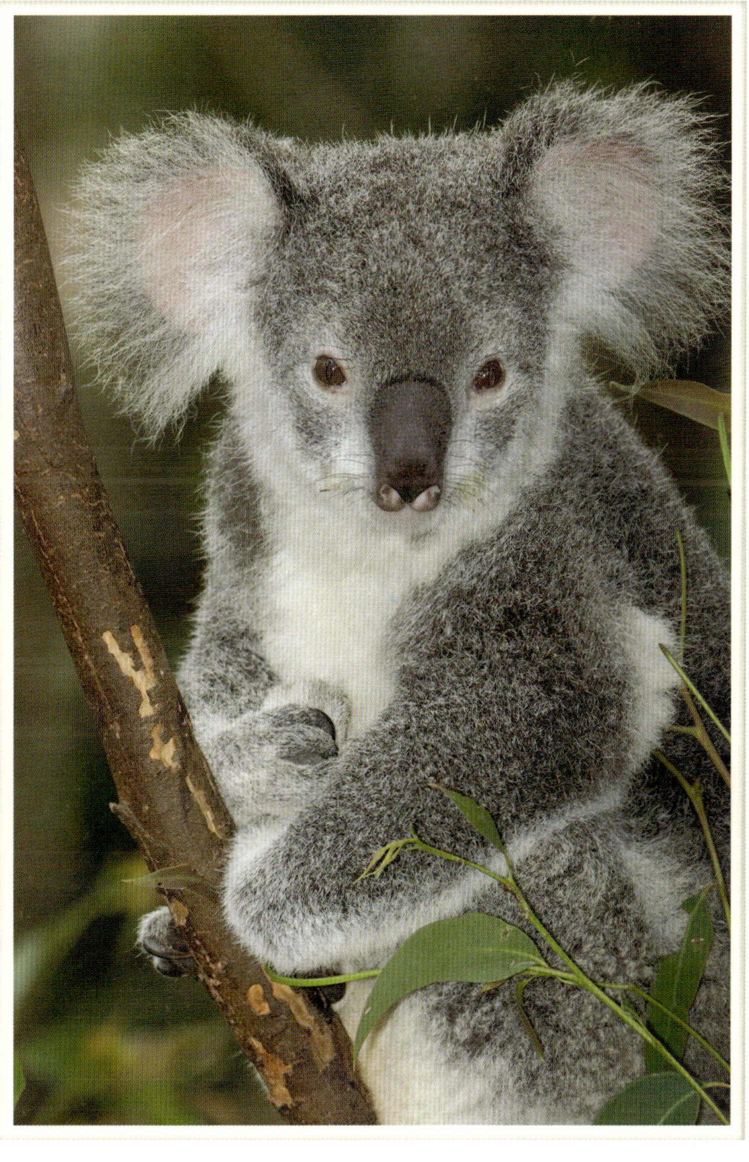

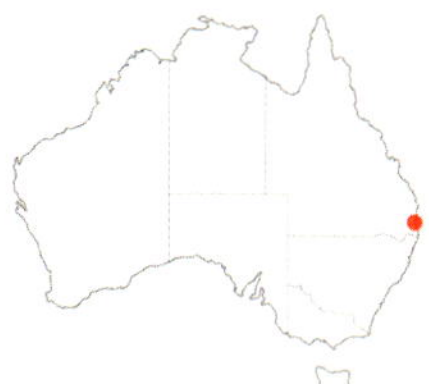

Andrew Teakle

KOALA

Lone Pine Koala Sanctuary, Brisbane, QLD

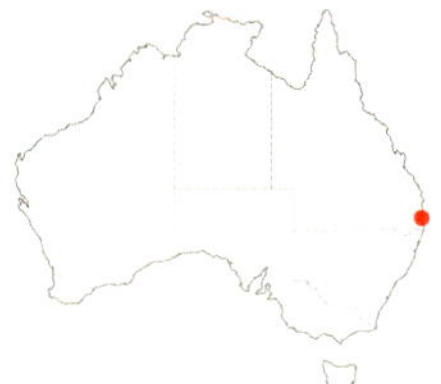

78

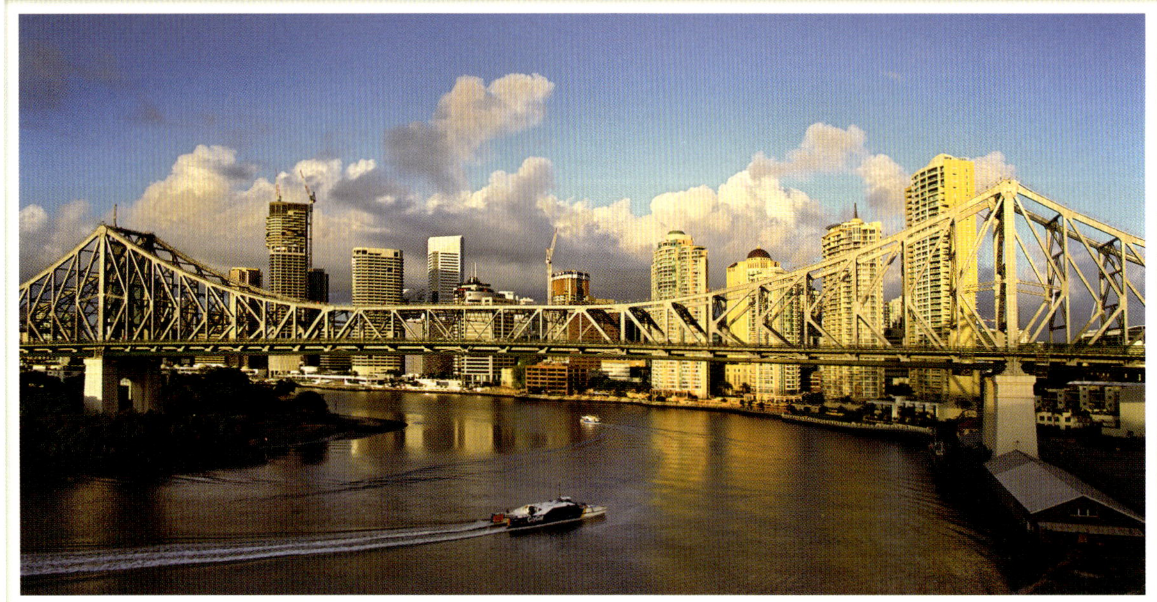

STORY BRIDGE OVER BRISBANE RIVER
Brisbane, QLD

Debra Doenges

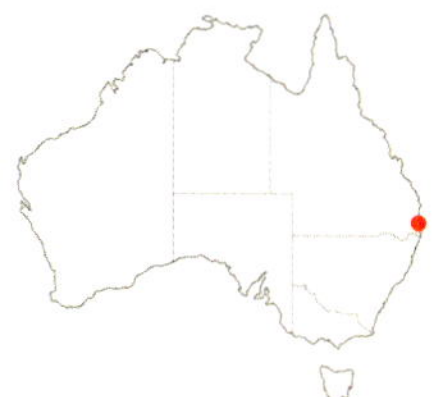

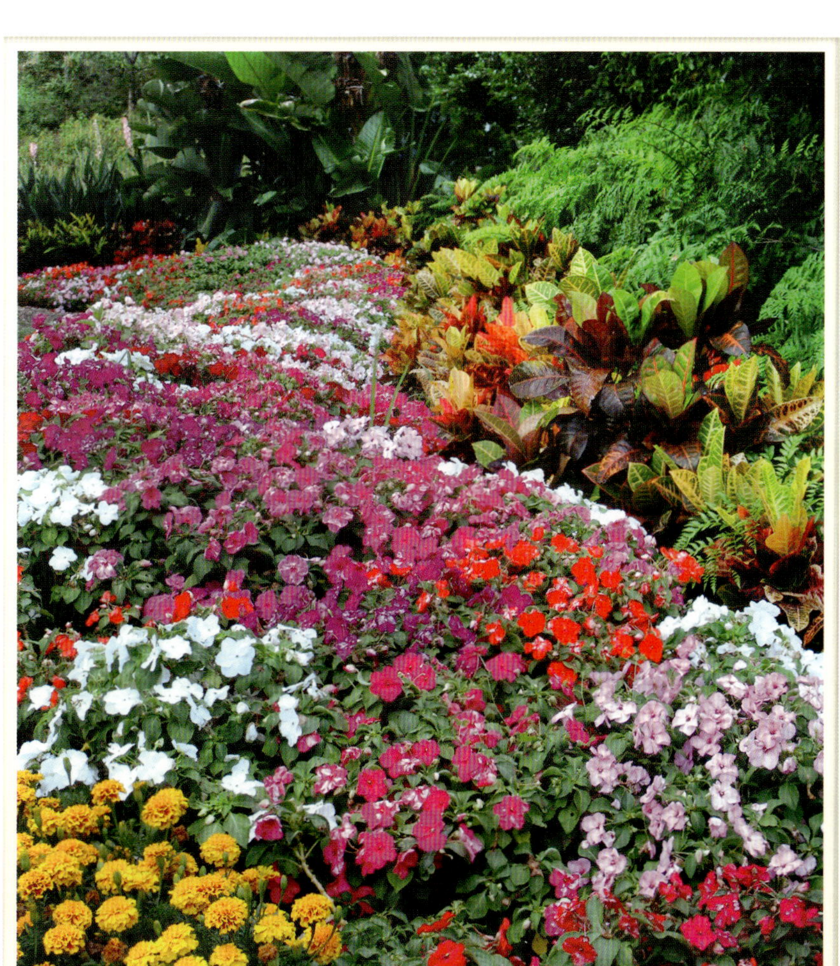

Debra Doenges

ROMA STREET GARDENS
Brisbane, QLD

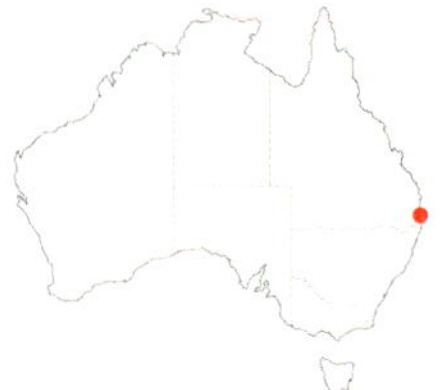

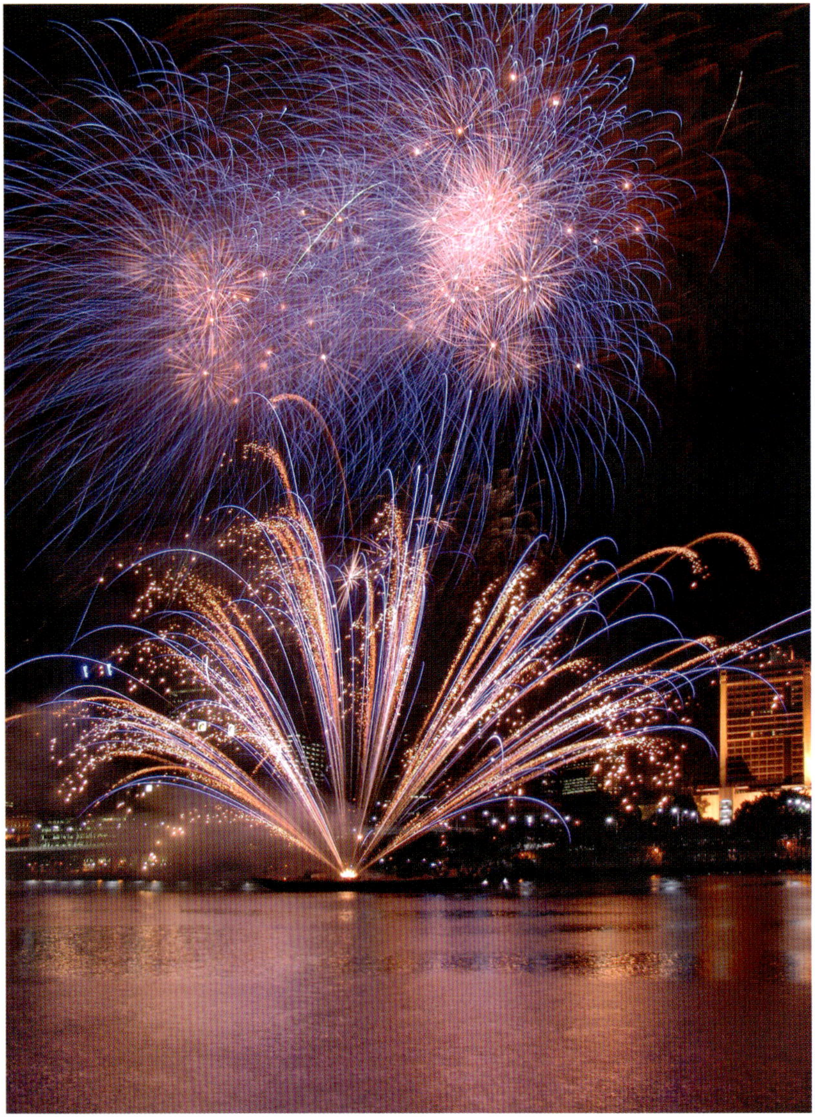

AUSTRALIA DAY FIREWORKS
Brisbane, QLD

Andrew Teakle

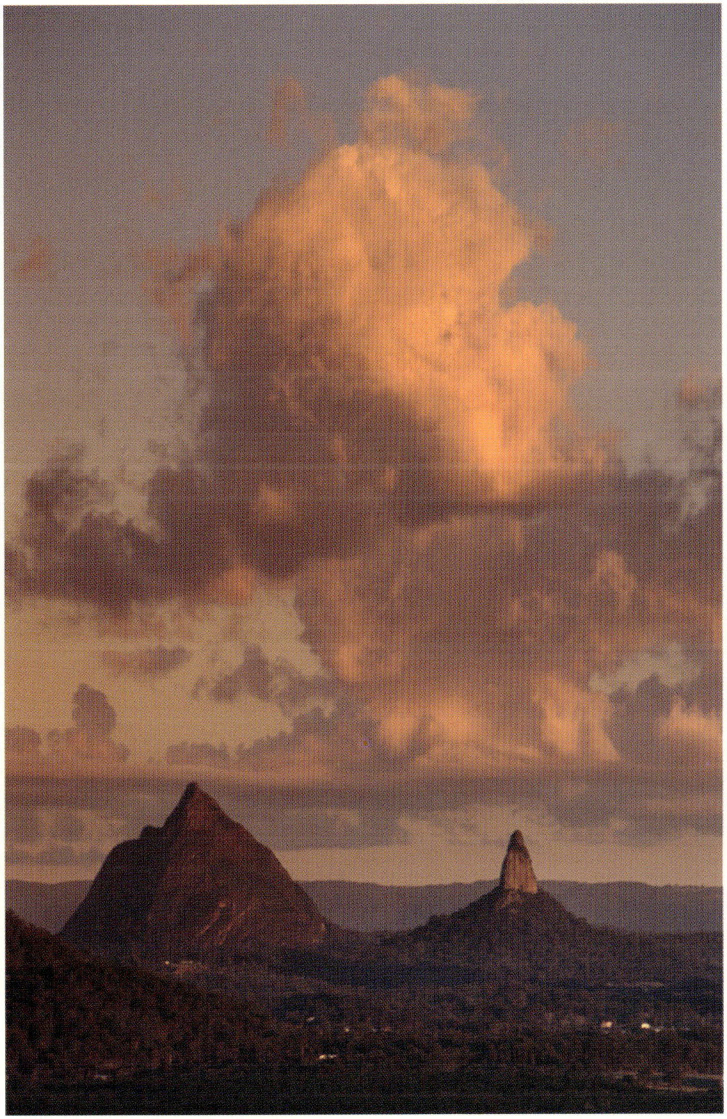

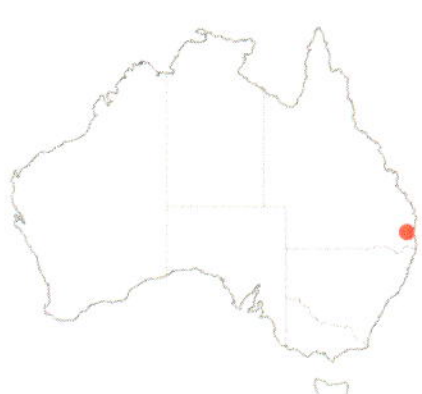

Andrew Teakle

GLASS HOUSE MOUNTAINS

Sunshine Coast Hinterland, QLD

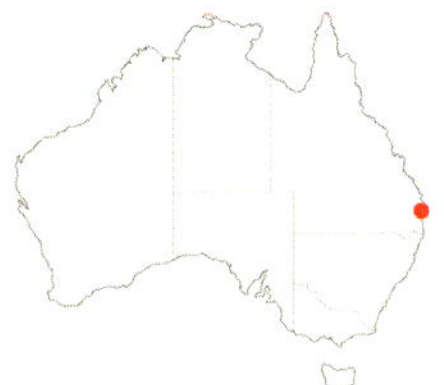

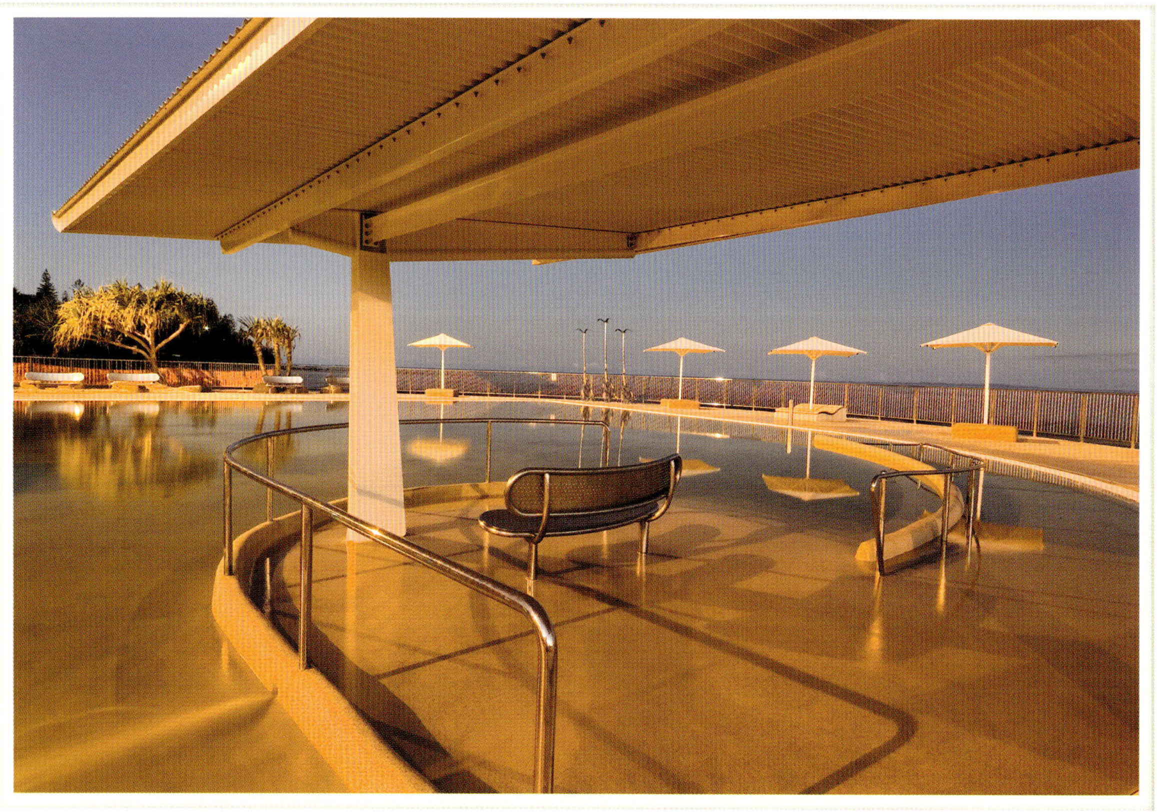

SWIMMING POOL AT KINGS BEACH

Caloundra, Sunshine Coast, QLD

Andrew Teakle

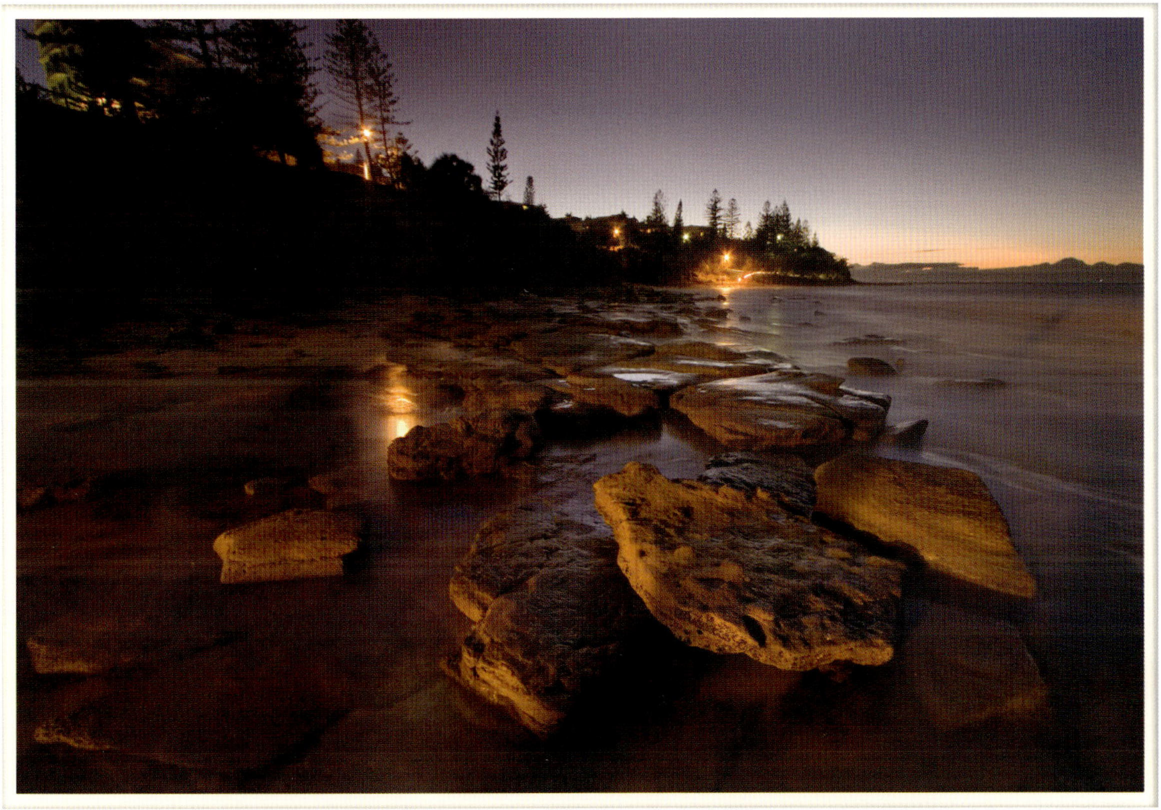

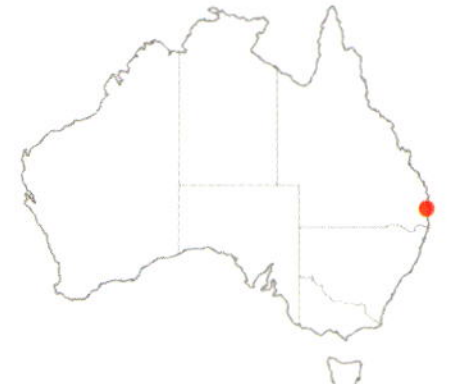

Andrew Teakle

DAWN OVER KINGS BEACH

Caloundra, Sunshine Coast, QLD

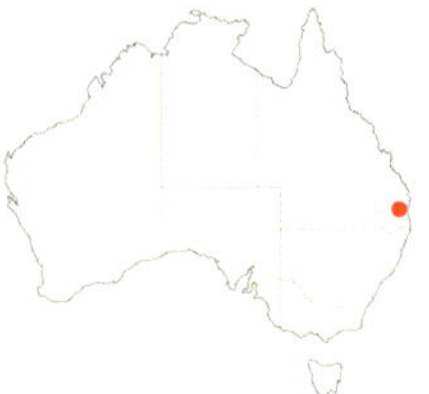

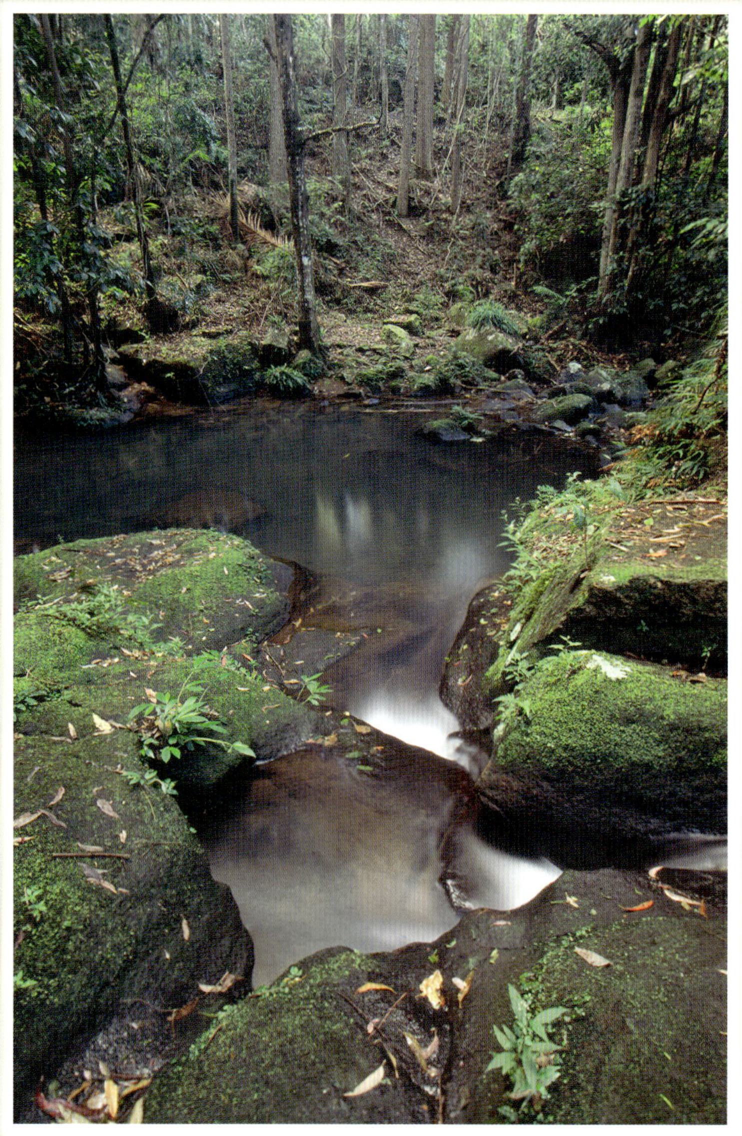

PICNIC CREEK
Kondalilla Falls National Park, QLD

Andrew Teakle

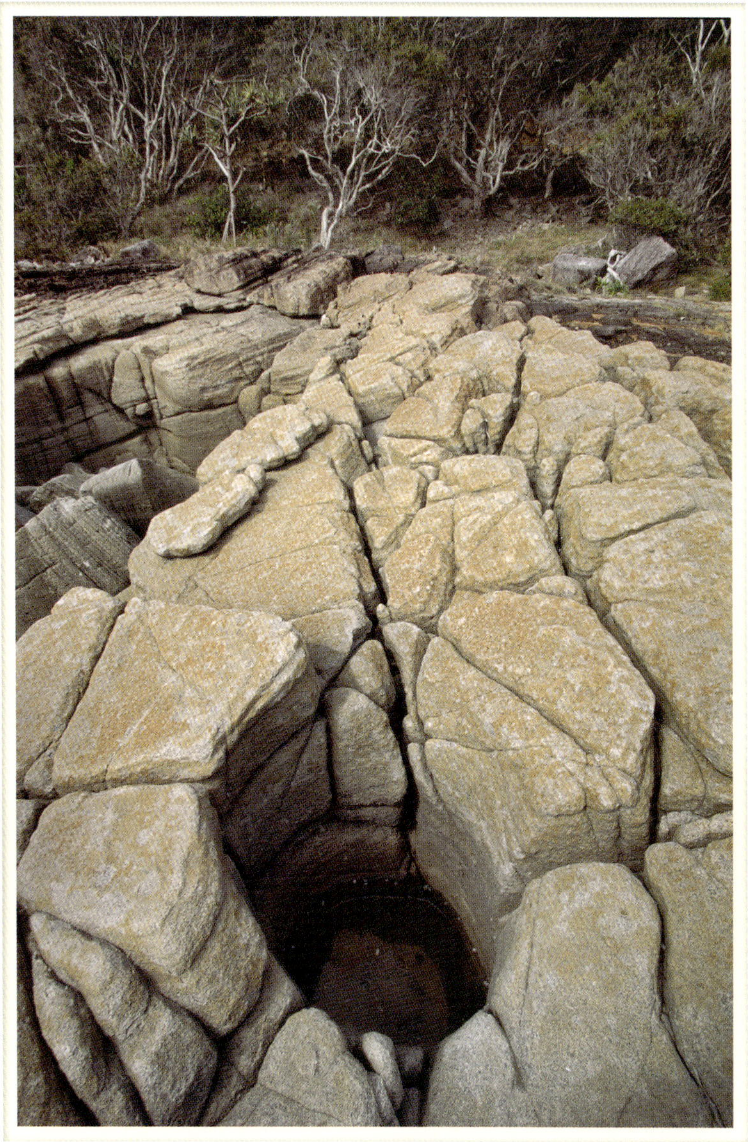

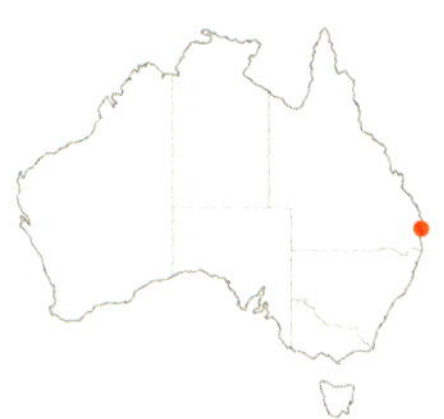

Andrew Teakle

TEA TREE BAY

Noosa National Park, QLD

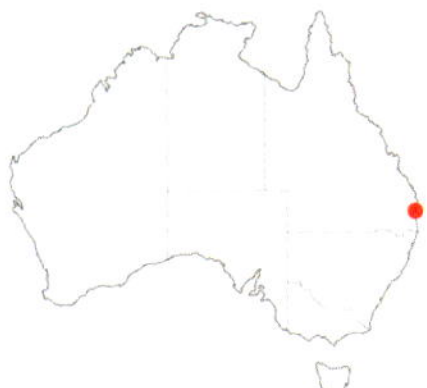

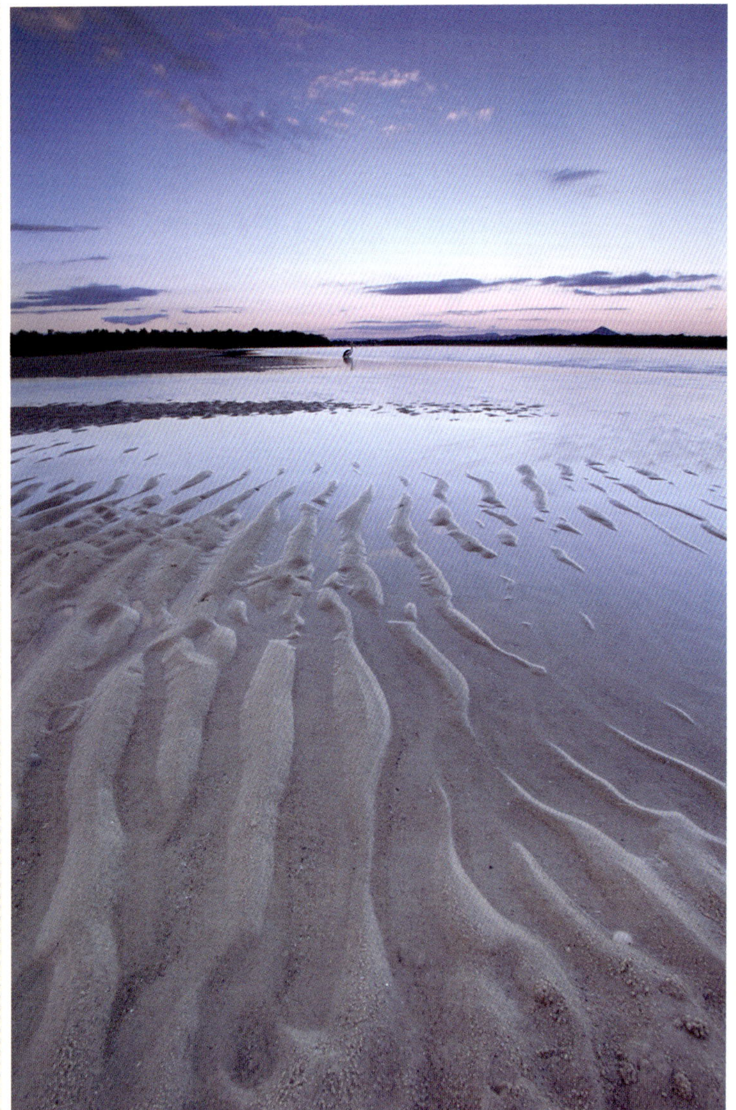

NOOSA SPIT

Noosa, Sunshine Coast, QLD

Andrew Teakle

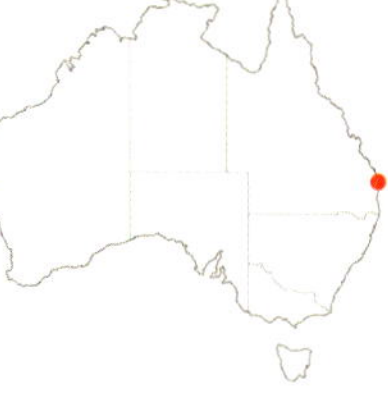

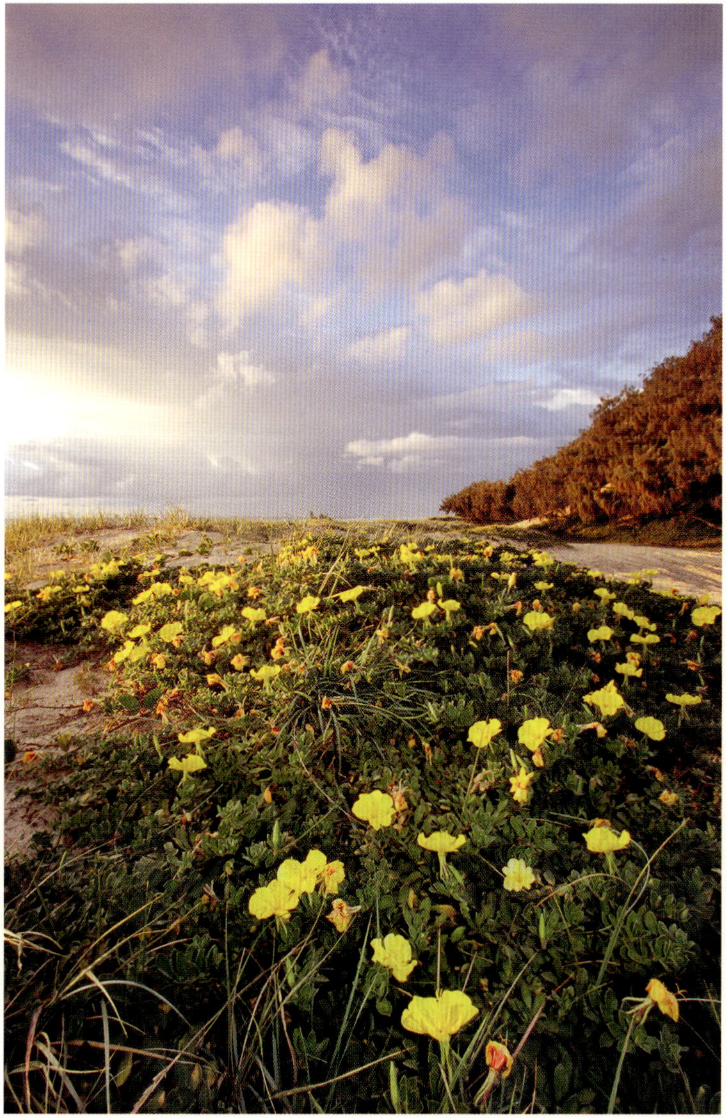

Andrew Teakle

TEEWAH BEACH MORNING
Cooloola Coast, Great Sandy National Park, QLD

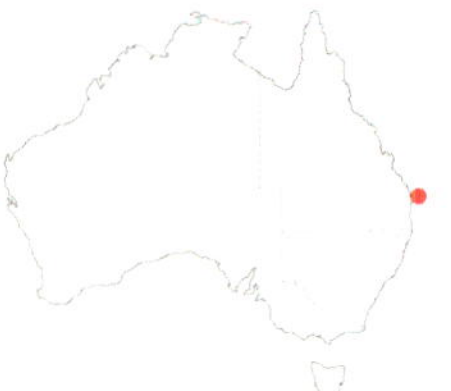

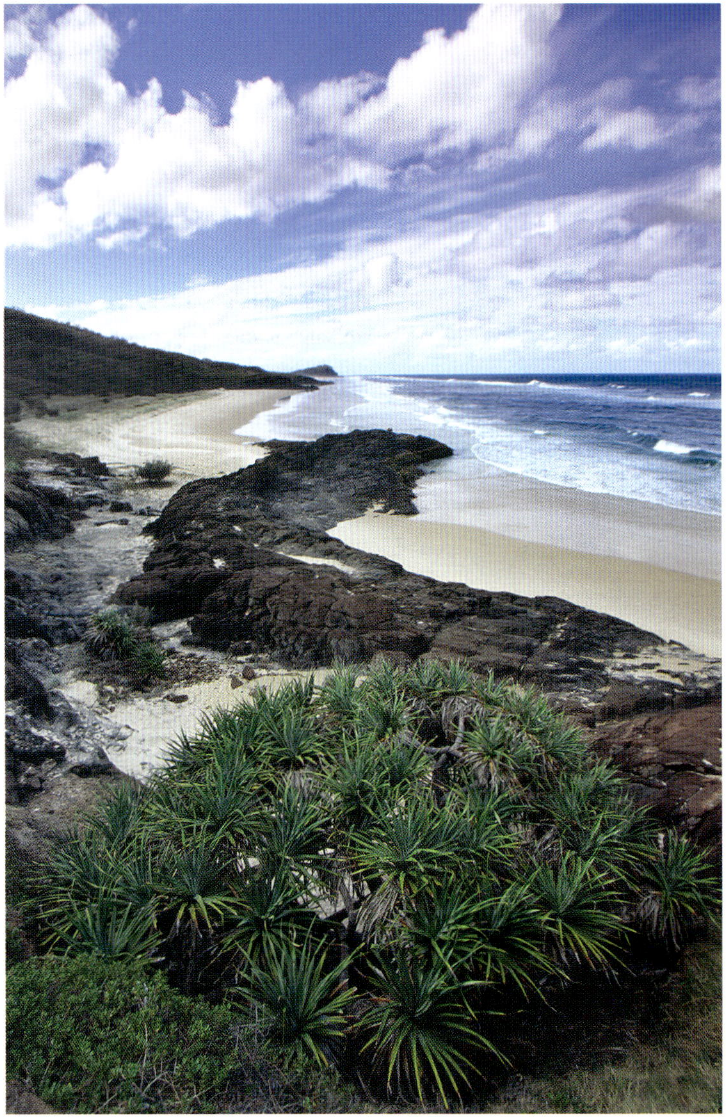

MIDDLE ROCKS

Andrew Teakle

Fraser Island, Great Sandy National Park, QLD

LAKE ALLOM

Fraser Island, Great Sandy National Park, QLD ▶

Debra Doenges

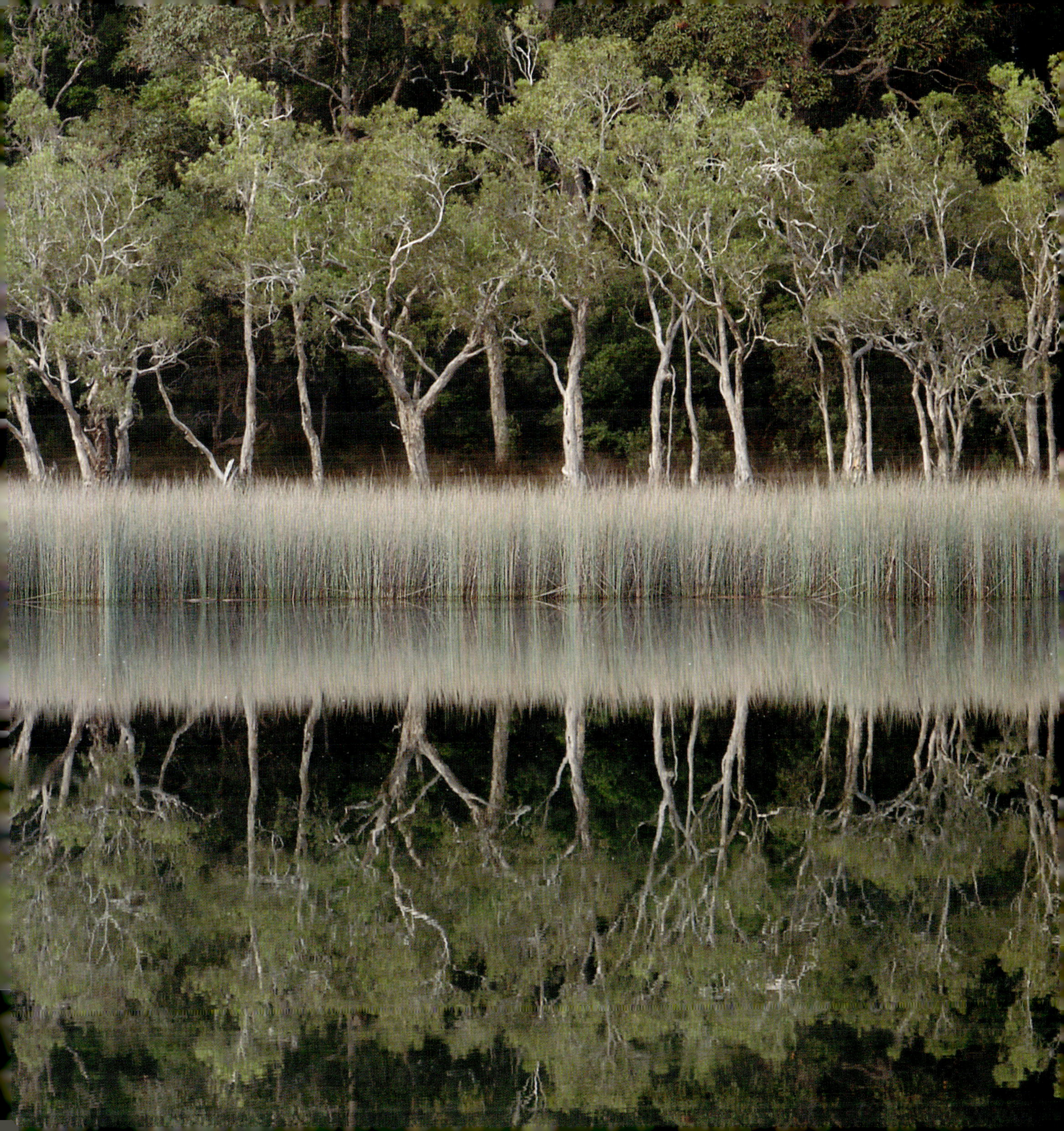

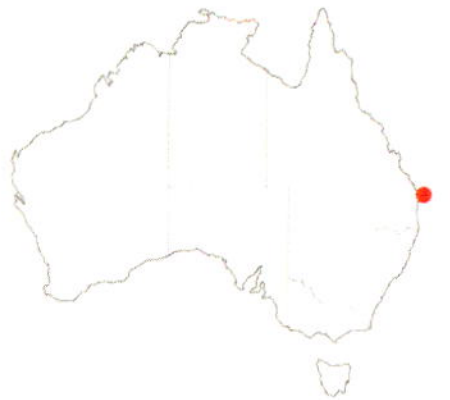

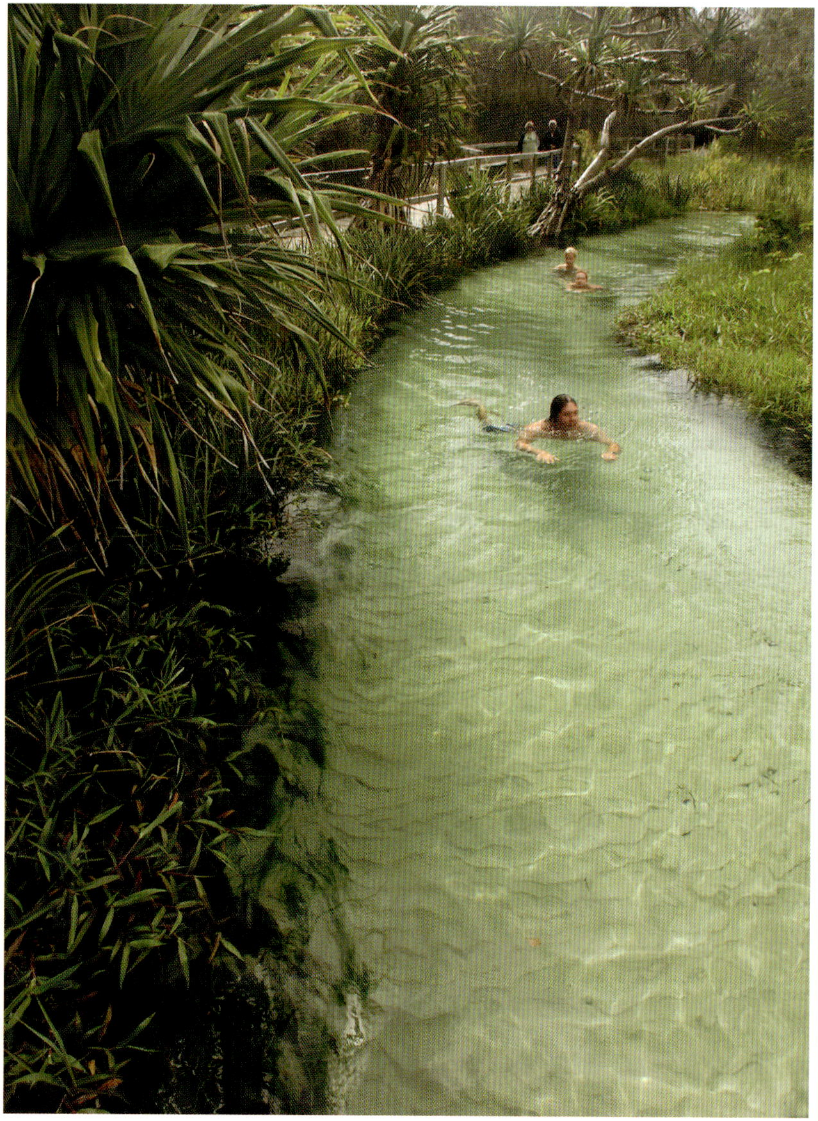

ELI CREEK

Debra Doenges & Andrew Teakle

Fraser Island, Great Sandy National Park, QLD

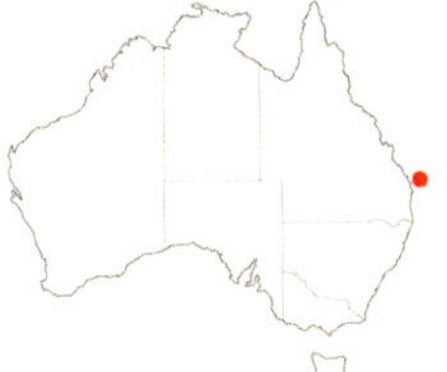

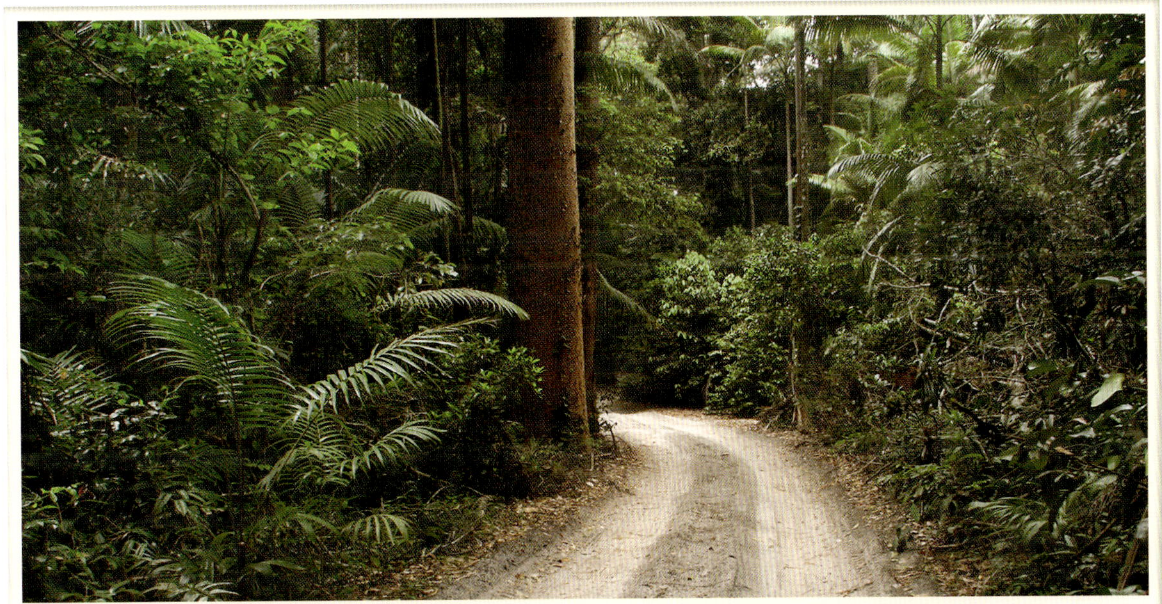

91

Debra Doenges & Andrew Teakle

RAINFOREST DRIVE

Fraser Island, Great Sandy National Park, QLD

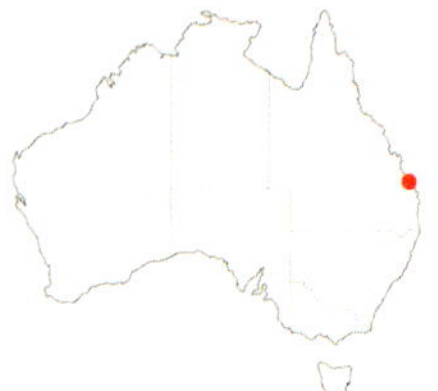

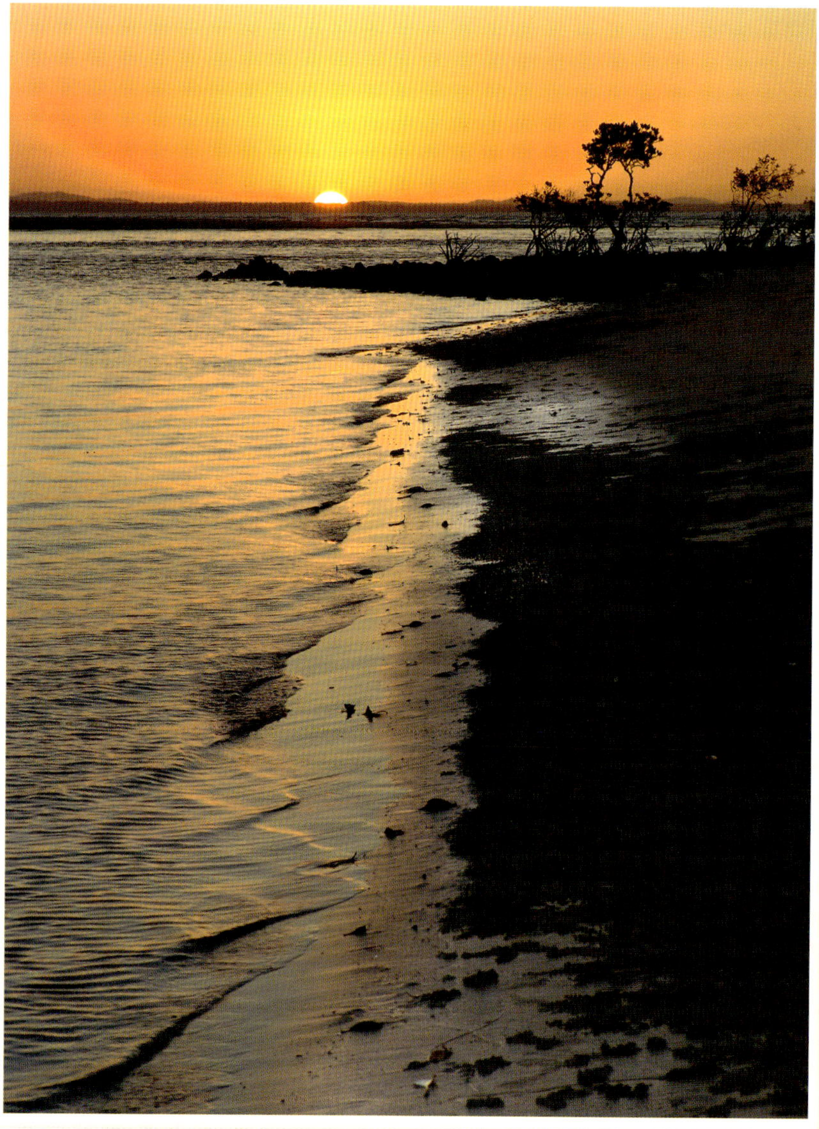

BUSTARD BAY SUNSET
Town of 1770, QLD

Debra Doenges

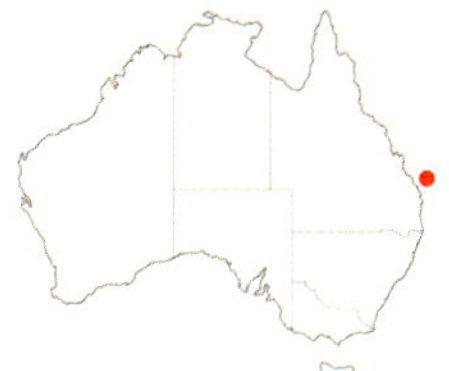

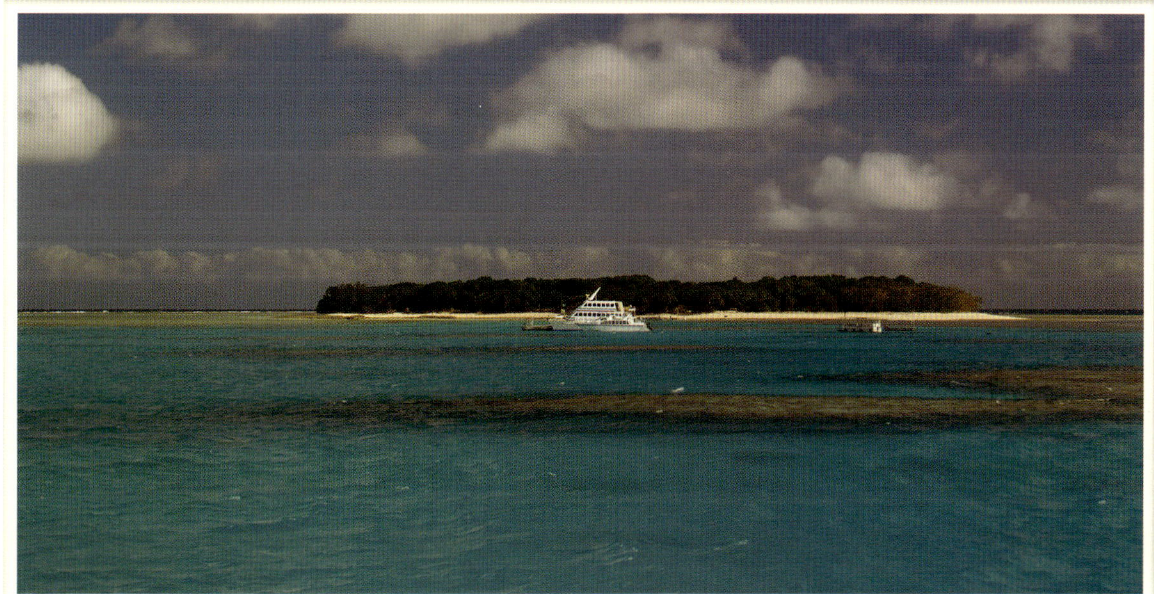

Debra Doenges & Andrew Teakle

CRUISING LADY MUSGRAVE ISLAND

Great Barrier Reef Marine Park, QLD

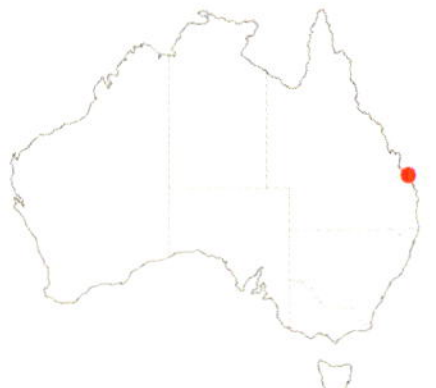

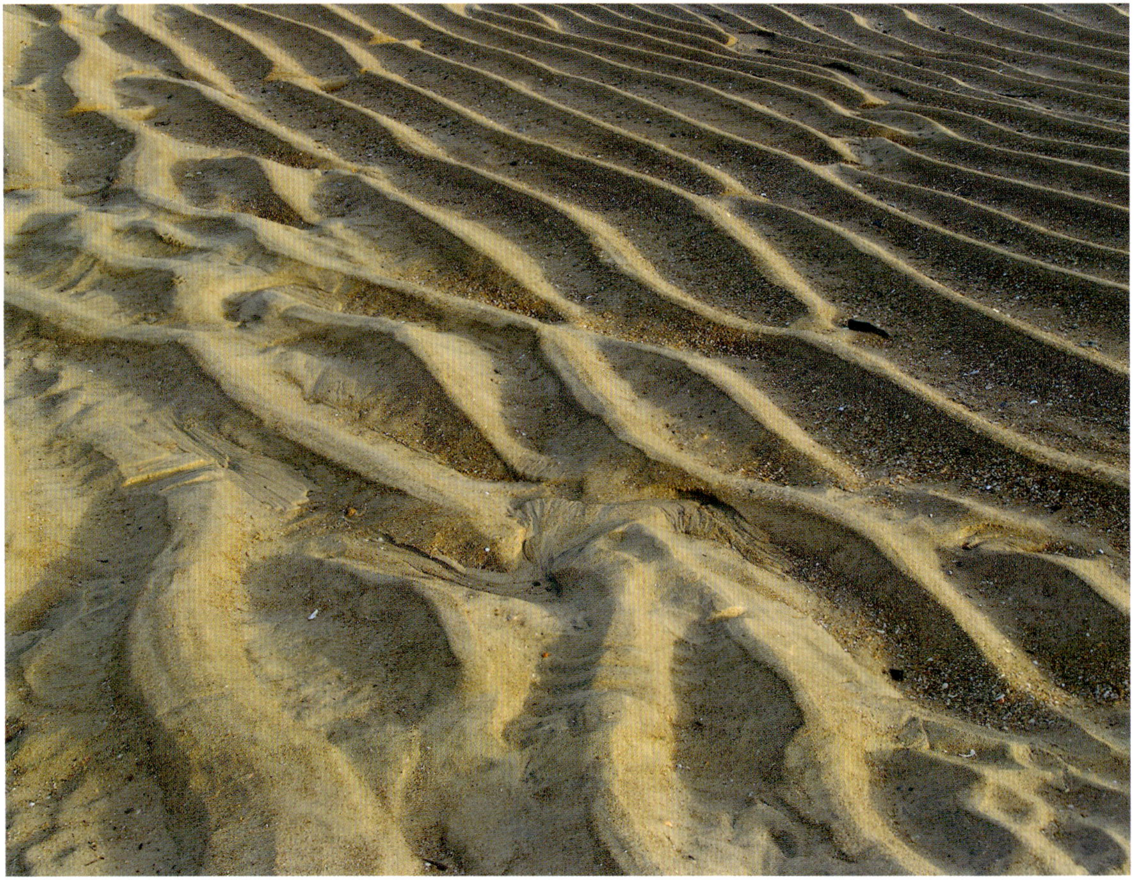

TIDAL SAND PATTERNS

Tannum Sands, QLD

Debra Doenges

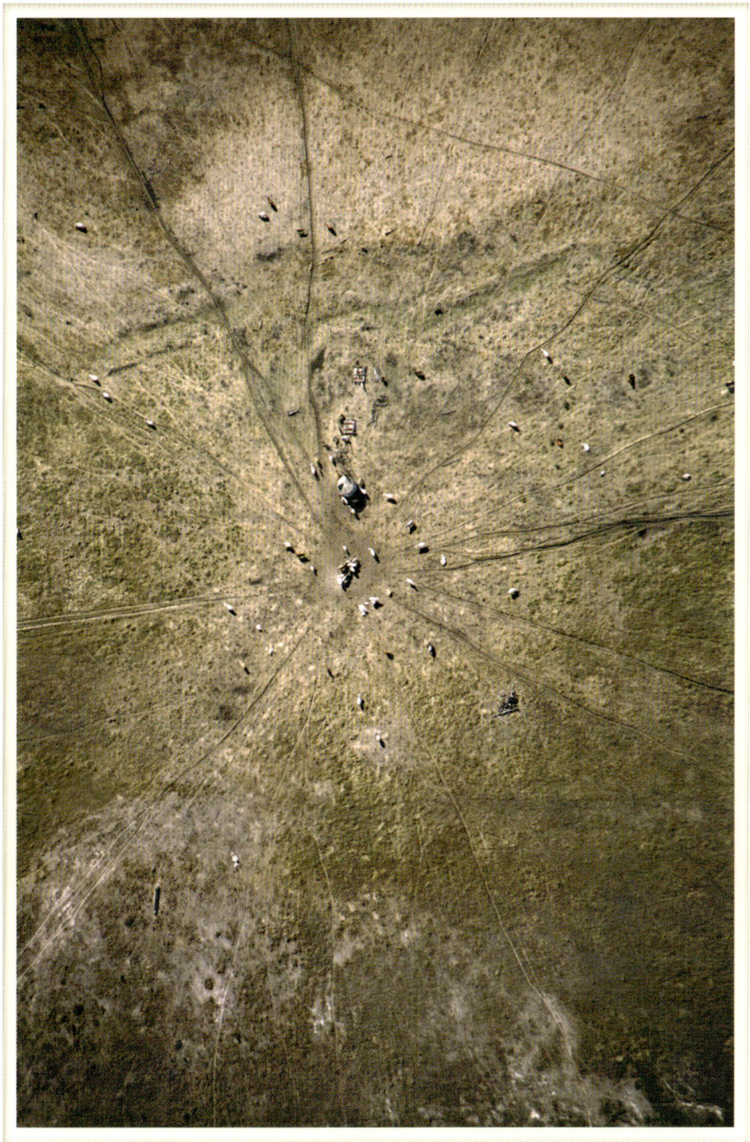

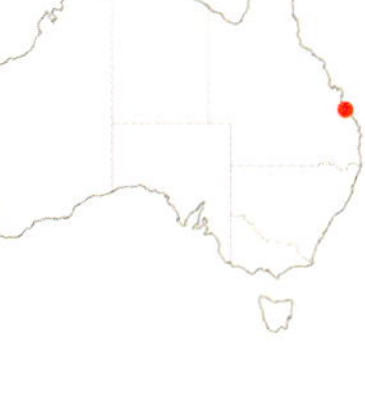

Andrew Teakle

CATTLE WATERING

Rockhampton, QLD

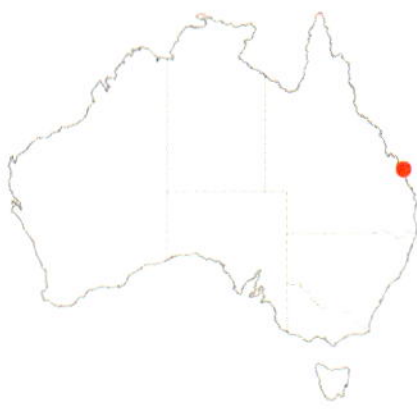

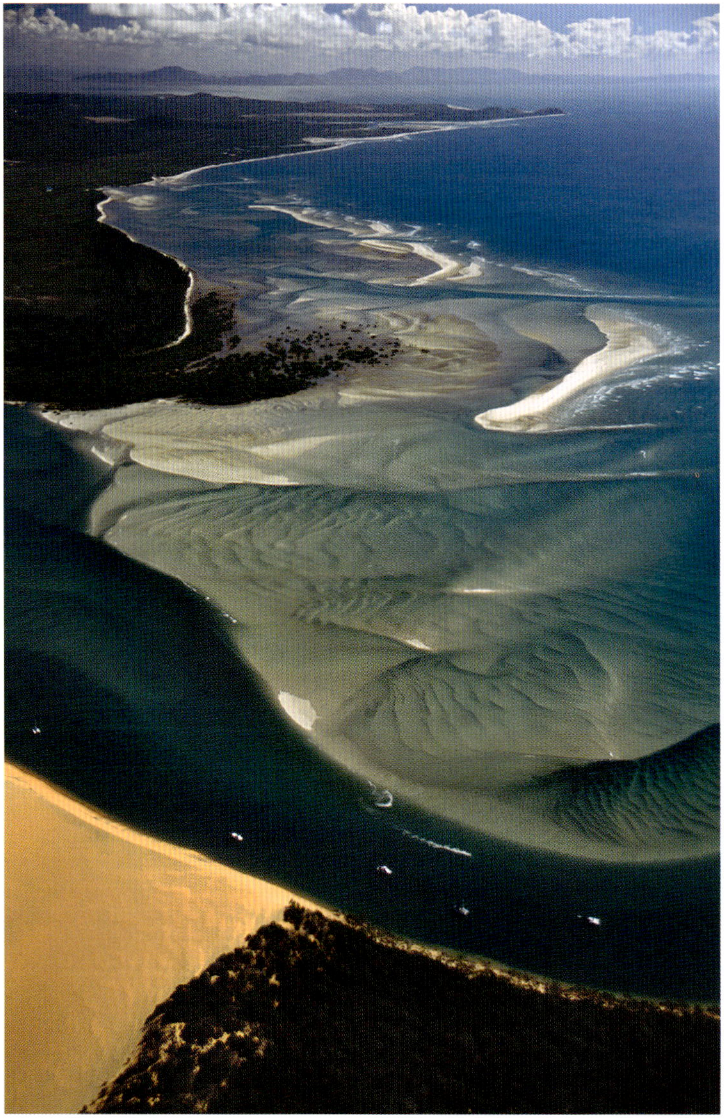

FITZROY RIVER

Keppel Bay, Capricorn Coast, QLD

Andrew Teakle

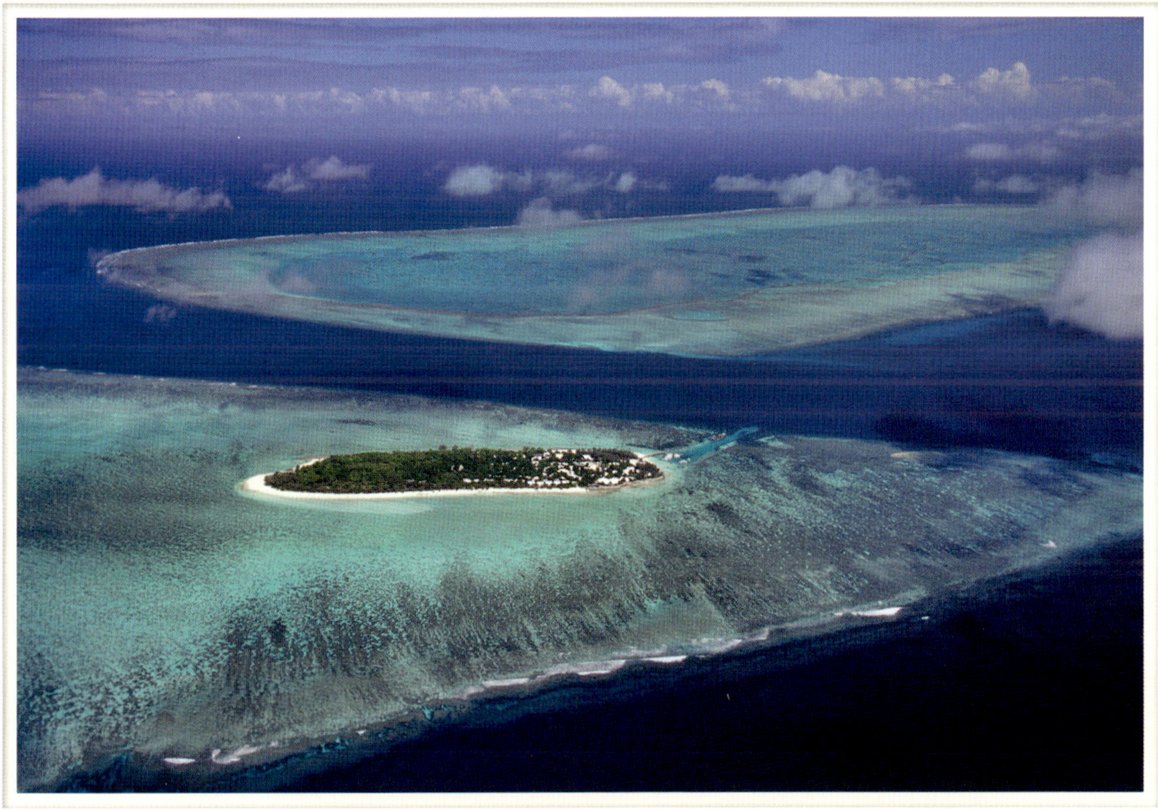

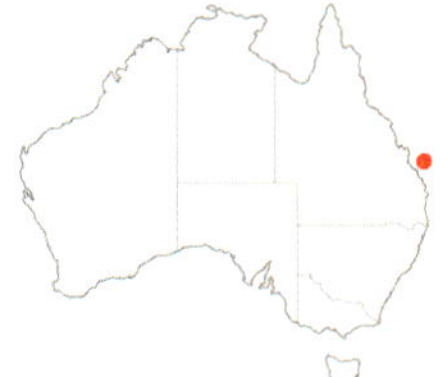

Andrew Teakle

HERON ISLAND

Capricorn Coast, Great Barrier Reef, QLD

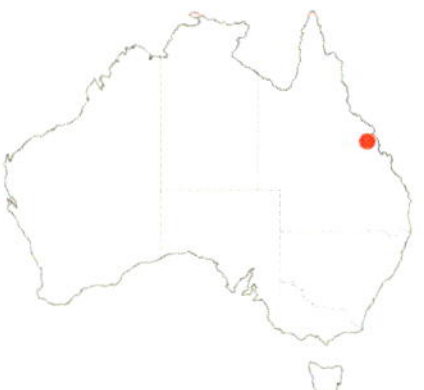

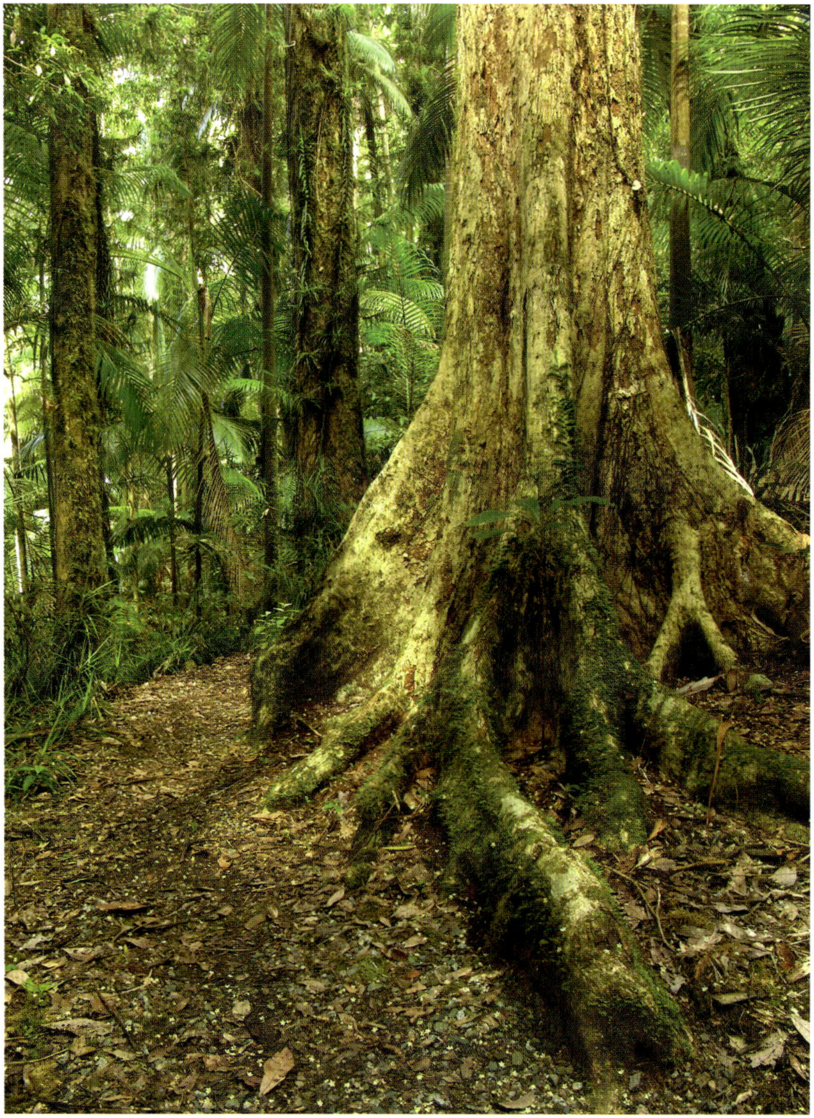

MACKAY TULIP OAK TREE
Eungella National Park, QLD

Debra Doenges

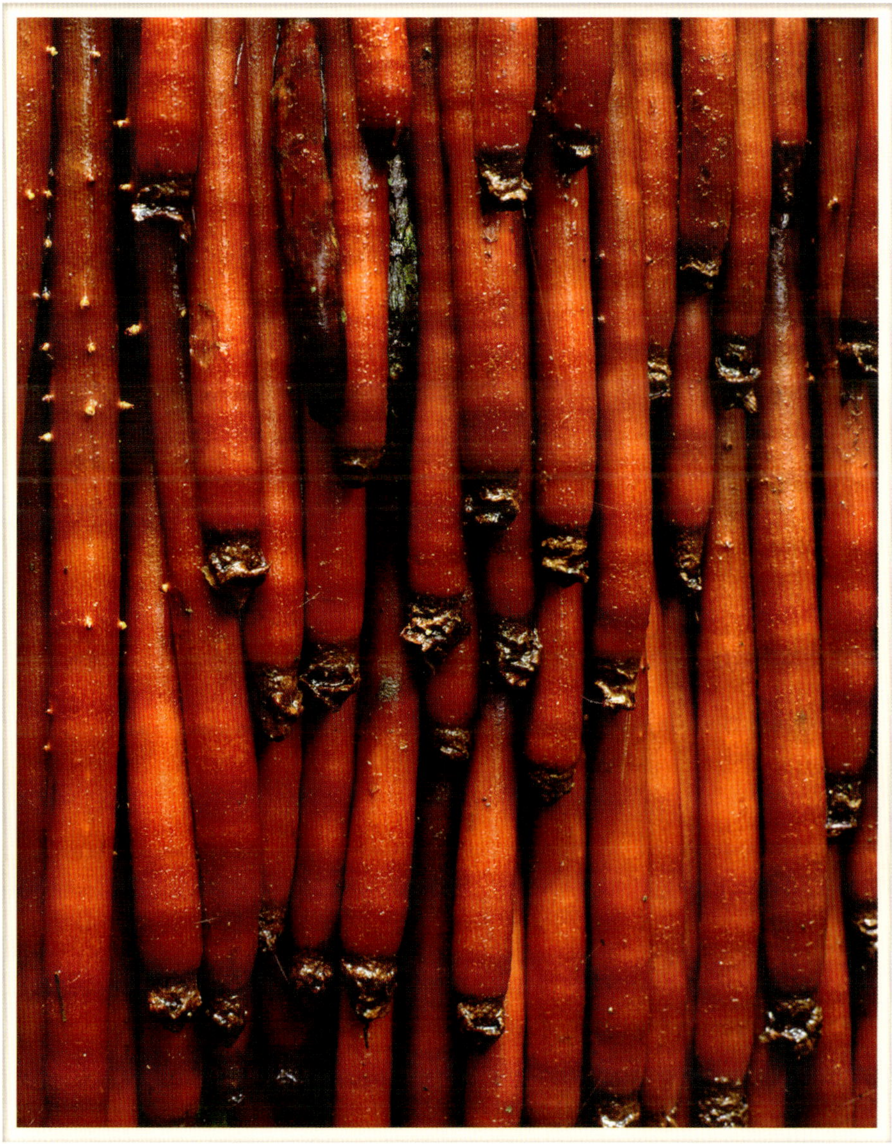

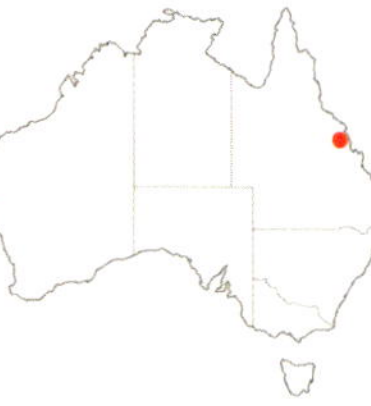

Debra Doenges

PALM ROOTS
Eungella National Park, QLD

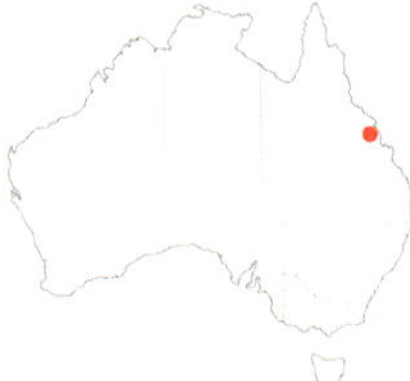

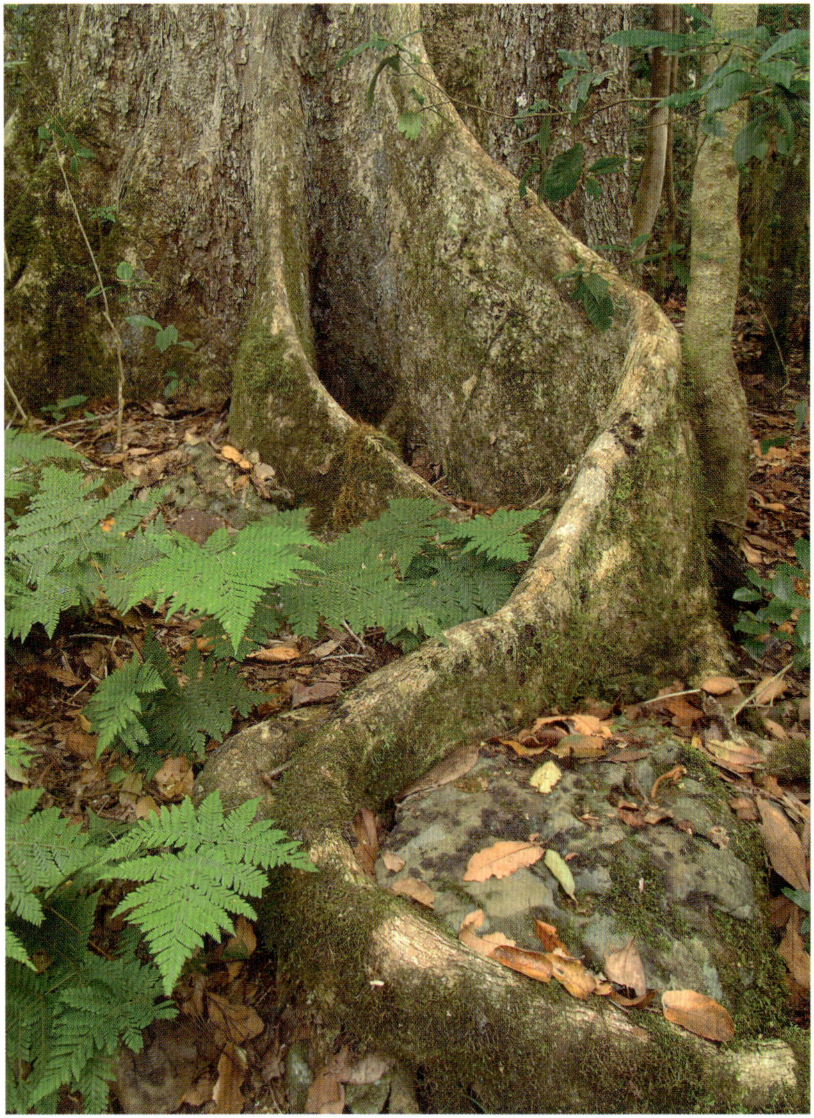

RAINFOREST BUTTRESS ROOTS
Eungella National Park, QLD

Debra Doenges

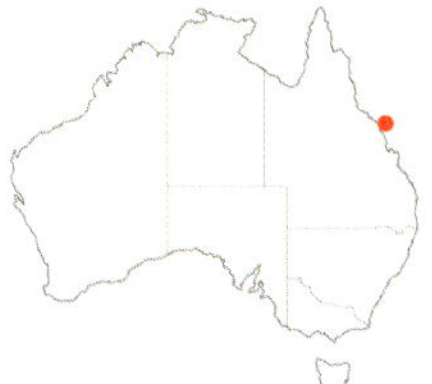

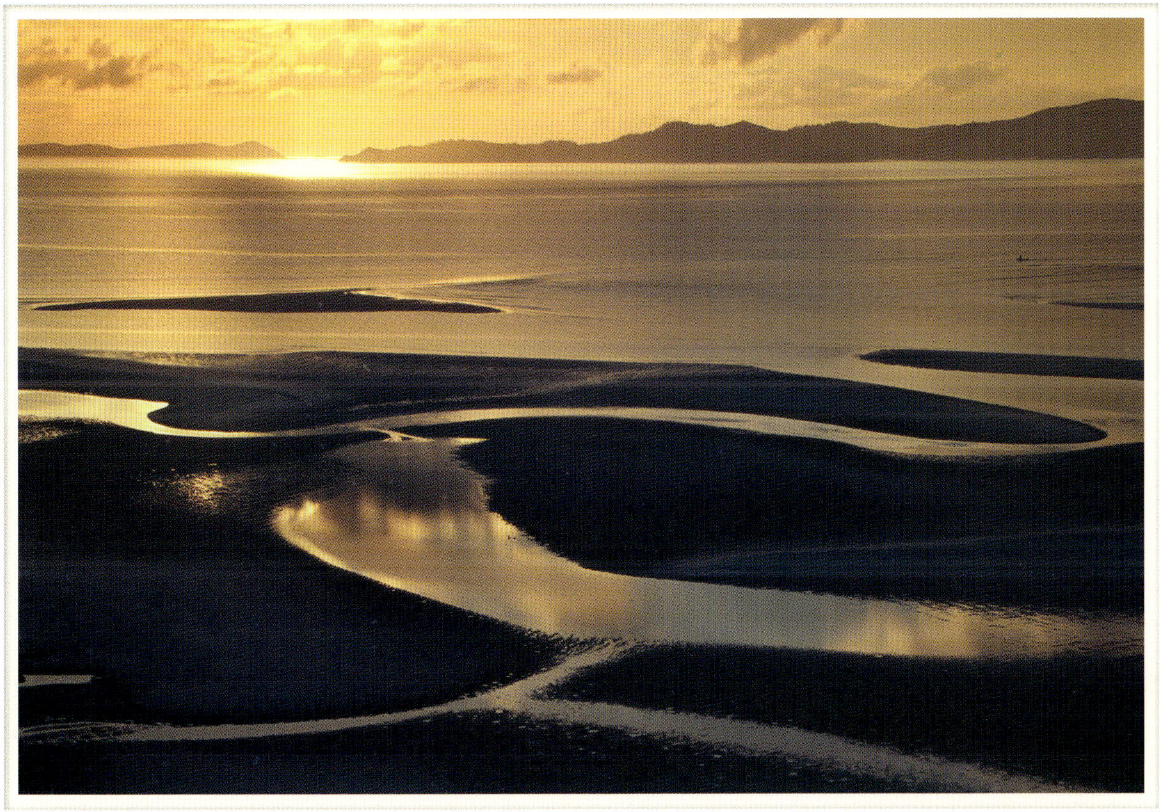

Andrew Teakle

SUNRISE OVER TONGUE LOOKOUT

Whitsunday Islands, QLD

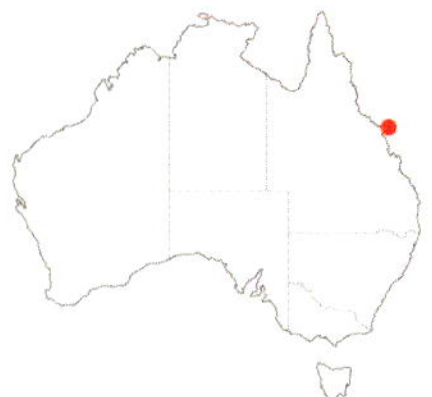

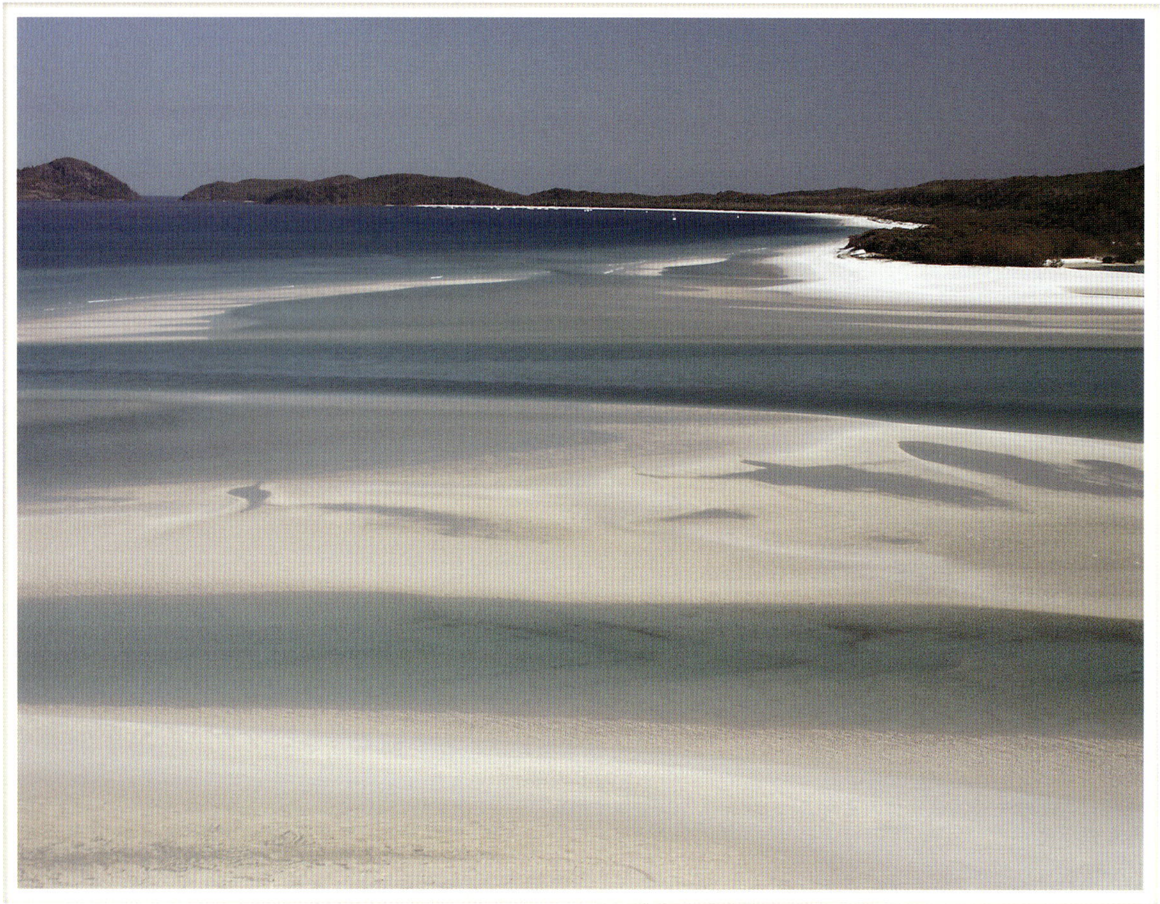

WHITEHAVEN BEACH
Whitsunday Islands, QLD

Debra Doenges

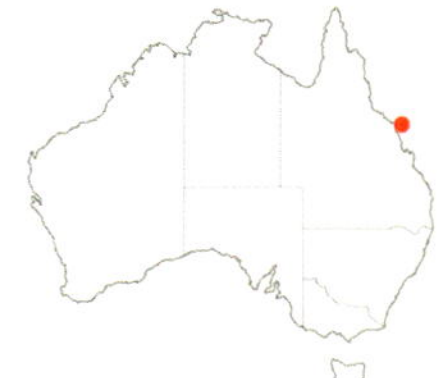

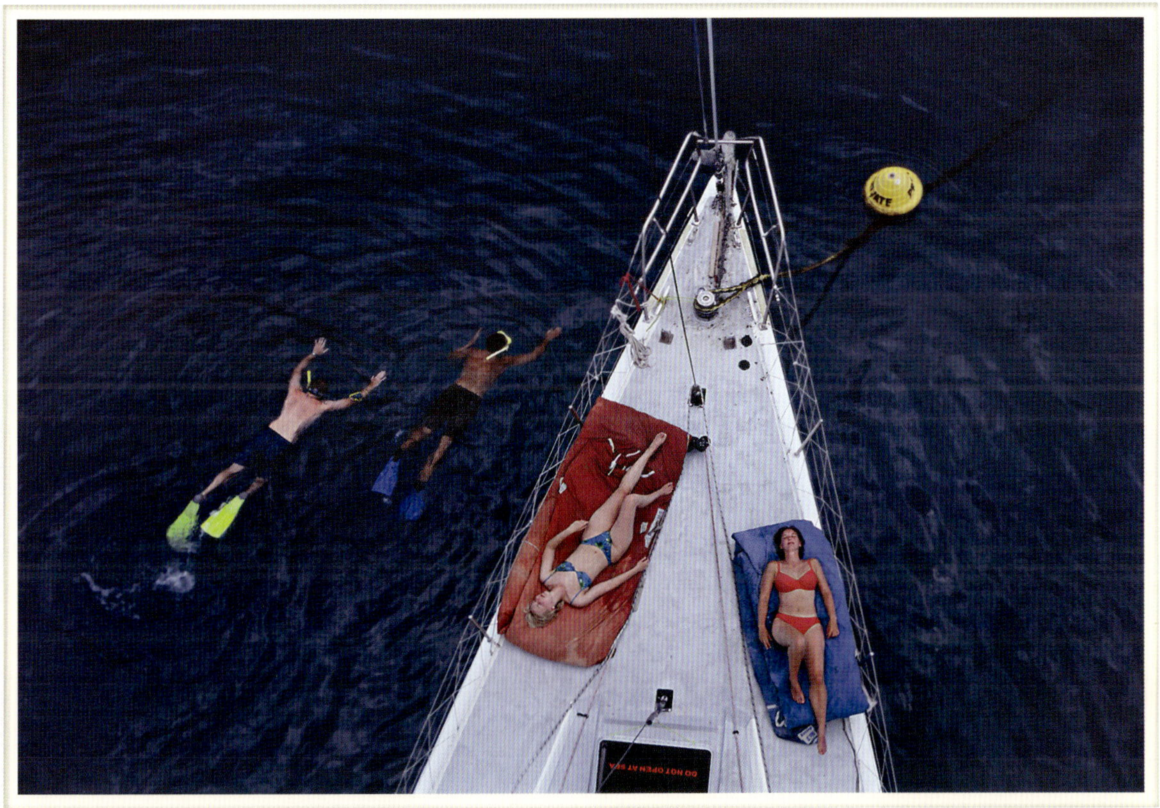

Andrew Teakle

SUNBATHERS & SNORKELLERS
Whitsunday Islands, QLD

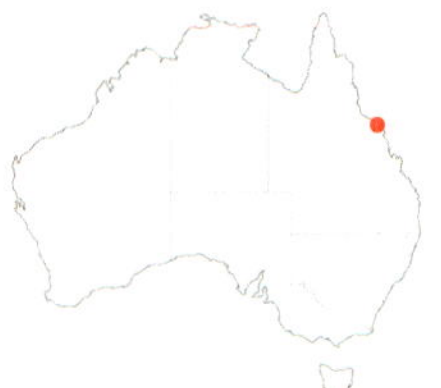

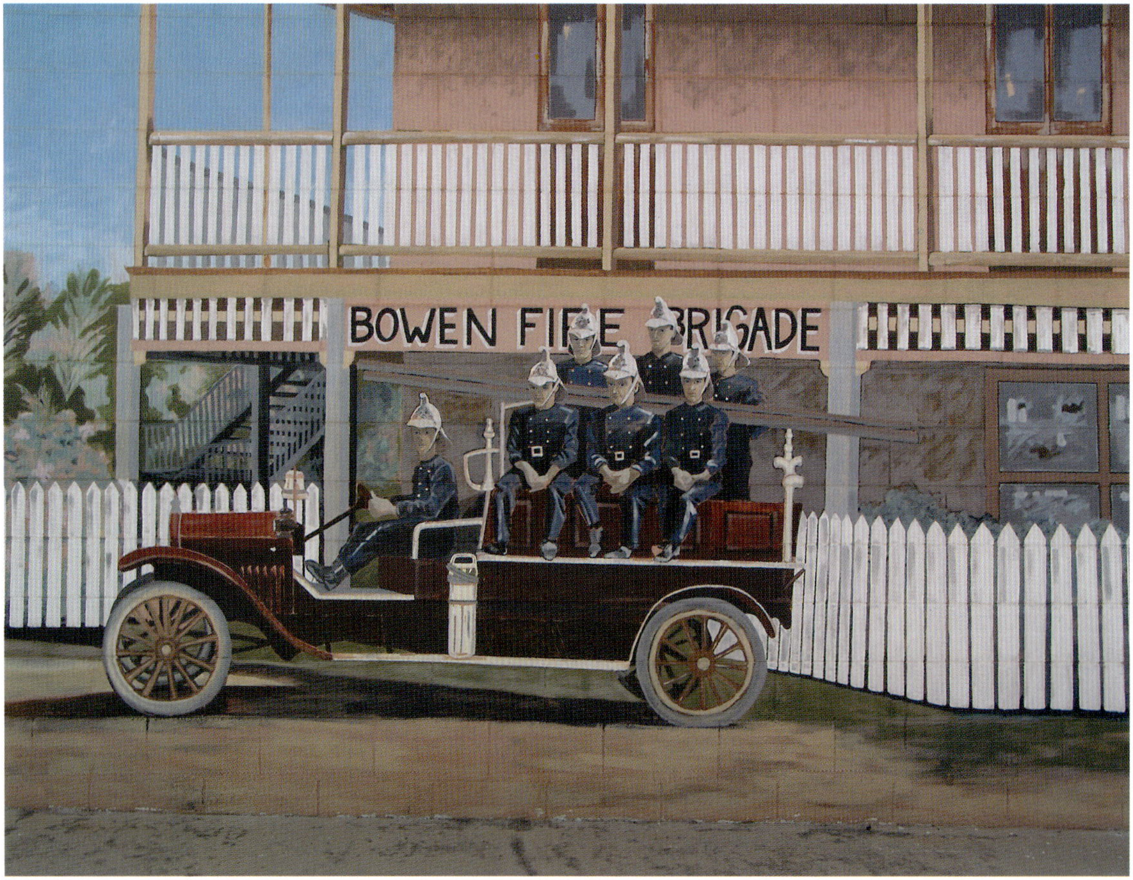

FIRE BRIGADE MURAL
Bowen, QLD

Debra Doenges

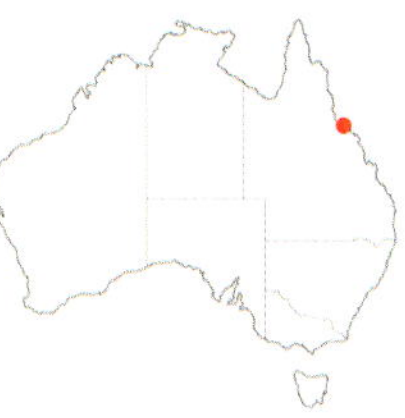

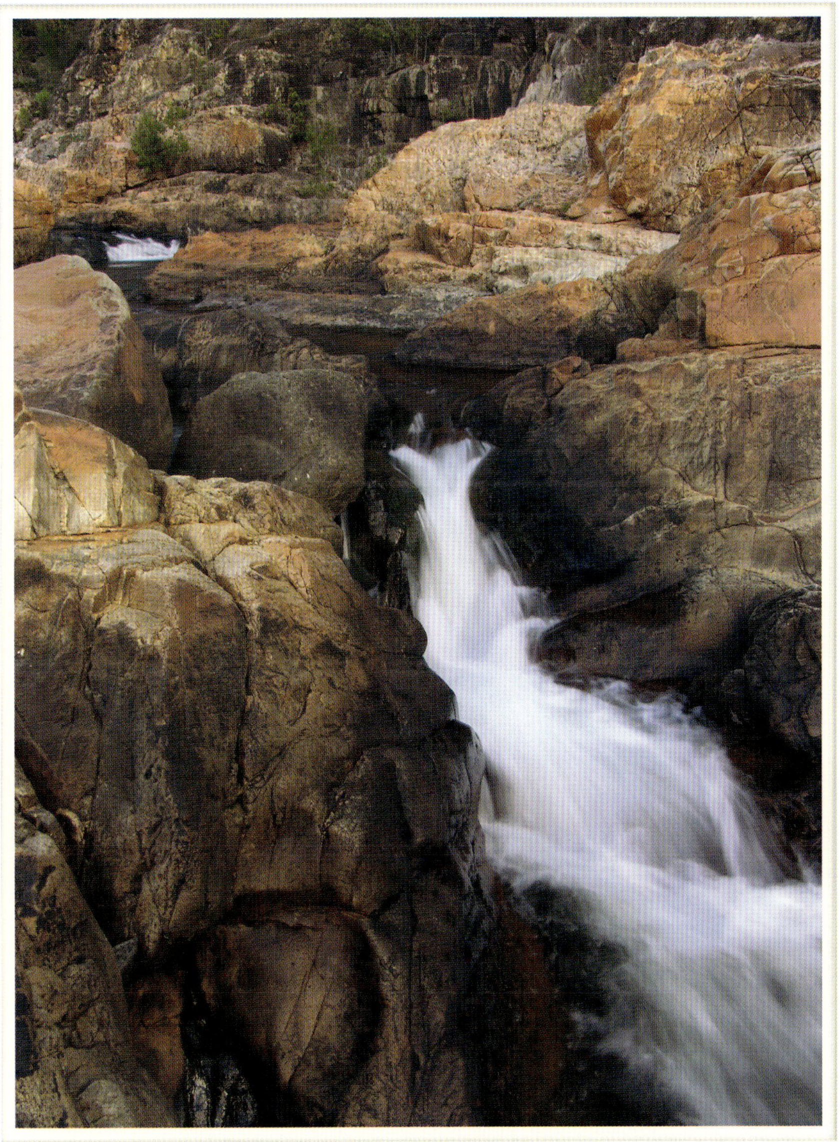

Debra Doenges

ALLIGATOR CREEK

Bowling Green Bay National Park, QLD

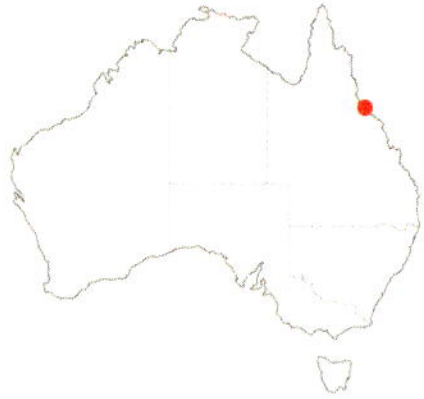

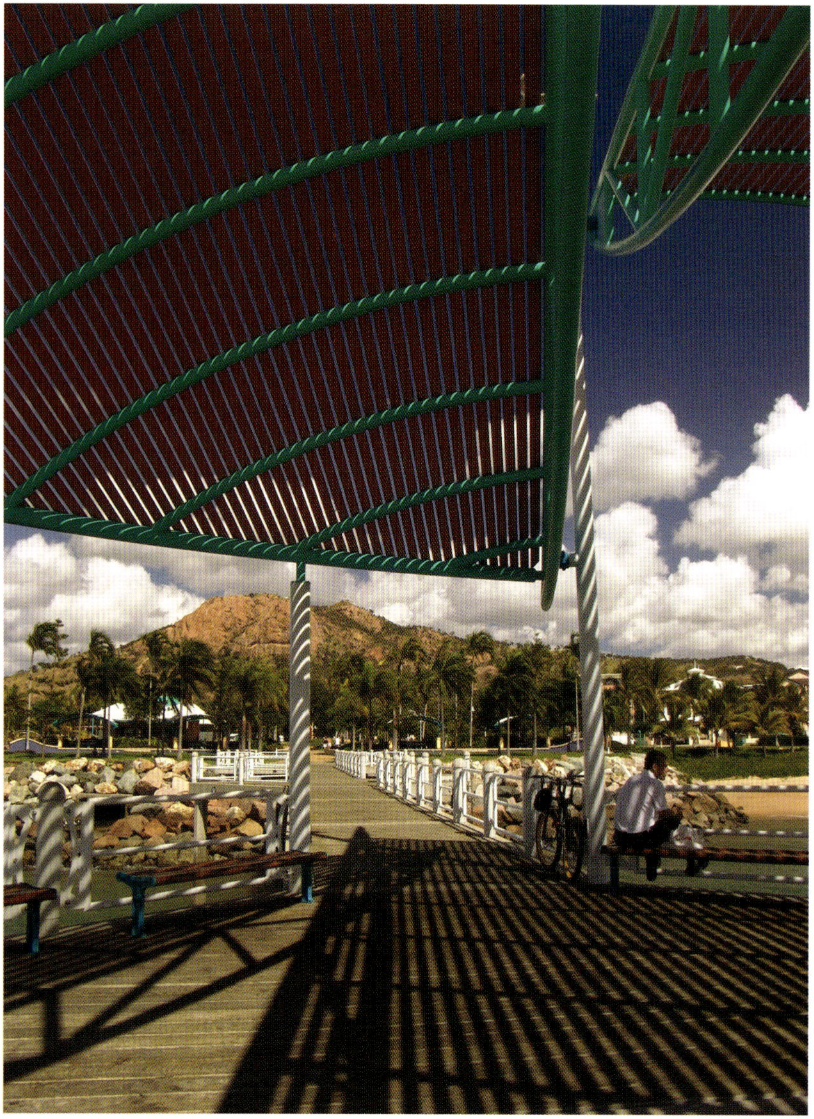

THE STRAND & CASTLE HILL

Townsville, QLD

Debra Doenges

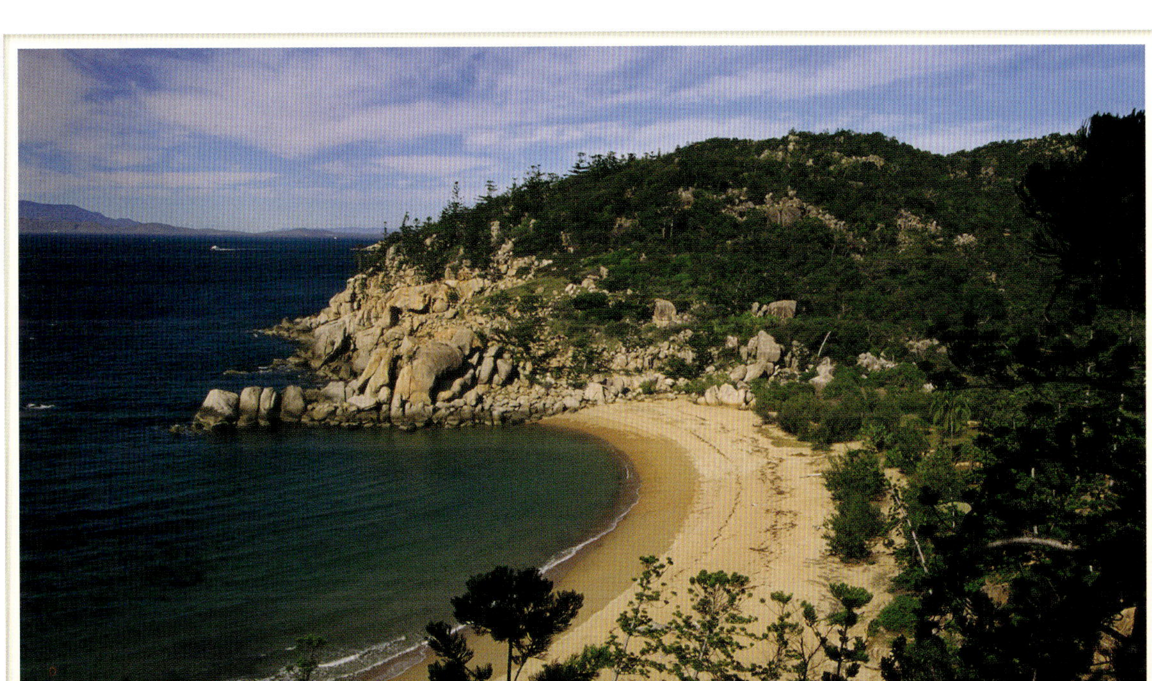

Andrew Teakle & Debra Doenges

ARTHUR BAY

Magnetic Island National Park, QLD

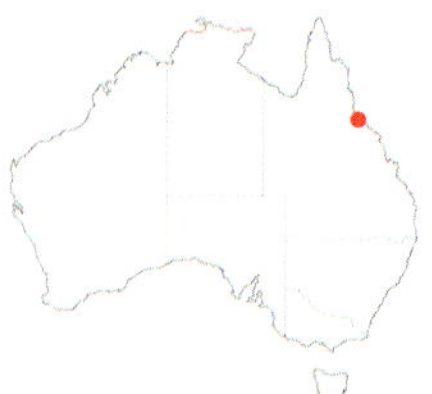

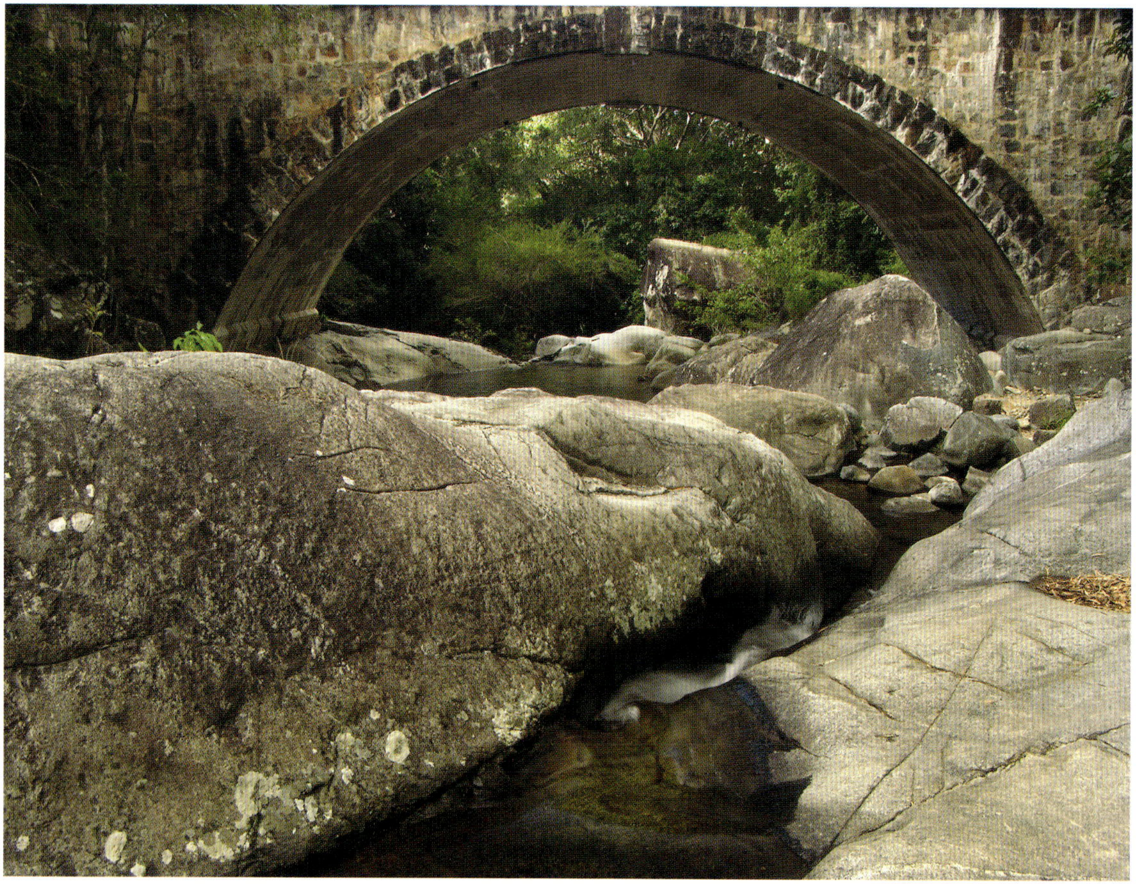

LITTLE CRYSTAL CREEK
Paluma Range National Park, QLD

Debra Doenges

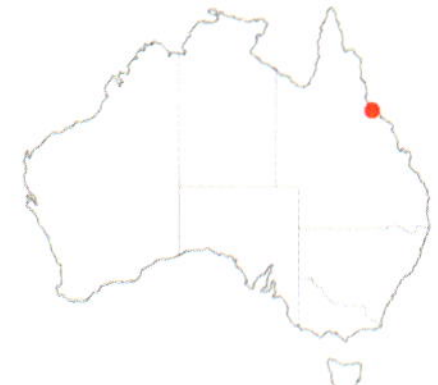

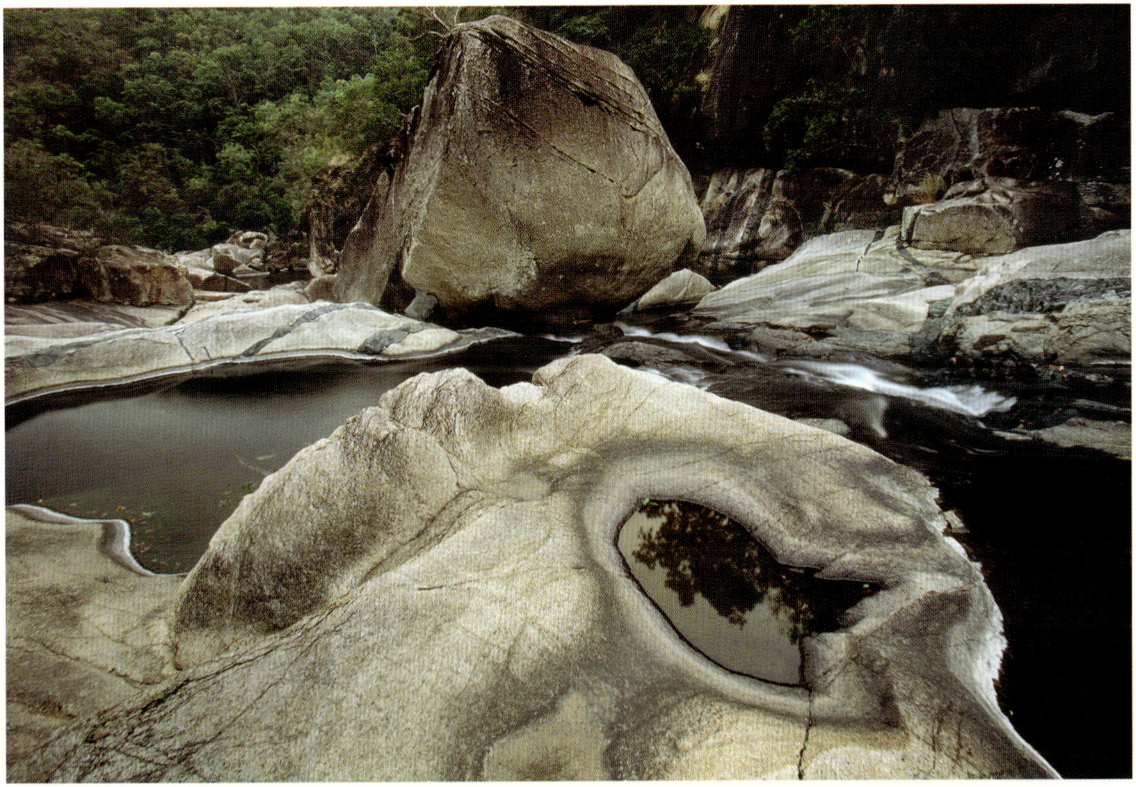

Andrew Teakle

WATERVIEW CREEK

Jourama Falls, Paluma Range National Park, QLD

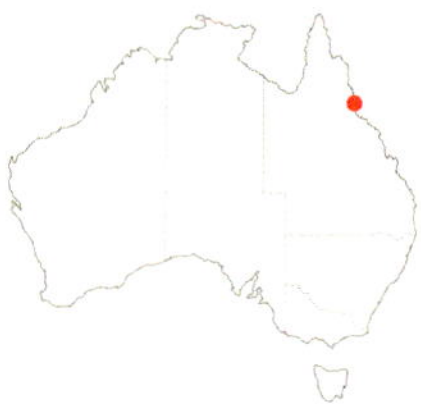

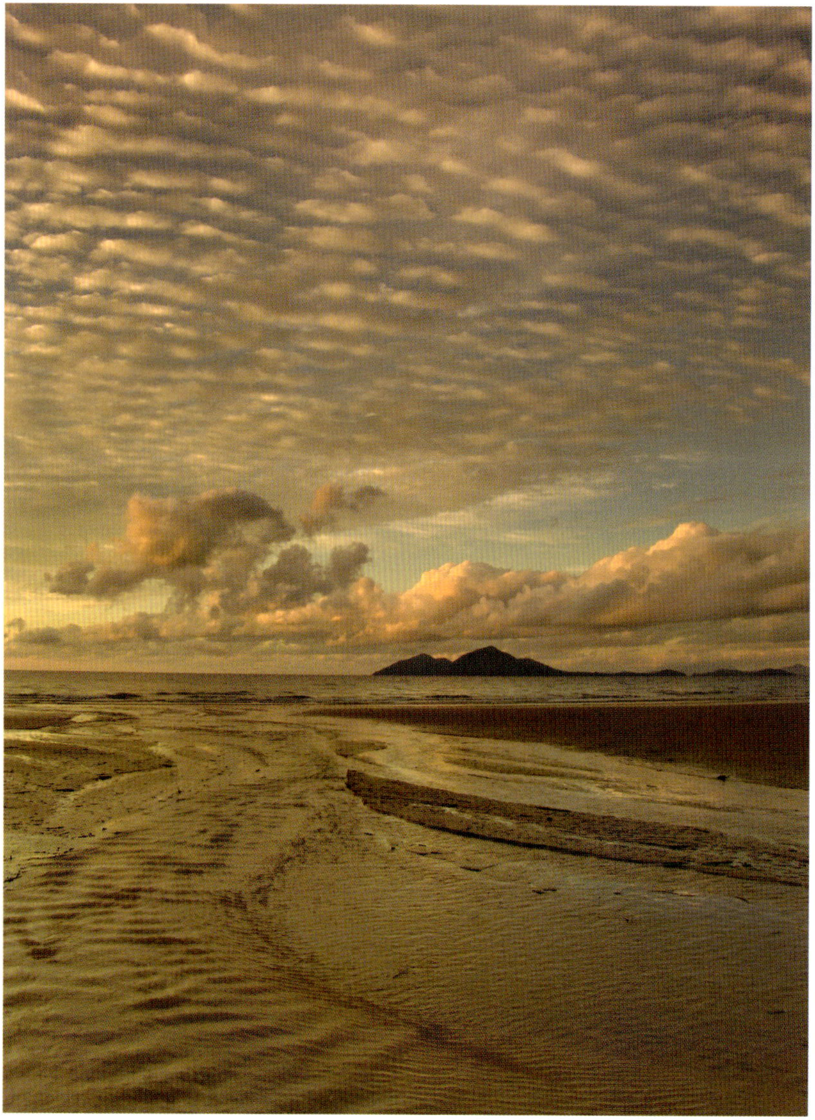

DUNK ISLAND
Mission Beach, QLD

Debra Doenges

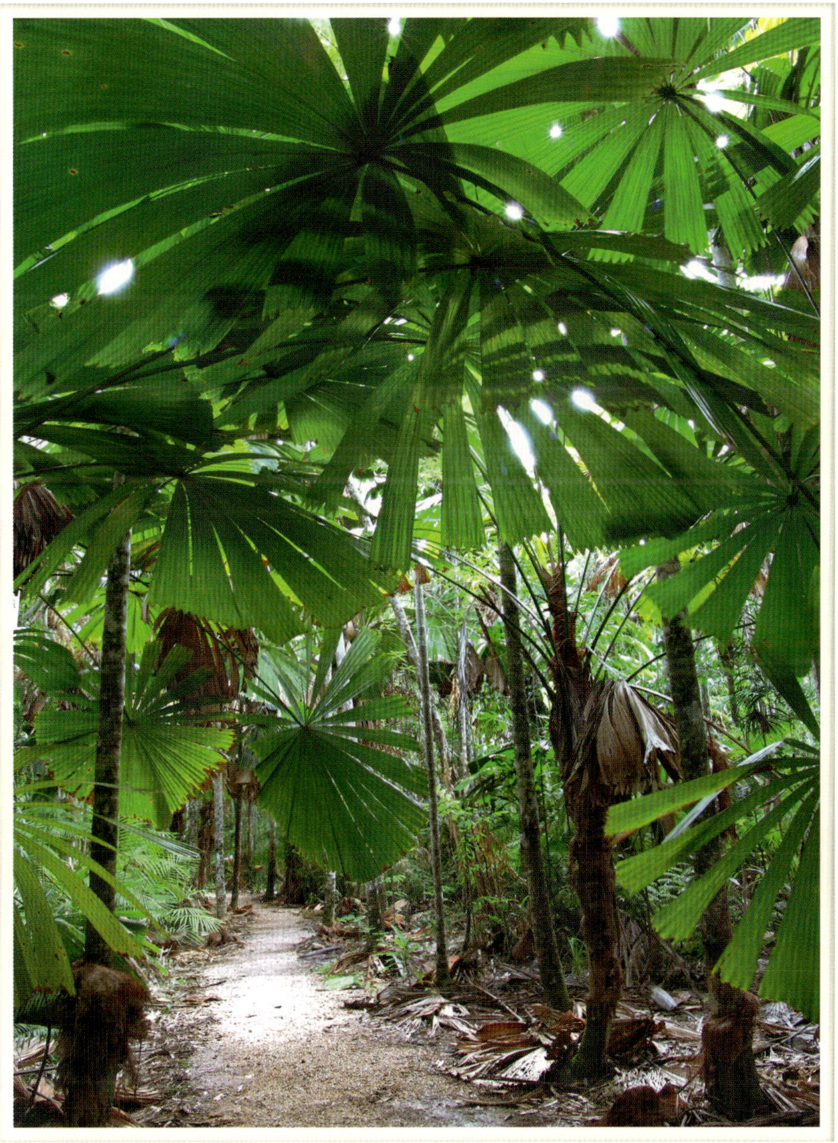

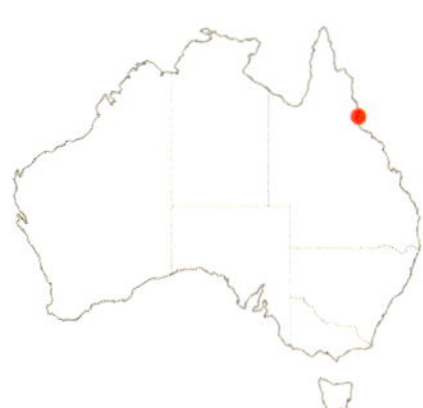

Debra Doenges

FAN PALM WALK

Licuala State Forest, Mission Beaach, QLD

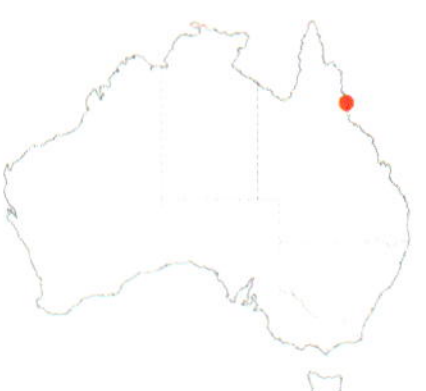

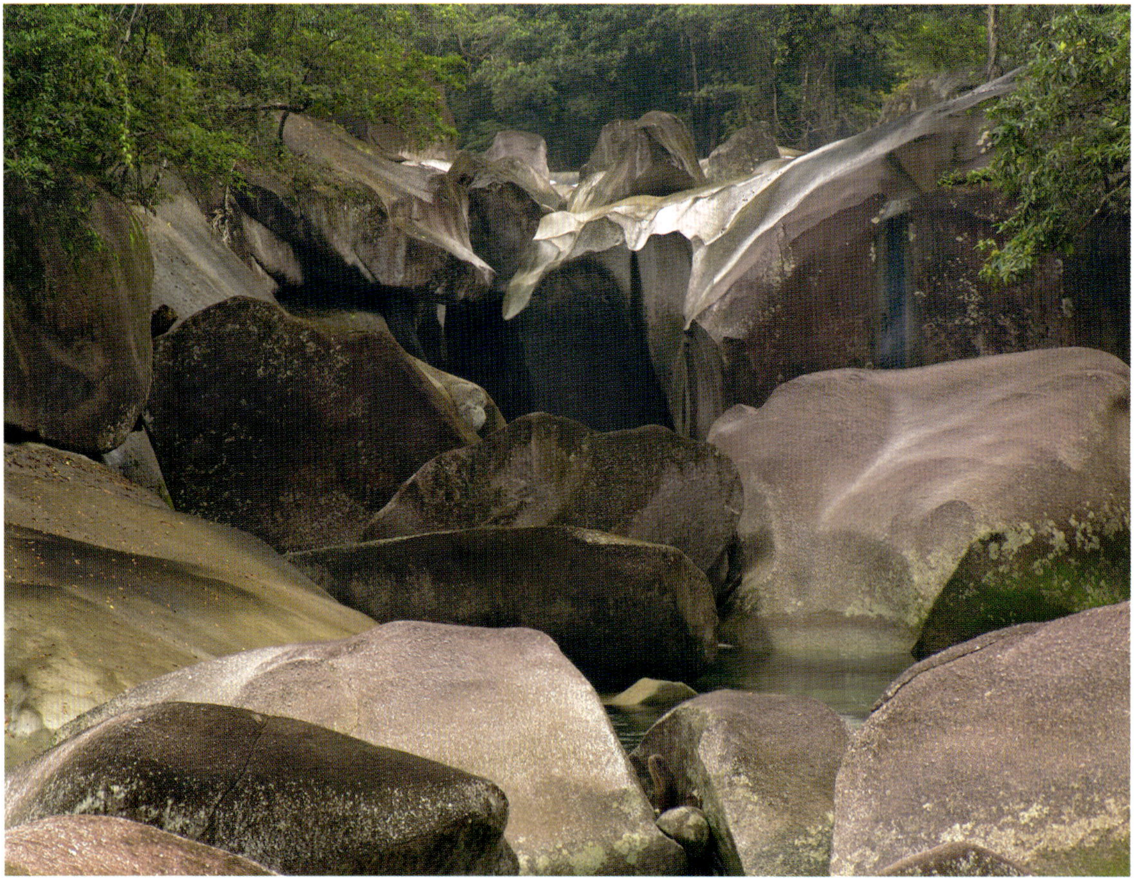

THE BOULDERS

Babinda Creek, Wooroonooran National Park, QLD

Debra Doenges

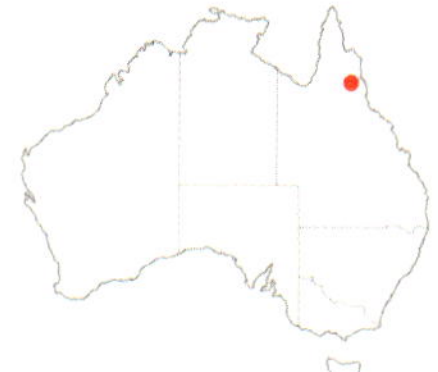

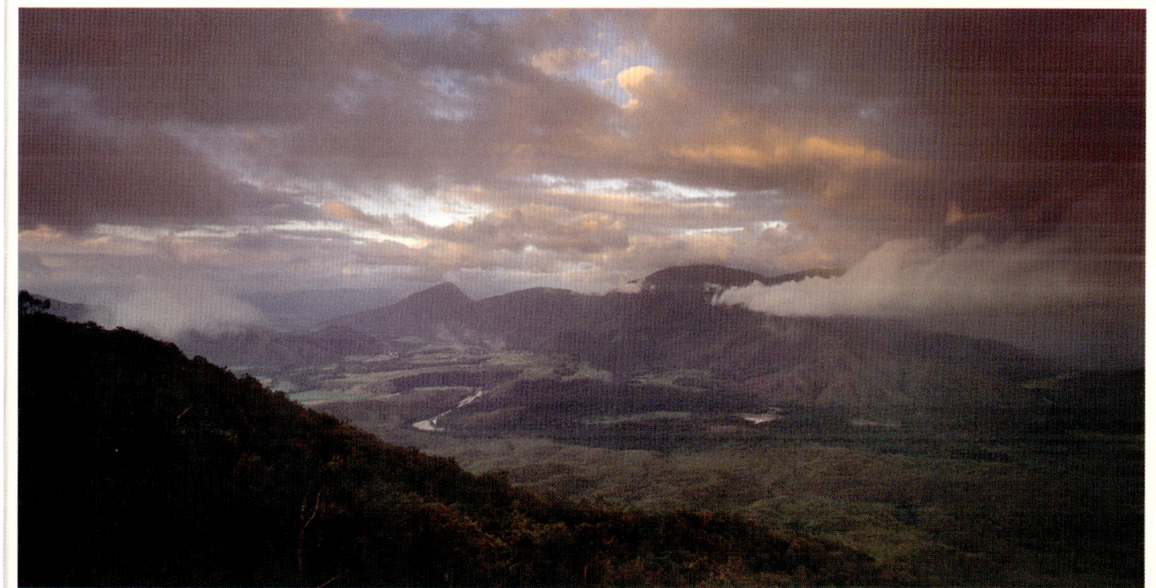

Andrew Teakle

MUSGRAVE VALLEY & BELLENDEN KER

Atherton Tablelands, QLD

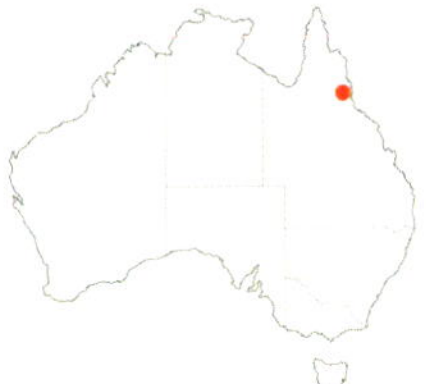

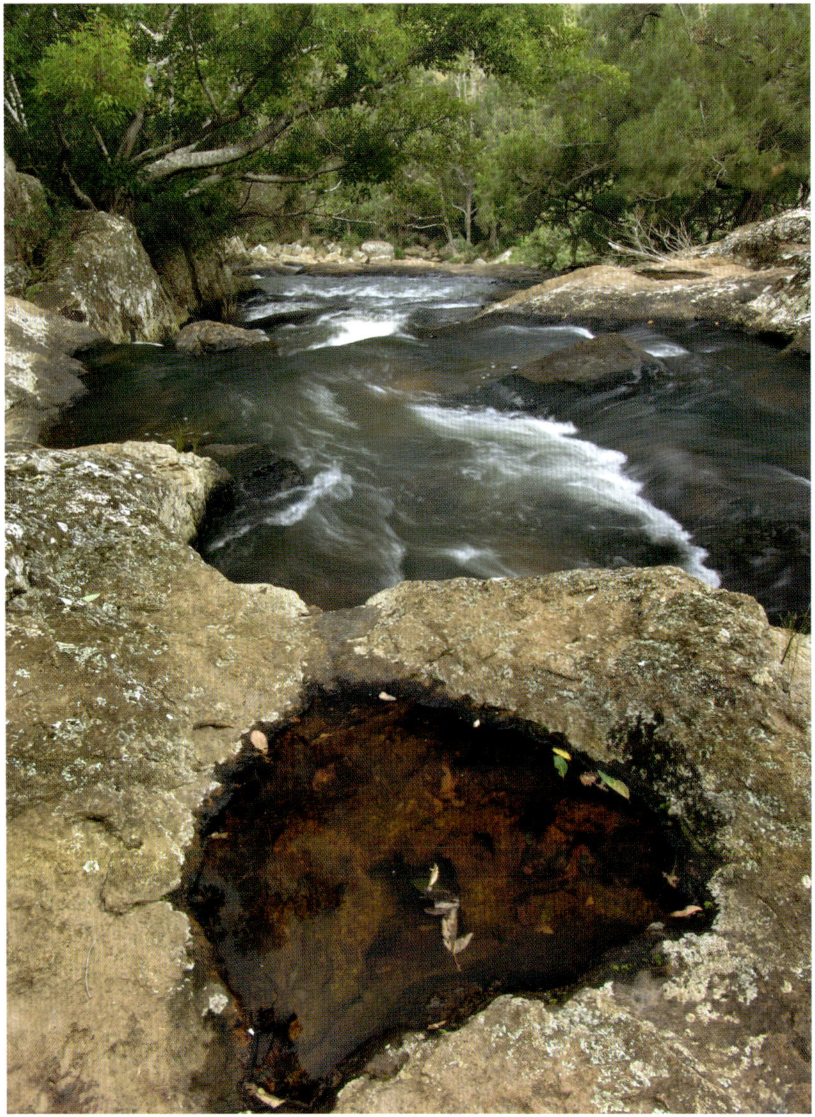

UPPER LITTLE MILLSTREAM FALLS

Debra Doenges

Ravenshoe, Atherton Tablelands, QLD

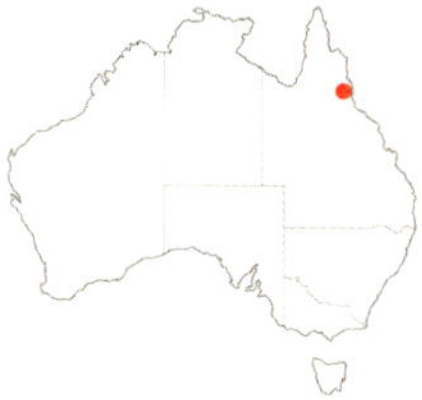

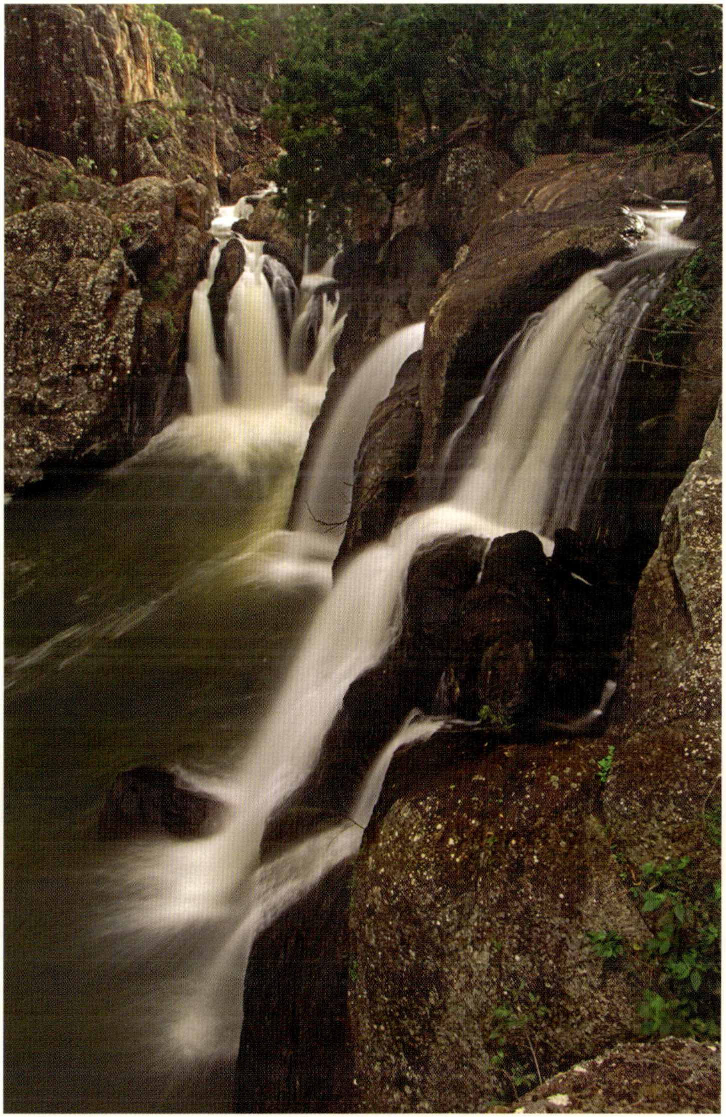

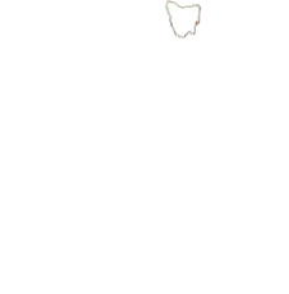

Andrew Teakle

LITTLE MILLSTREAM FALLS
Ravenshoe, Atherton Tablelands, QLD

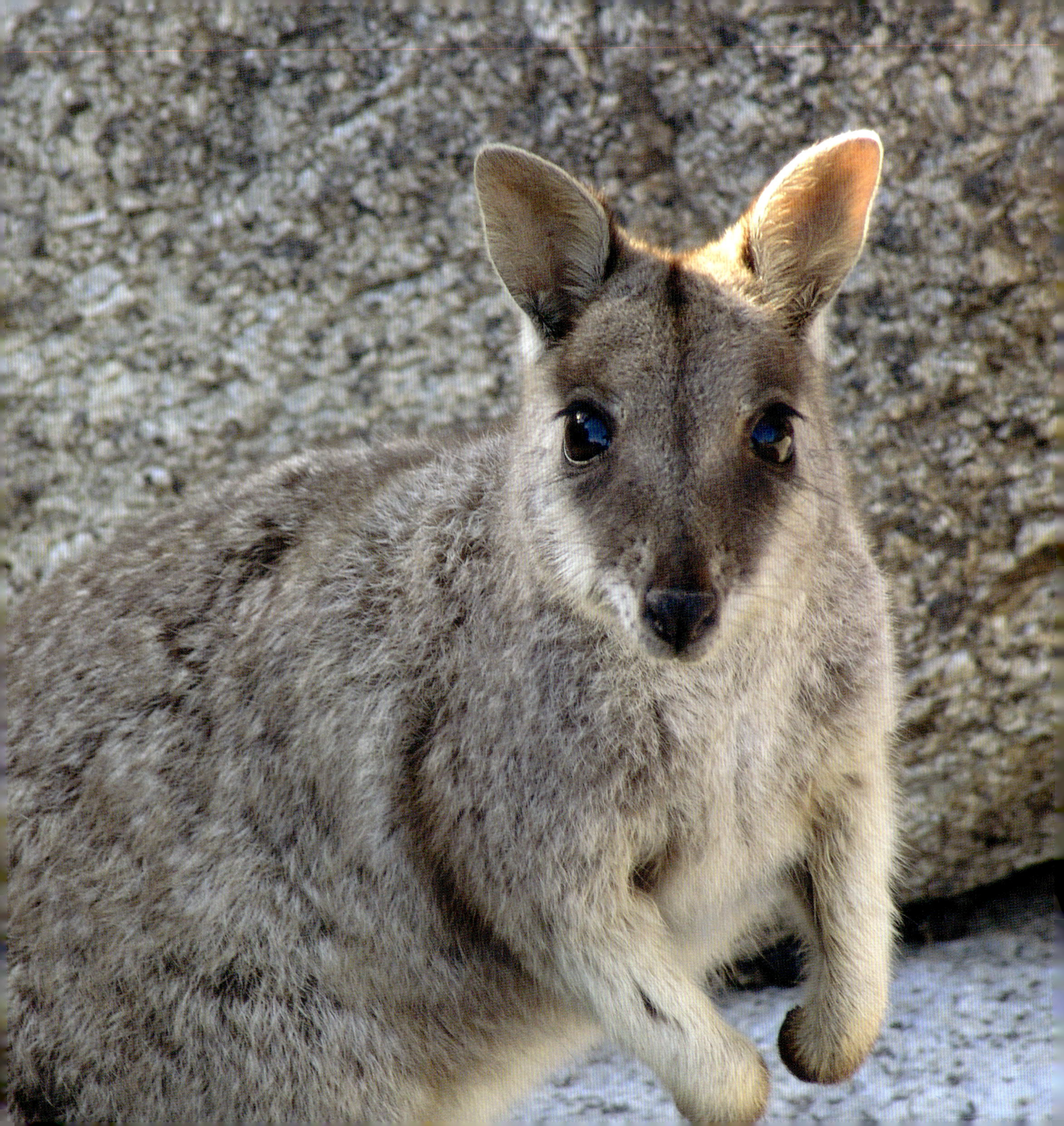

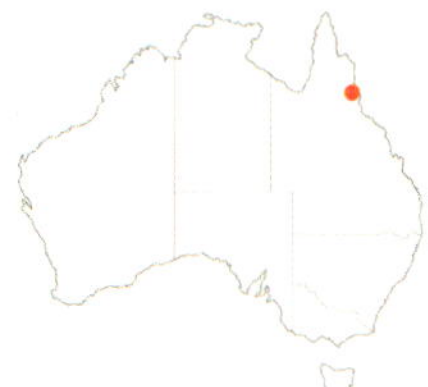

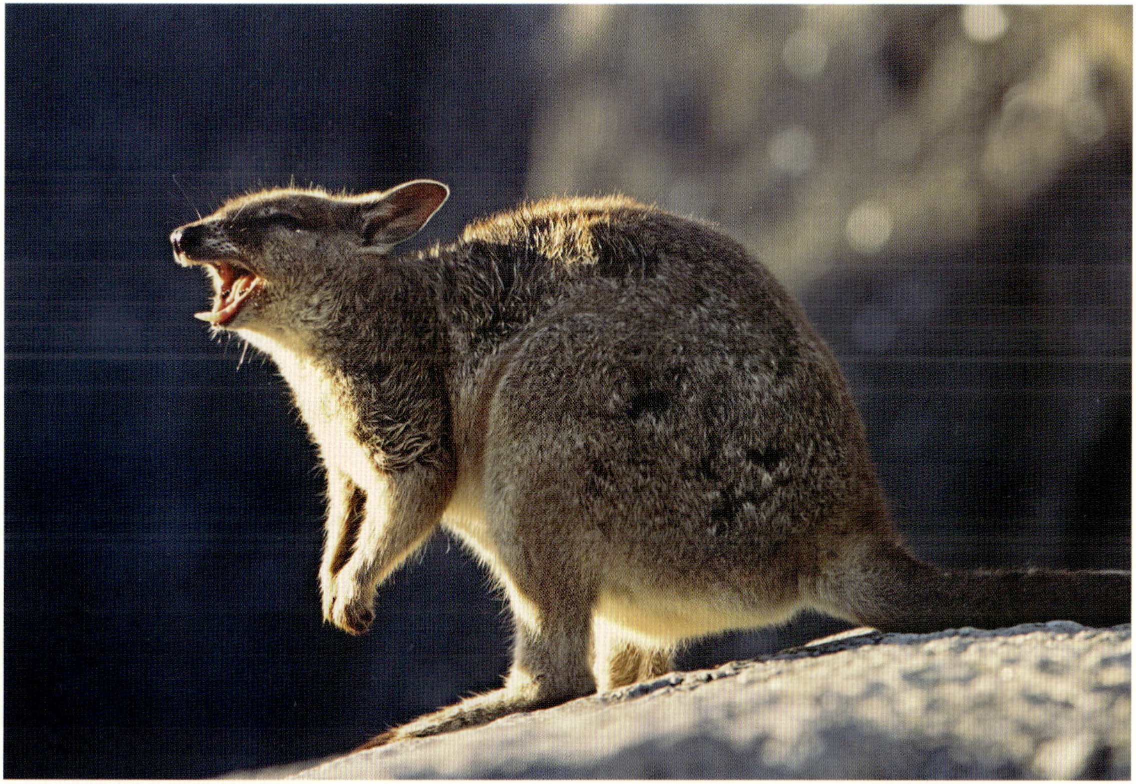

Andrew Teakle

ROCK WALLABY
Granite Gorge, Atherton Tablelands, QLD

ROCK WALLABY

◀ Granite Gorge, Atherton Tablelands, QLD

Debra Doenges

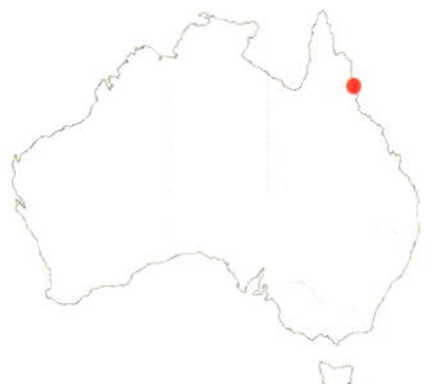

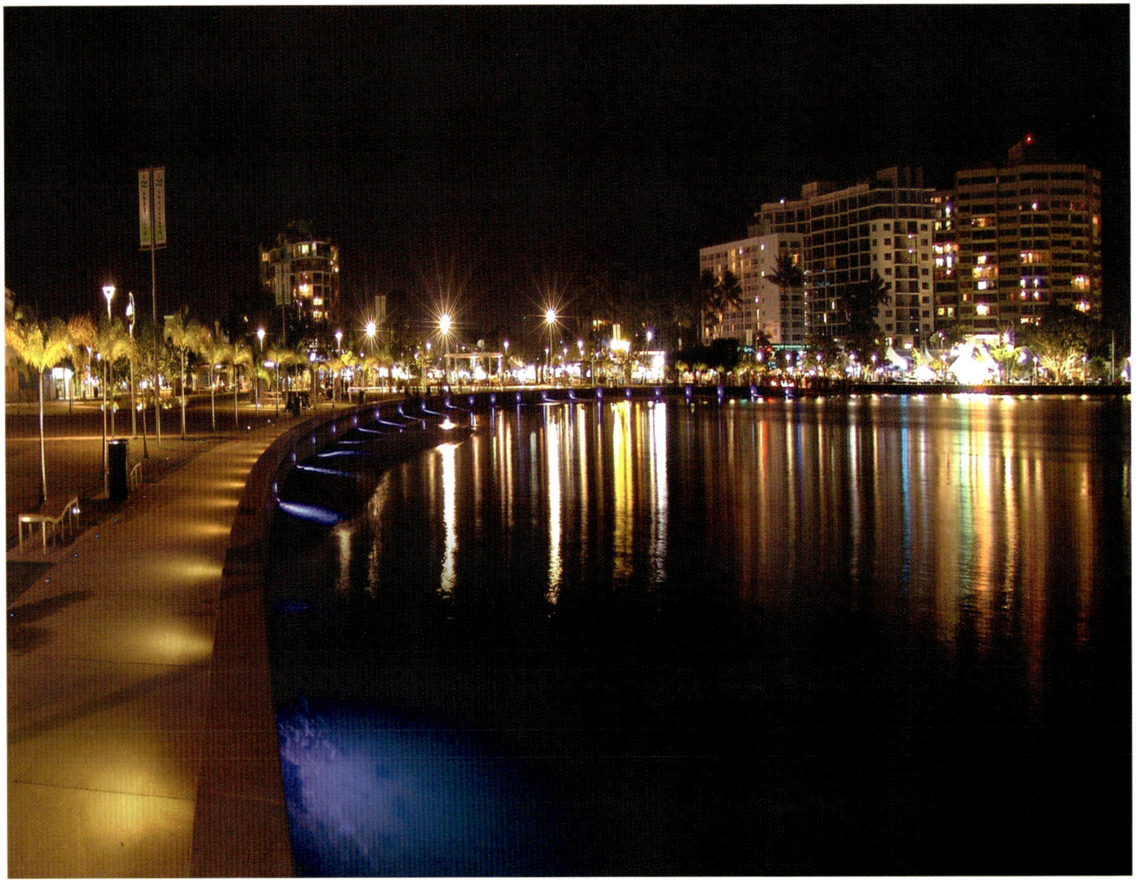

TRINITY BAY
Cairins, QLD

Andrew Teakle & Debra Doenges

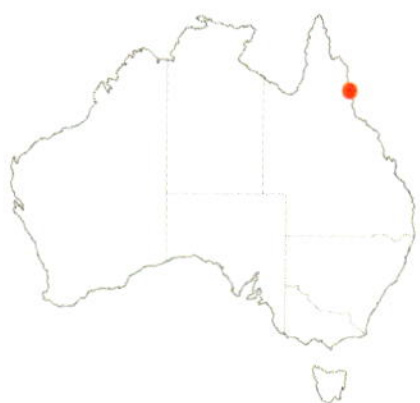

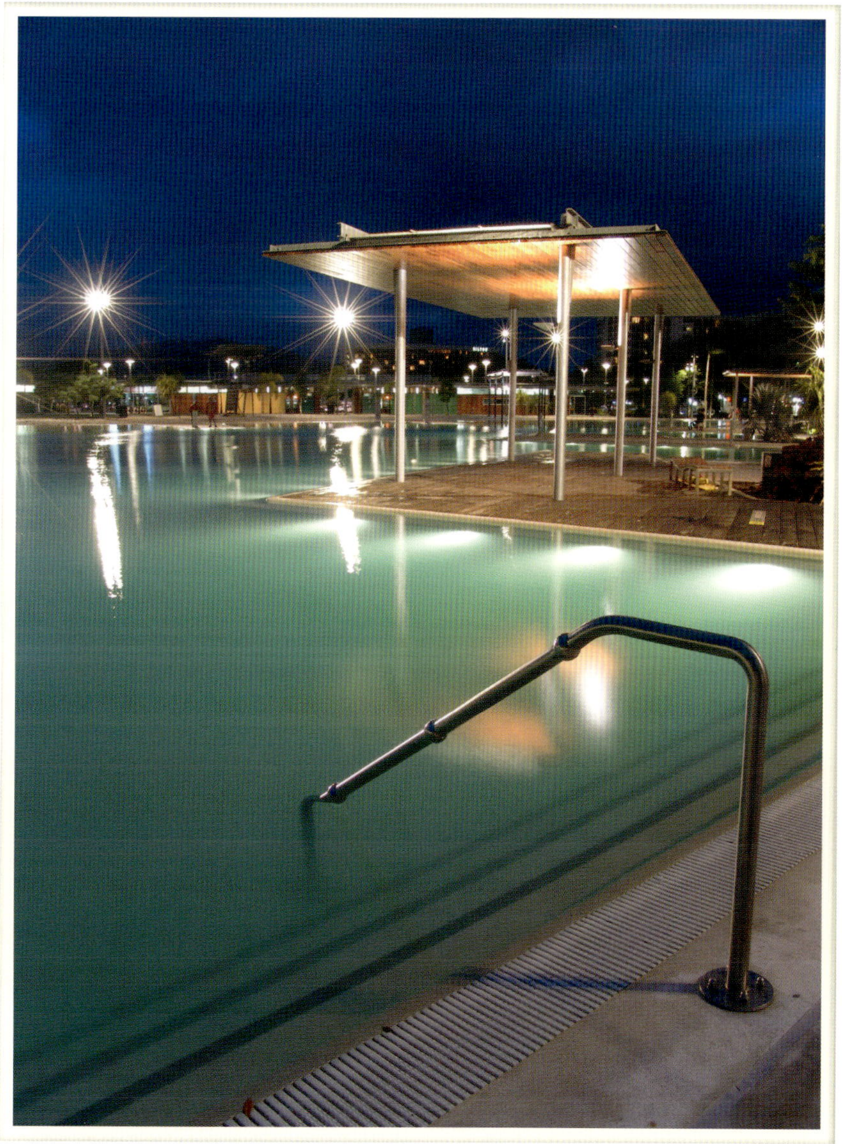

Andrew Teakle & Debra Doenges

THE LAGOON

Cairns, QLD

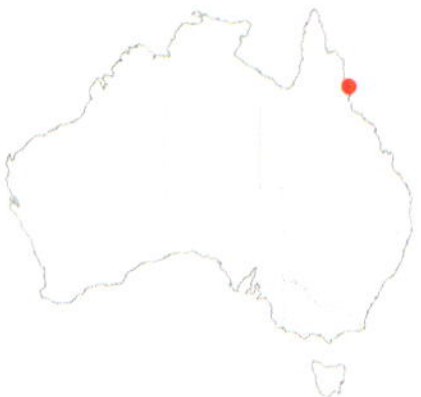

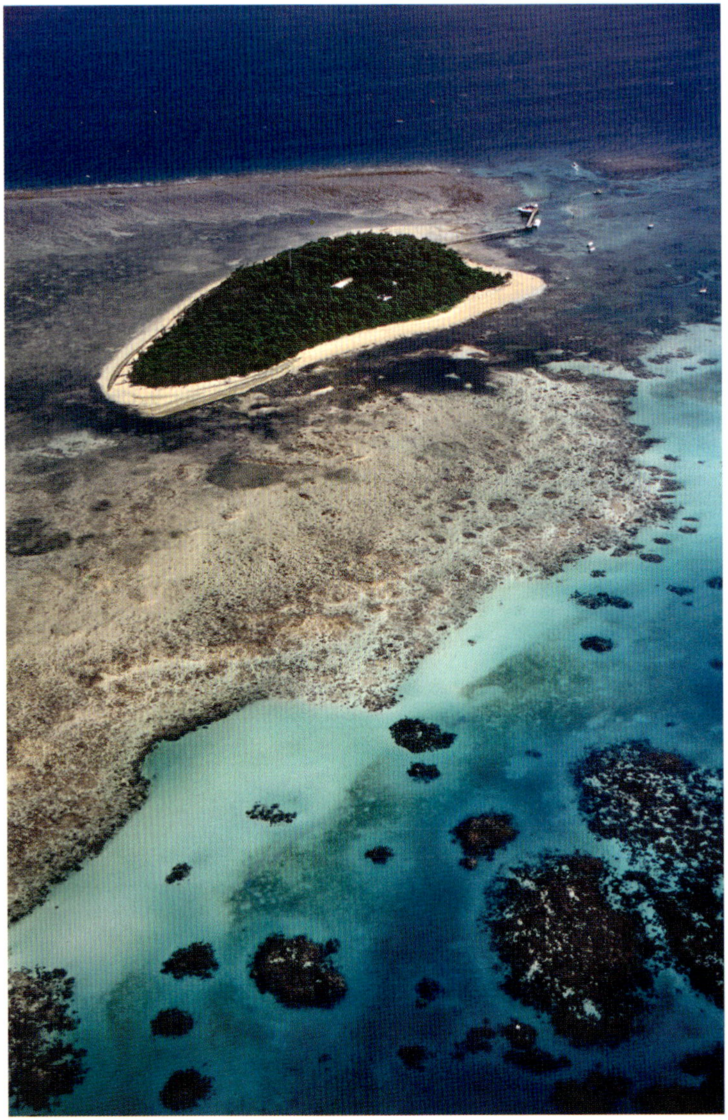

GREEN ISLAND

Great Barrier Reef, Cairns, QLD

Andrew Teakle

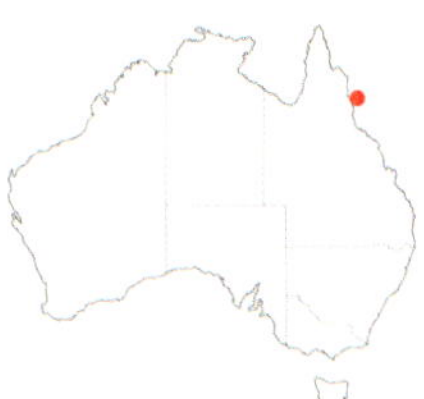

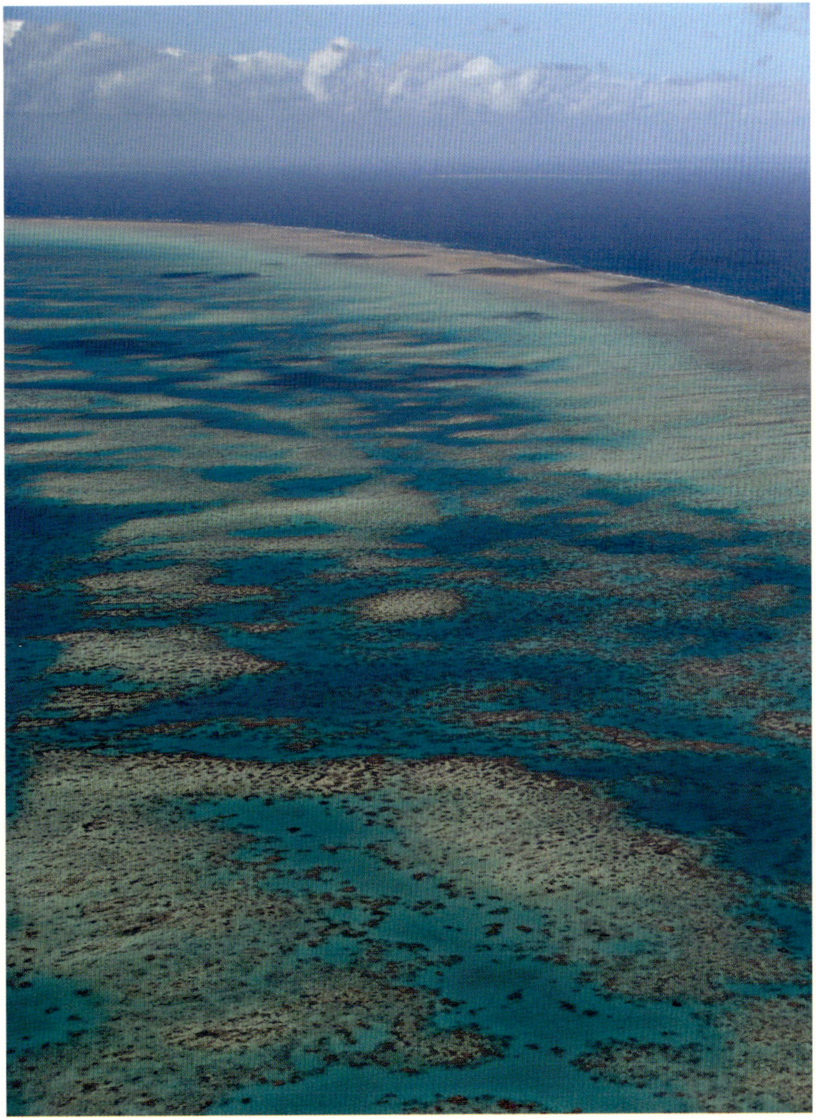

Debra Doenges

ARLINGTON REEF

Great Barrier Reef, off Cairns, QLD

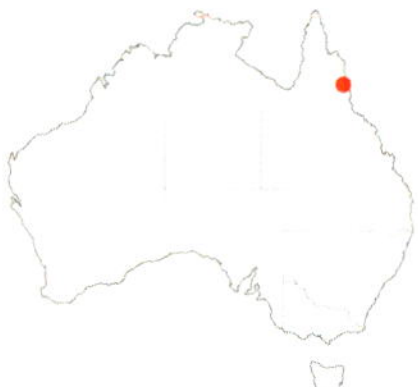

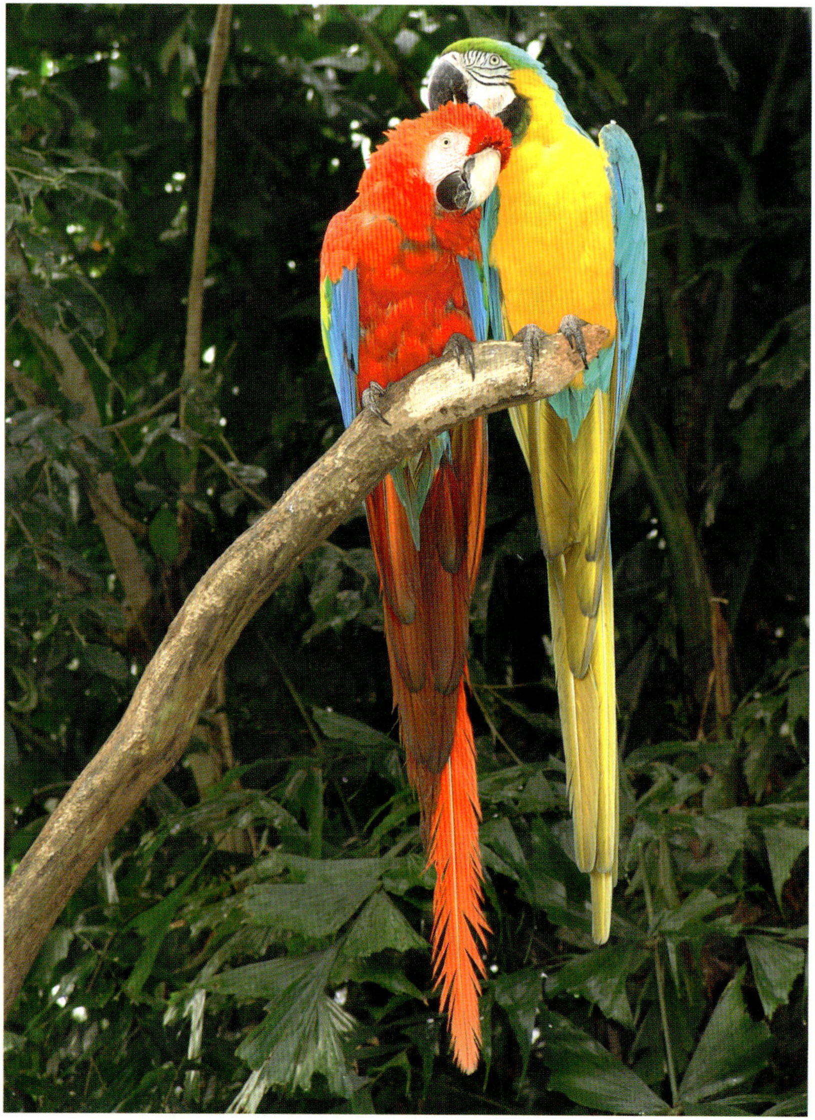

SOUTH AMERICAN MACAWS
Birdworld, Kuranda, QLD

Debra Doenges

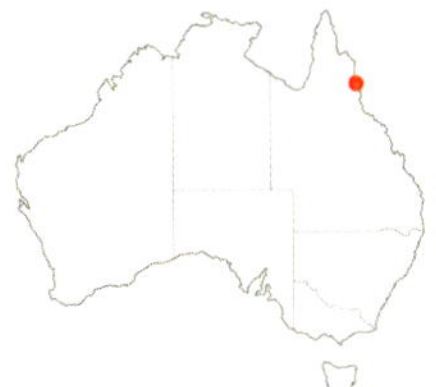

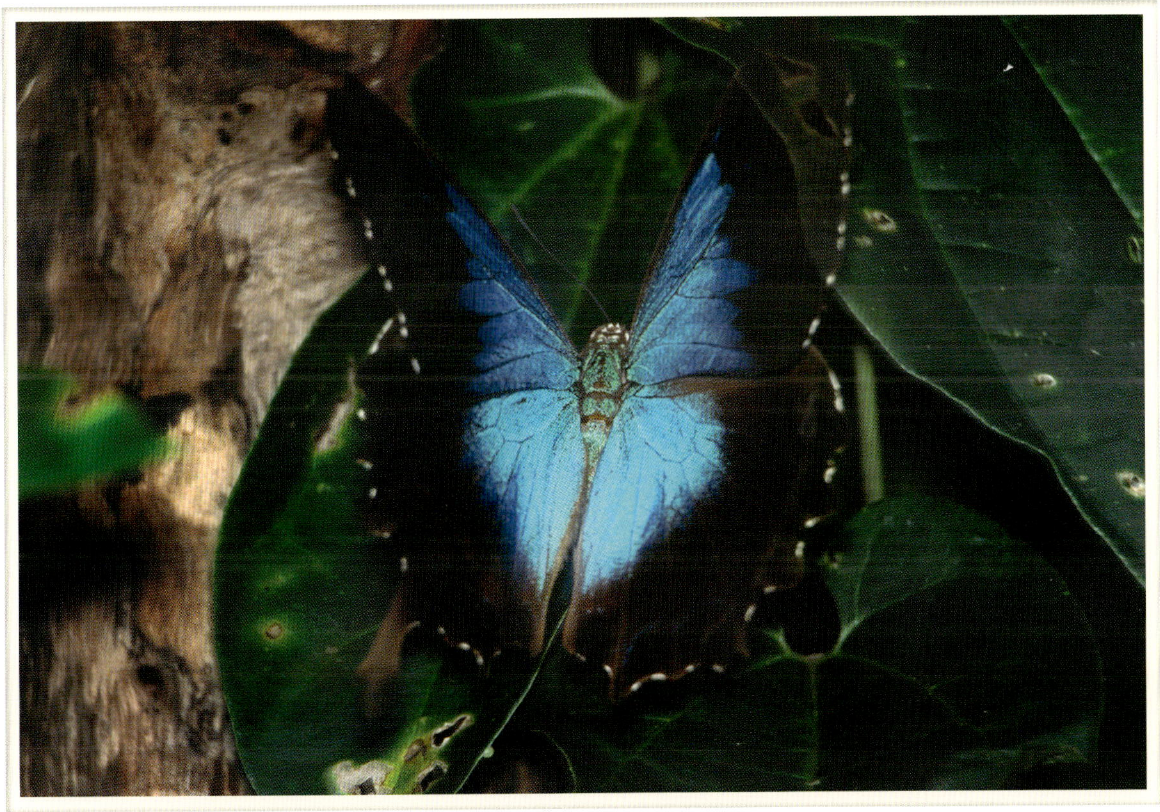

Andrew Teakle

ULYSSES BUTTERFLY

Australian Butterfly Sanctuary, Kuranda, QLD

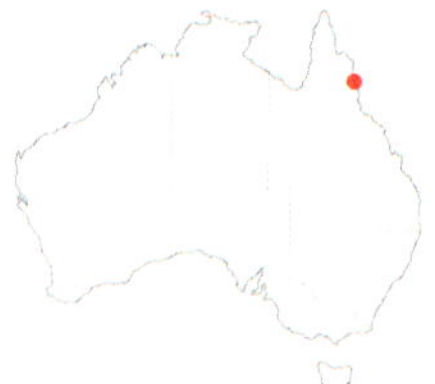

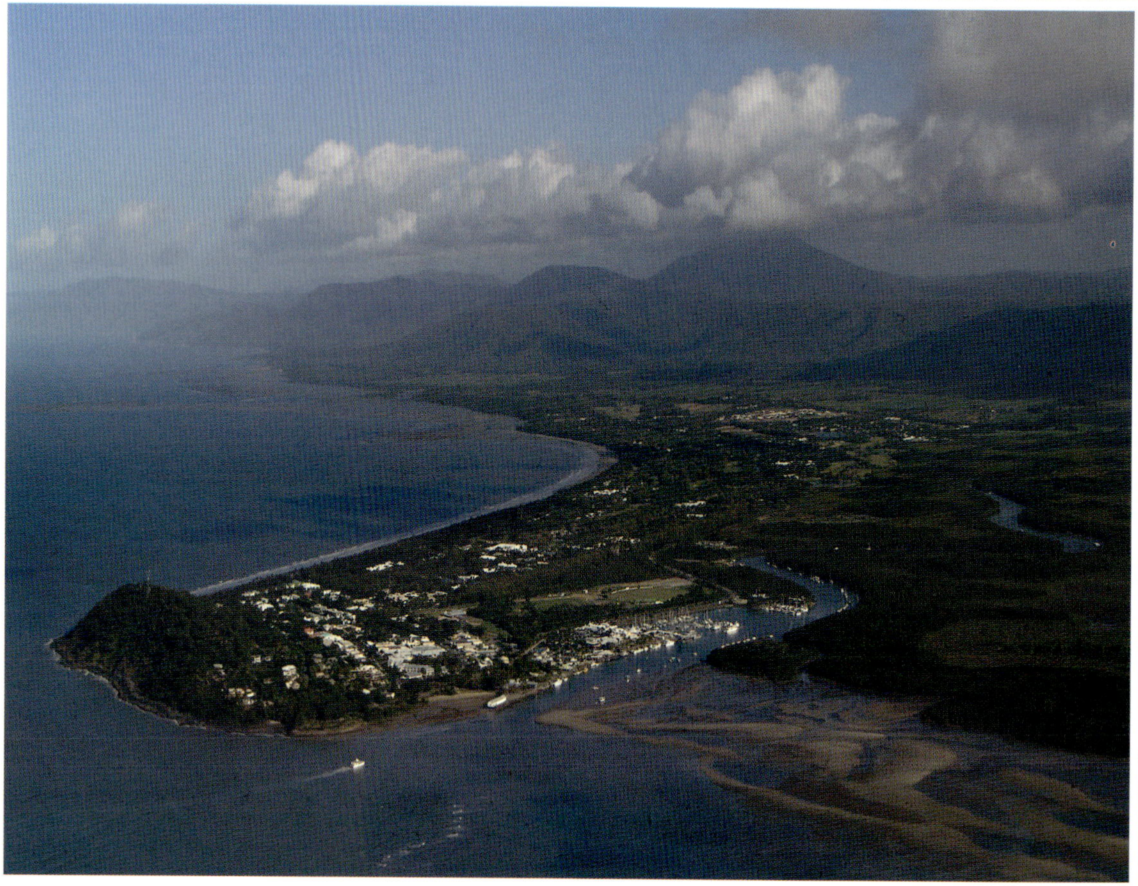

PORT DOUGLAS
Port Douglas, QLD

Debra Doenges

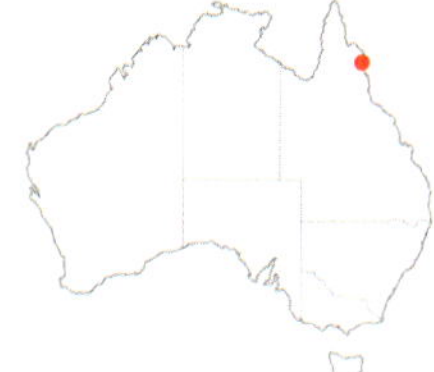

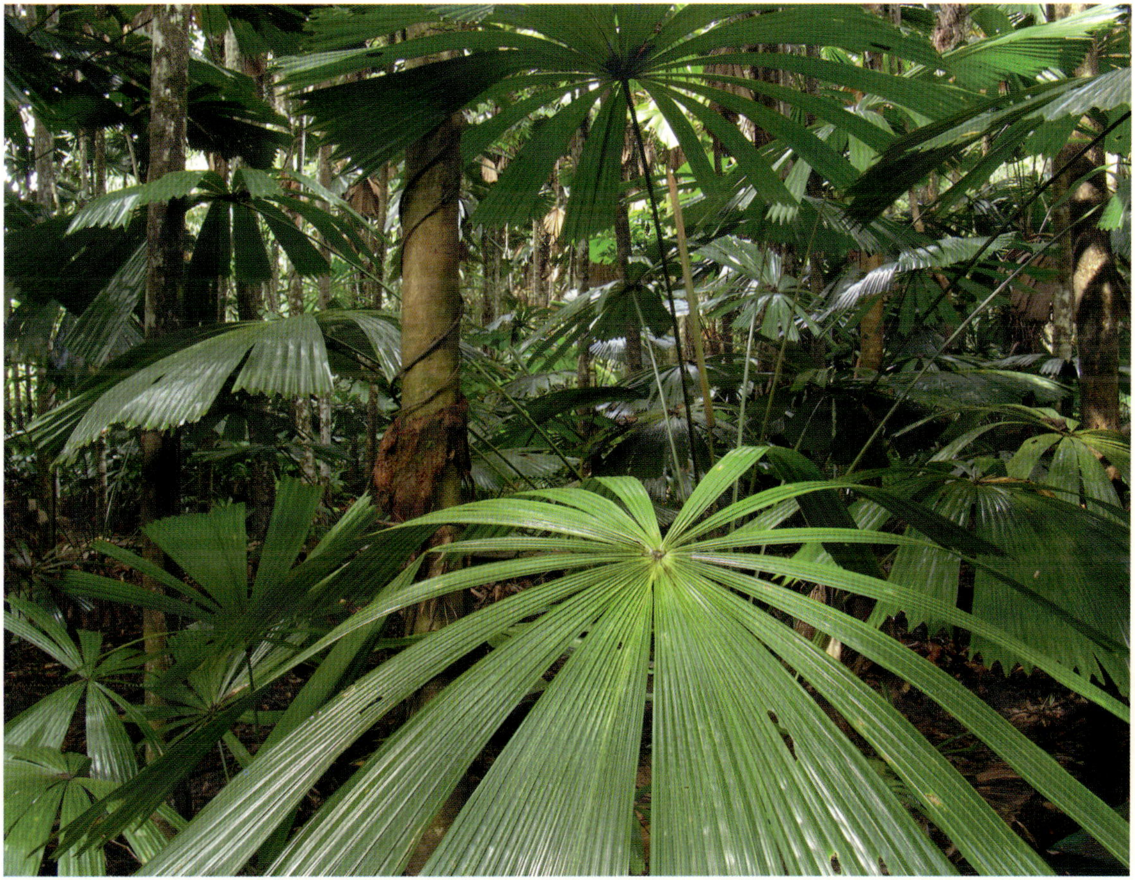

Debra Doenges

FAN PALM RAINFOREST
Daintree National Park, QLD

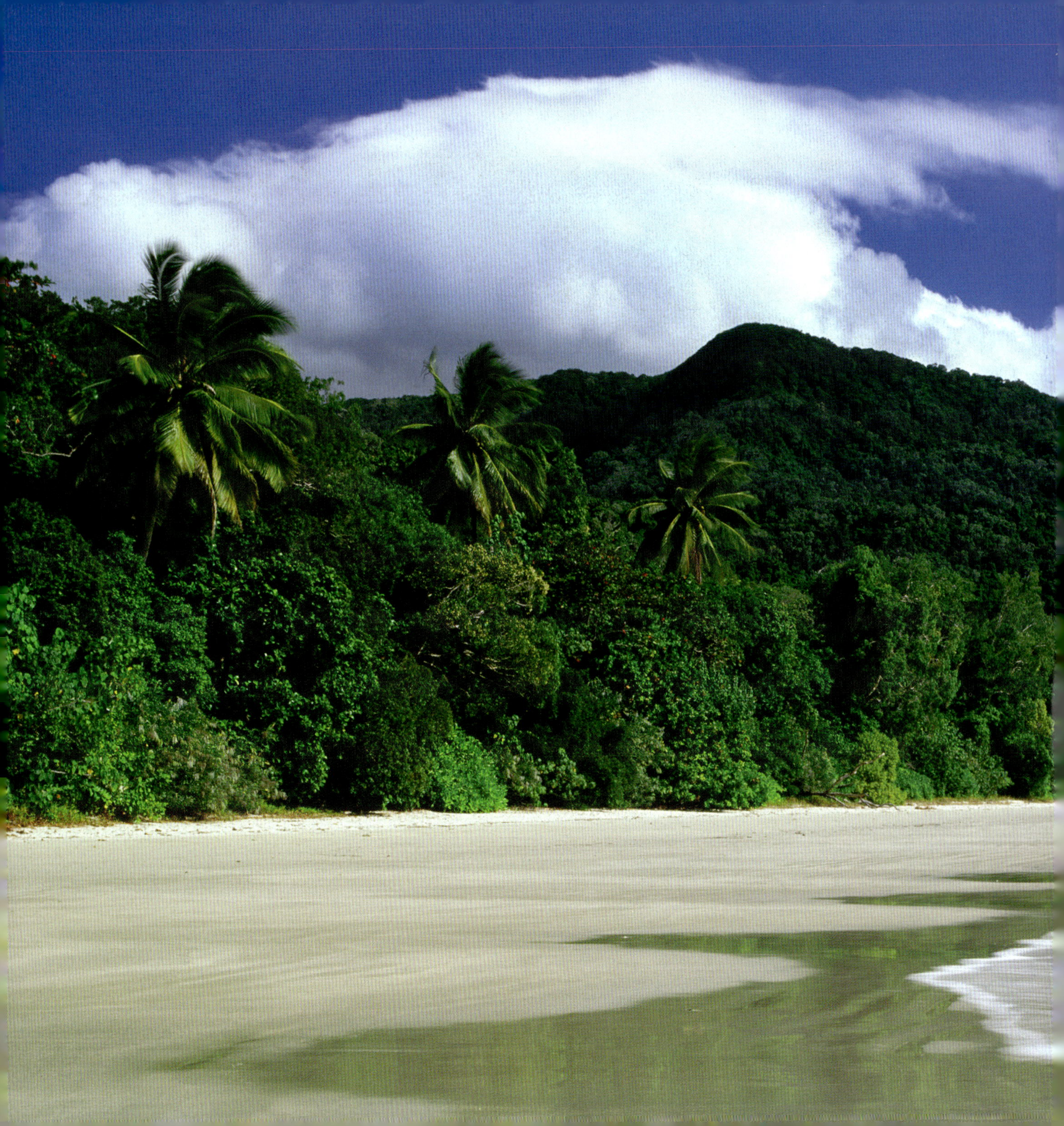

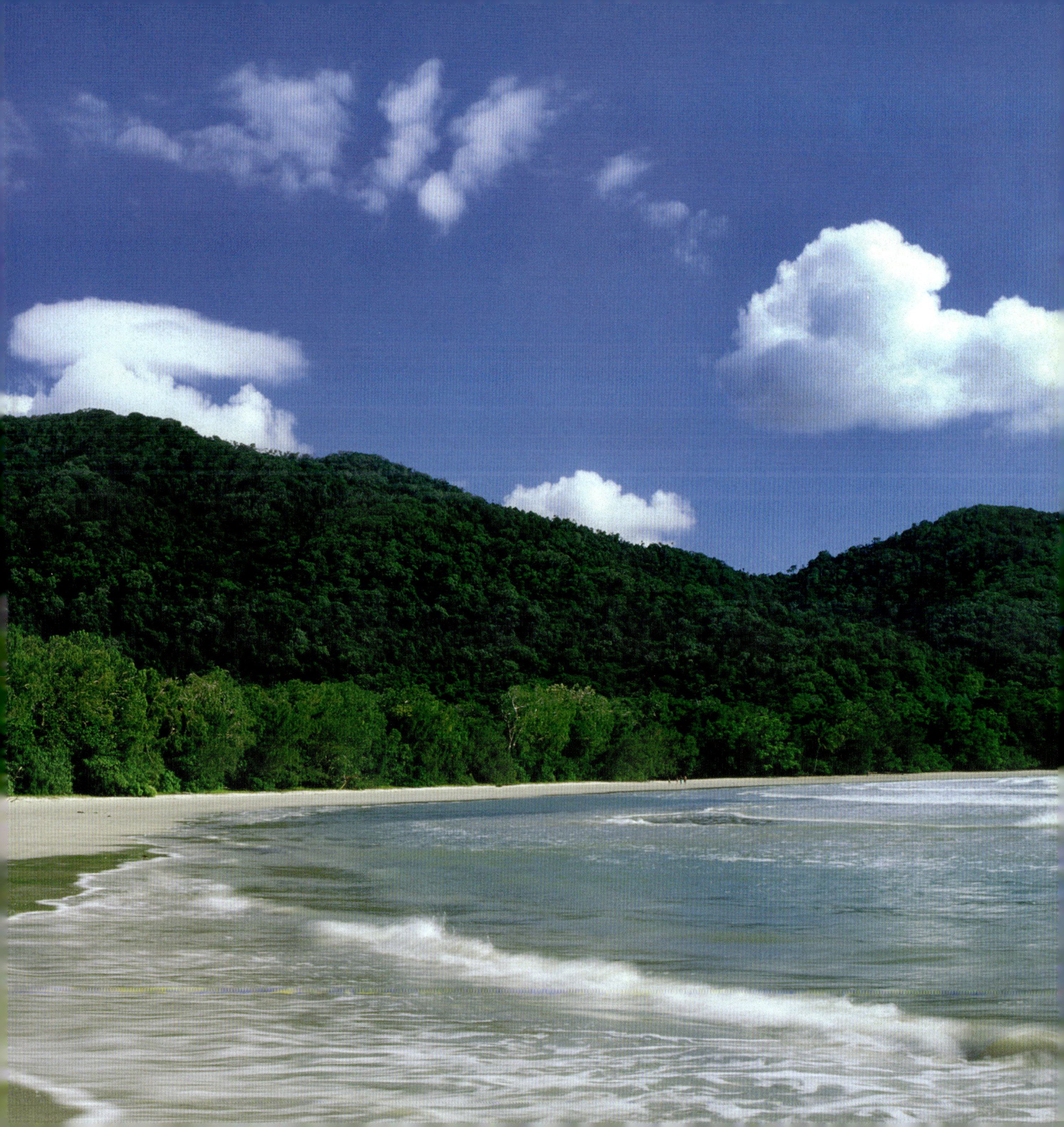

CAPE TRIBULATION DAWN

Daintree National Park, QLD

Andrew Teakle

EMMAGEN BEACH

Daintree National Park, QLD

Debra Doenges

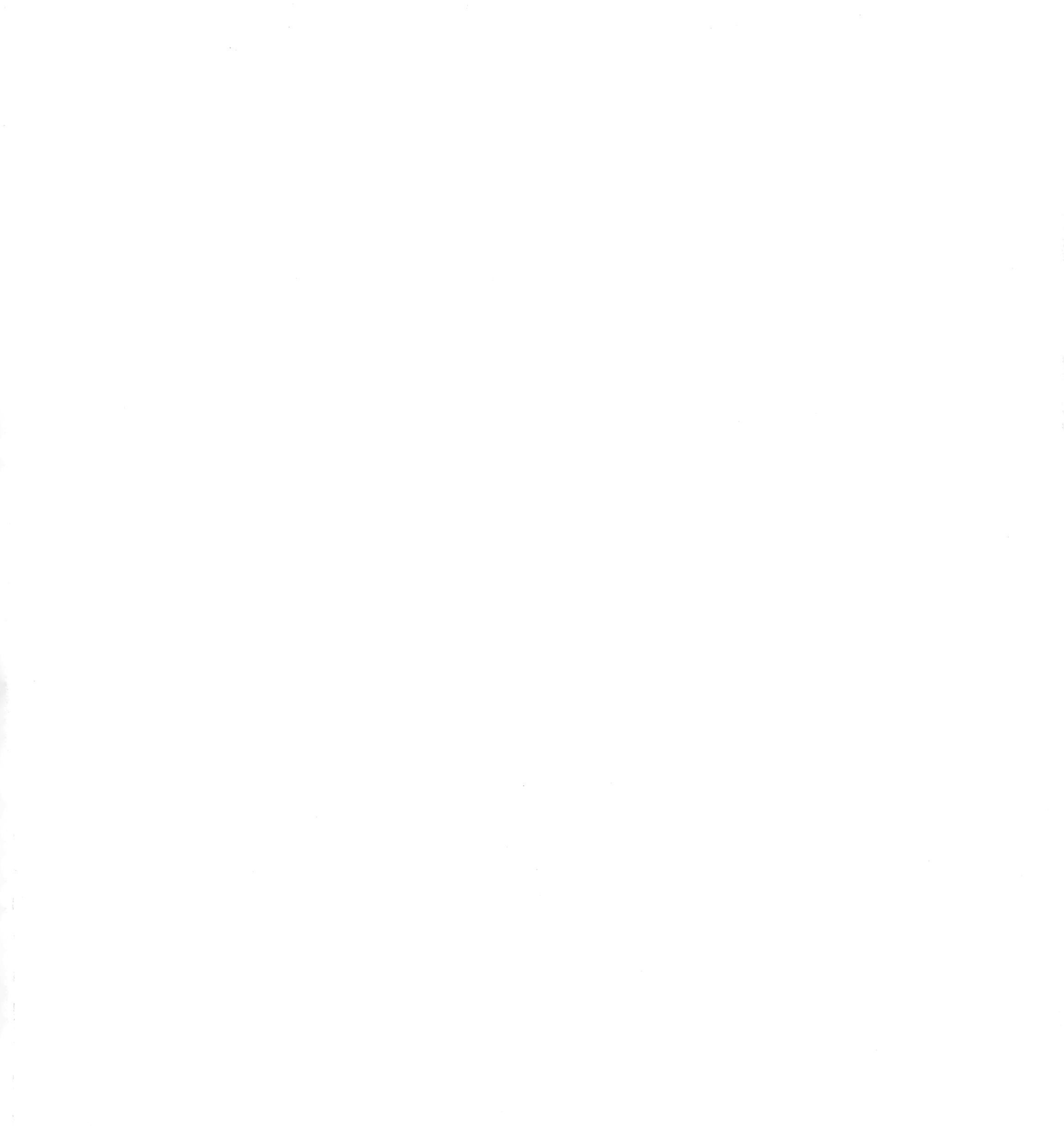